INTERIOR PEDESTRIAN PLACES

INTERIOR PEDESTRIAN PLACES

MICHAEL J. BEDNAR, AIA

WHITNEY LIBRARY OF DESIGN
an imprint of Watson-Guptill Publications, New York

To my wife, Mary, and my children,
Richard Earl, Matthew Scott, and Rachel Catherine

First published in 1989 by Whitney Library of Design
an imprint of Watson-Guptill Publications
a division of BPI Communications, Inc.
1515 Broadway, New York, N.Y. 10036

Library of Congress Cataloging-in-Publication Data
Bednar, Michael J.
    Interior pedestrian places : arcades, galleries, markets,
atria, winter gardens, skywalks, and concourses / Michael J. Bednar.
        p. cm.
    Includes index.
    ISBN 0-8230-3161-6
    1. Pedestrian facilities design.   2. Interior architecture.
I. Title.
NA2543.P4B43   1989
729—dc20   89-5798
                                                  CIP

Manufactured in U.S.A.

First printing, 1989

1 2 3 4 5 6 / 94 93 92 91 90 89

The completion of this book was made possible by a grant from the Graham Foundation for Advanced Studies in the Fine Arts. The research necessary to prepare the manuscript was conducted during the fall of 1987 as a sesquicentennial associate at the Center for Advanced Study of the University of Virginia.

My appreciation is graciously extended to the colleagues and critics who generously took time to comment on portions of the manuscript: Warren Boeschenstein, Robert F. Brown, Eric Kuhne, Roger Lewis, William Lucy, Barry Maitland, Richard Saxon, Richard Guy Wilson, and William H. Whyte. My students at the School of Architecture of the University of Virginia were helpful as reactors to the ideas contained herein. Starling Keene and Paul Thompson carefully prepared most of the graphic illustrations for the text. Janet Cutright diligently completed the volumes of correspondence.

A note of thanks is extended to the staff members of numerous architectural firms and city-planning departments who generously provided photographs, drawings, and information throughout the book. Special appreciation goes to my editors at the Whitney Library of Design and their staff: Julia Moore who initiated and encouraged this project and Cornelia Guest who assiduously carried it through to successful completion. ■

CONTENTS

PREFACE

Of the changes that have occurred in urban pedestrian life since World War II, the most significant is the result of the burgeoning development of interior urban places. These enclosed pedestrian environments offer protection from the weather—a valuable attribute at certain times in virtually all climates. Since the means of enclosure are usually transparent, direct and reciprocal perception of outside and inside is readily available. The controlled climate allows pedestrians to utilize interior places and their amenities freely throughout the day and between seasons. The continuity of exterior to interior space enables free, fluid movement and perceptual simultaneity (outside-inside and inside-outside), which are stimulating experiences for the twentieth-century pedestrian. But enclosure also can have unwarranted consequences through the privatization of pedestrian space, the result of which is limited access and controlled use.

In the nineteenth century, the opportunities for creating new types of interior pedestrian places were greatly expanded with the introduction of glass-and-steel enclosure systems. Architects could design and build spaces completely protected from the weather but with the visual transparency and daylight availability of exterior spaces. A period of extensive invention and development followed—resulting in many interior-place types: galleries, conservatories, exhibition halls, train sheds, indoor markets, and winter gardens. Many were of grand scale and/or complex form; all provided extensive opportunities to develop a public pedestrian life.

In the last quarter century, the nineteenth-century precedent of interior pedestrian places has been rediscovered. The result is a resurgence of interest in the design and development of interior places. New place types have been created, based on the needs of complex, high-density urban development, and aided by improved technologies. New retail galleries, shopping centers, festival market places, multiuse centers, public atria, winter gardens, skyways, and concourses are dramatically changing the contemporary pedestrian's use and experience of the city.

This book is about the design of interior pedestrian places—spaces in the city center enclosed from the weather for use by people on foot. Although significant pedestrian places are located outside of city centers, the concern here is with the relationship between interior urban places and traditional exterior urban places and their role in the life of the pedestrian. The places investigated here are intended for public uses—whether publicly or privately owned or managed.

After a quarter century of sustained growth and development, it is time to make an assessment of the interior pedestrian place as a form of urban architecture: What design concepts have been utilized and how well are they working? Have the precedents for these place types been acknowledged in the development of new forms? How well do they fit into the existing city in terms of massing, appearance, and streetscape? How are they experienced, accessed, and used by pedestrians? What are the sociological, political, and economic effects brought about by the rapid introduction of interior places in the city center? What future design directions can be suggested based on this assessment?

This book is organized into six chapters that present, analyze, and evaluate the design of interior pedestrian places of the past, present, and future. Chapter 1 defines the reasons for the contemporary resurgence of interest and development of this place type. Since commerce is one of the main purposes of a city, many interior pedestrian places are devoted to this use. Four types of commercial places are considered in chapter 2: arcades and gallerias, urban shopping centers, festival marketplaces, and multiuse centers. The design characteristics of public atria, as they relate to known building types—such as hotels, office buildings, government buildings, museums and institutions, and leisure-related buildings (winter gardens)—are the subject of chapter 3. The method of analysis in both chapters 2 and 3 is to study the nineteenth-century origins of each place type to form a basis for analyzing the twentieth-century examples. Chapter 4 delves into the urban phenomena of skyways and concourses—that is, extensive pedestrian networks above and below ground that link together commercial places and public atria. The integration of interior pedestrian places within existing urban contexts is discussed in chapter 5, through the presentation of four urban-design case studies: Chester, England; Washington, D.C.; Toronto; and Philadelphia. Chapter 6 outlines recommended urban-design criteria and concepts.

The critiques of the example projects are presented from both the perspective of the pedestrian user and the design critic. The pedestrian is more concerned with the activities at hand, easy way finding, and enjoying the experience of the people and the environment. The designer is more concerned with how well the design problem has been solved and executed. He or she asks, How is the scheme organized in plan and section? How is it built? What are the aesthetic results? The pedestrians' and designers' perspectives can be mutually reinforcing, but this is not always the case. (Although the viewpoints of the developer, the owner, and the tenants are important to the success of any project, this book does not include an in-depth consideration of their perspectives.)

The methods I used to develop this book are an eclectic assortment: direct experience; focused observation; analysis of drawings; photography; discussions with designers; conversations with pedestrians; and extensive consultation of books, journals, articles, and reports. My interest in the subject grew out of the research and writing of *The New Atrium* (1986), which is devoted to the design development of the atrium building and includes examples of public atria.[1] My orientation throughout is that of the reflective professional—that is, the architect who is constantly trying to understand the how and why of urban architecture. The results are not definitive because the subject is new and complex, but there is a clear attitude. Interior urban places are not inherently good or bad. Their value depends on how well they are planned and designed.

This study is intended to contribute to the larger question confronting our era. How can we once again *positively* inhabit urban public places? I assume that the need and motivation to undertake this habitation remains strong. Thus, the question focuses on the forms and places of this habitation. I strongly suggest that interior urban places have a significant role to play in resolving this issue—for they offer opportunities for public activities in transformed public settings. ∎

CHAPTER 1

RATIONALES

Cities of many eras have had sheltered pedestrian places. The center of the Greek city, for example, was formed by extensive ranges of *stoa*—detached, roofed colonnades that served social, political, and economic purposes. The *porticus* of the Roman city was extended to connect houses, temples, and shops in a system of covered pedestrian passages. In the medieval and Renaissance eras, systems of street arcades were extended throughout many Italian cities, thus enabling the inhabitants to traverse undercover to all districts. The most developed of these systems is located in Bologna, Italy; it reaches twenty miles throughout the city, surrounds the great university, and leads up to the mountain sanctuary of the Madonna di San Luca. In all cases, these sheltered places were considered adjuncts to the streets and squares that formed the matrix of the city. Sheltered pedestrian places afforded protection from the weather, safety from wheeled traffic, opportunities for strolling, and locations for social conduct.

The invention and development of the covered commercial arcade in France and England at the beginning of the nineteenth century was the result of a specific set of economic and social conditions. Industry had developed the ability to produce a large variety of luxury goods, thus necessitating new methods and means of marketing and sales. The covered arcade, through its grouping of stores with ample window-display space, created a competitive atmosphere for continuous, undisturbed shopping. This paved pedestrian place was protected both from the climate and the inhospitable street—with its traffic, noise, and dirt. But the arcade was also a social space, a promenade, and a place of public meeting. This freely accessible public space supported the concept of a democratic society with a thriving public life.

In the middle of the twentieth century, another set of economic and social conditions in the United States led to the development of the enclosed, suburban shopping mall. After World War II, the suburbs surrounding large cities rapidly grew in population in conjunction with the extended use of private automobiles. The initial built form of the suburban commercial center was a group of stores around an open-air pedestrian mall surrounded by vast parking lots. In its subsequent form, the mall was covered by a roof with skylights; and the grouping of the stores was compacted horizontally but was expanded vertically to two or three stories. Thus, the nineteenth-century urban arcade was transformed into its twentieth-century counterpart with similar economic and social advantages. Small stores were arranged in rows between large department stores, thus creating a layout that induced shopping and sales within a conducive environment. Moreover, the new shopping centers supplanted the historic role of the central business district and became the public social centers for the new suburbs—places for exhibitions, performances, and gatherings.

Since the 1970s, the cities of North America have become the sites for a new phase in the design transformation and development of the interior pedestrian place. This renewed interest was generated by the economic desire to revitalize urban centers through increased commercial and entertainment activity. Although office buildings had been built in great numbers in the central business districts since World War II, the activity in these districts usually ended when the office workers went home. The opportunity for other kinds of activities had been lacking. The most recent trend in urban redevelopment has emphasized provision for retail, entertainment, and cultural activities along with office uses, in order to once again make downtown the vital center of public social life.

Interior pedestrian places are spaces enclosed from the weather for the use of people on foot. They are intended for public use, even if they are owned or managed by private or philanthropic entities.

The present era is one of unprecedented interest in the design and development of these places. New forms and types have been invented and built in the last two decades, and they have been organized into pedestrian systems of spatial richness and vitality. The suburban shopping mall has been transformed into an urban counterpart of greater density, connected to existing stores with ready access to parking garages and public-transit systems. Public atria, with their added amenities, have been built that enclose plazas and gardens—creating new kinds of settings for public activity. These spaces often are associated with multiuse centers, which include offices, hotels, apartments, and cultural institutions. In many cities, pedestrian-linkage systems composed of skyways and concourses have been built between these interior places.

The rationales for creating interior pedestrian places are important to understand in order to evaluate their present and future effects upon the design development of the urban center. They include the experiential rationale, the pedestrianization rationale, the sociological rationale, the interiorization rationale, and the privatization rationale. Together, these five rationales form a basis for understanding the motivations for and the consequences of creating interior urban places. An analysis of the pedestrian experience serves as a point of departure. ■

When Giovanni-Battista Nolli drew his now-famous figure-ground map of Rome in 1748, he represented exterior and interior public places together. A prevalent contemporary reason for this unique graphic depiction was given by urban designer Edmund Bacon, "In the mind of Nolli and his contemporaries the exterior and interior public spaces were inextricably integrated into a singleness of thought and concept."[1] Nolli's graphics depict white pedestrian spaces carved from the dark building blocks of the city, which constitute all of the private spaces (figure 1.1). Private outdoor spaces, such as courts, cloisters, and gardens, also are shown but with little detail. This black-white, solid-void, abstract image of the city creates a strong impression—for it is not the architect's aerial view nor is it the cartographer's street system. It is a spatial image in which the uniform depiction of public pedestrian spaces in white, de-

void of surface detail, causes the spaces to be read as a continuous network.

The density of baroque Rome provided the designers of that city with a substantial urban fabric with which to create this series of defined spaces. (It would be more difficult to achieve Nolli's vision in a more diffuse city.) The creation of positively shaped exterior public spaces was seen as a desirable goal in large part because Italian baroque culture placed a high value on a well-developed public life. The interlocking of exterior and interior rooms reached such a historic zenith during the baroque era that a reciprocity of design intention existed between the outside and the inside. This is illustrated by the plan of S. Ignazio, wherein the aisles and nave of the church were extended into the piazza to shape the house walls that define the piazza.

Nolli's revolutionary image of Rome's spatial structure has continued to in-

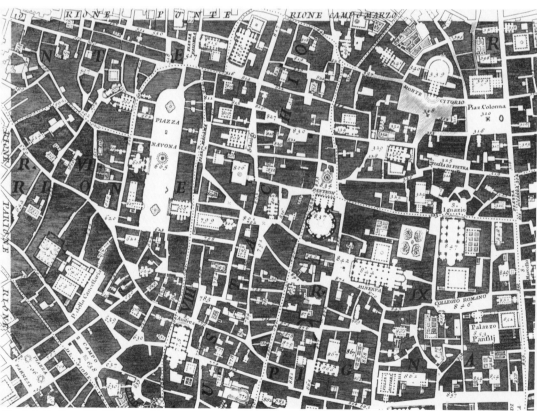

Fig. 1.1. Portion of Nolli's map of Rome.

trigue urban designers because it represents an idealized vision of the pedestrian's experience of the city as a connected series of exterior and interior spaces. The pedestrian in the city moves freely between these two realms, whether these spaces are public or semipublic. The pedestrian understands their inherent difference as openness and enclosure. In memory and experience the two realms become entwined. Articulated transitions in the form of porticoes, foyers, entries, and narthexes help to distinguish both realms; but in the last analysis, the spatial experience becomes unified. Streets, squares, courts, gardens, naves, and rotundas—each distinct in form and shape—are connected together through physical movement and mental image.

An area of twentieth-century midtown Manhattan represented as a "Nolli map" provides some important revelations about the nature of modern pedestrian places: First, the vast majority of public space is in the form of wide streets given over to motorized traffic. Streets are laid out in a geometric grid that isolates blocks of land occupied by buildings. Pedestrian sidewalks follow each street on both sides and often penetrate the blocks, thus forming passages between buildings and/or through them. Most of the interior space at street level is private or semipublic. Although some of Manhattan's buildings have a formal sequence of entry and procession, as did buildings in baroque Rome, the movement into and through many of them is unstructured.

The two urban blocks between Fifth Avenue, Madison Avenue, 55th Street, and 57th Street can serve as a specific example of contemporary pedestrian space (figure 1.2). These blocks contain the Corning Glass Works, the AT&T Building, the IBM Building, and Trump

Fig. 1.2. Two blocks in Manhattan drawn as a "Nolli map."

Tower. In addition to the perimeter sidewalks, the only exterior spaces are three small corner areas, which are not real plazas. The base of the AT&T Building has a generous amount of arcaded, paved area, mostly treated as passage but also utilized for seating (figure 1.3). A glass-covered arcade, lined with shops, at the rear of the building creates a formal mid-

Fig. 1.3. View of street arcades, AT&T Building. New York City.

Fig. 1.4. AT&T Building arcade. New York City.

block passage (figure 1.4). At Fifth Avenue, a formal entry to Trump Tower leads via a two-story interior passage to an opulent, six-story retail atrium (figure 1.5). The atrium is joined to a triangular, enclosed plaza-garden at the rear of the IBM Building. This place of tranquility, full of pedestrian amenities and large bamboo trees, is New York City's twentieth-century equivalent of a Roman piazza (figure 1.6). Additional enclosed exhibition spaces and lobbies can be found in the bases of the IBM Building, the AT&T Building, and the Corning Glass Works. Unfortunately, the design of these separate spaces is not well coordinated; and, therefore, they do not form an integrated ensemble. The baroque achievement of a direct relationship between interior and exterior space is somewhat evident in each separate project. For example, the entrance to the IBM Building is from a triangular plaza that leads through the elevator lobby to the triangular, enclosed plaza-garden—which, in turn, relates to another corner plaza. But overall, the concept of spatial reciprocity has not been well implemented.

Although the form, scale, and quality of public space has changed vastly from seventeenth-century baroque Rome to twentieth-century Manhattan, the contemporary spatial experience is quite similar. The perceptual and physical movement from exterior to interior is one of fluidity and continuity. The horizontal walking surface is significant, due to its functional, tactile role. Large areas of glass have increased greatly the experience of literal transparency—one can see through these spaces both horizontally and vertically. However, memory must still be utilized to relate separated spaces. Defined places of repose are still important to give a sense of orientation.

The critical disruption in the contemporary experience of spatial continuity between exterior and interior occurs at the entrance. In climates that are either

Fig. 1.5. Interior view, Trump Tower atrium. New York City.

Fig. 1.6. Interior view, IBM Plaza Garden. New York City.

cold and windy or hot and humid, the conditioned interior needs to be separated from the unconditioned exterior. This usually necessitates a wind lobby or a revolving door—creating a break in pedestrian movement. The glass curtain wall, with its sets of doors, is psychologically uninviting. The spaces within do not appear to be public, and the pedestrian must rely on sign graphics to determine accessibility. At the IBM Plaza Garden, there is an ingenious technical solution to the climate-separation problem. Exhaust air from the office tower's air-conditioning system is channeled through the garden, enabling the 33-foot-high (10-meter-high) glass sliding doors to remain open much of the time. Indoors and outdoors are thus directly linked without an intervening barrier. Another solution is an air door, which is proposed for many such schemes but often is eliminated due to energy costs. The problem of climate separation is significant in the design of most interior pedestrian places and must receive creative attention to improve the pedestrian's experience of continuity.

Perhaps the most dramatic difference between the seventeenth and twentieth centuries is in the nature and quality of the public spaces themselves. The technology of roof glazing has made possible the creation of places that are experientially interior but perceptually exterior. Such places are simultaneously interior-exterior—that is, closed and open. The atrium in Trump Tower and the IBM Garden Plaza are two examples. Moreover, mechanical means of conveyance, in the form of escalators and elevators with glass-walled cabs, have enhanced perception through vertical movement. Vantage points from high balconies and bridges are available in spaces with soaring ceilings made possible by steel space frames. Glass-enclosed public places provide a new range of spatial experience unavailable to previous generations of urban pedestrians. ∎

In 1490 Leonardo da Vinci envisioned an idealized city in which pedestrian walkways would be located above service streets and canals in order to promote efficiency and safety.[2] Although the conflict between traffic and pedestrians was not a great problem in da Vinci's era, it has certainly become one today; thus, da Vinci's solution increasingly is employed. However, it remains a difficult and costly system to utilize because the system requires specific points of connection between the pedestrian and the vehicular levels. (see pages 145–86).

Since the time of da Vinci, whenever conflicts between pedestrians and other forms of traffic have arisen, some planners have tried to separate them. According to Johann Friedrich Geist, this was one reason for the development of the nineteenth-century arcade:

> The arcade came into fashion because the street still existed in its medieval state. It had no sidewalk, was dirty, and was too dangerous for promenading and window shopping. Hence, around 1800 society was more developed than the public space at its disposal. The amount of traffic on the narrow Parisian streets took on dangerous and threatening proportions at this time. Carriages and carts battled pedestrians. This unequal conflict was fought on poorly paved streets without drainage which were transformed by rain into a sea of mud.[3]

In the twentieth century, the conflict became more serious—due to the amount and danger of motorized traffic. Cars, trucks, and buses killed and maimed pedestrians at an ever-increasing rate. Some utopian proposals were developed to separate pedestrians from traffic for their own protection, whereas the intention of other proposals was to speed the flow of traffic. Until the 1960s, however, the conflict between pedestrians and vehicles in city centers was not serious

enough to warrant physical solutions.

Pedestrianization is the creation of traffic-free zones exclusively for pedestrian circulation, use, and enjoyment. Every major city and most minor cities in Europe and North America now have downtown streets that have been closed to traffic to create pedestrian zones. This urban-design movement is thoroughly documented in Klaus Uhlig's *Pedestrian Areas*.[4] In Europe, pedestrian zones were established primarily to retain the cultural and commercial vitality of the central city. In America, pedestrianization was primarily a competitive reaction to the suburban shopping mall with its hazard-free pedestrian climate. In some cases, a street was simply closed to traffic, such as the Stroget in Copenhagen. In other cases, such as the Nicollet Mall in Minneapolis, the entire street was redesigned—with a new configuration, landscaping, and unique amenities (figure 1.7). The *malling* (the creation of pedestrian malls) of Europe and America has brought many pedestrians back to the downtown for shopping, culture, and entertainment.

The pedestrianization movement of the last three decades has had a profound impact upon the redevelopment of city centers. Once separated from their cars, people began again to recognize the joy of being pedestrians. The popularity of this type of leisure-time activity had been successfully demonstrated at suburban shopping malls and amusement parks. People could stroll at their leisure; they could stop to converse, to view sculpture, and to listen to performers. They could also window-shop or purchase something to eat or drink. Perhaps most importantly, people could once again begin to *see* their environment. The latter is significant because much of what people saw they did not like. Many architects had designed buildings devoid of detail, color, and texture that were to be viewed at a distance from automobiles. The historic buildings designed for pedestrians of ear-

Fig. 1.7. View of Nicollet Mall. Minneapolis.

lier eras had these qualities, and the public decided that such buildings should be saved and rehabilitated rather than torn down. The pedestrianization and preservation movements are thus undoubtedly related in their occurrence and intention.

The pedestrianization movement also forms the attitudinal background for the development of interior pedestrian places. Once people enjoy being pedestrians again, they can appreciate higher-quality pedestrian environments. These interior places, protected from the weather, offer a variety of amenities and a rich spatial experience. The experience of moving from a pedestrian zone into an interior place is more graceful than is coming in from a trafficked street—the spatial transition is not disruptive. In England, for example, most of the new enclosed shopping centers in urban areas are entered from previously established traffic-free zones. The Ridings Centre, in Wakefield, Yorkshire, is a good example, with its primary entry off of Kirkgate, the main pedestrianized shopping street opposite the historic cathedral precinct. The pedestrian can establish an orientation to the historic fabric before entering the new, somewhat disorienting, shopping center.

A new exterior-interior pedestrian zone should not be considered an island in the center city. Instead, the goal should be the creation of a totally conceived pedestrian environment. All aspects of urban planning that affect the pedestrian should be carefully considered, and the system should maintain complete continuity. Pedestrian areas can assume different forms—including covered but open passages, such as street arcades, and covered unenclosed spaces, such as markets. Squares are the nuclei within this urban pedestrian setting; they are places of activity concentration and spatial definition. Within the pedestrianization concept, interior places have a unique role. As Klaus Uhlig states:

Special forms of the covered city forum are more and more frequently being used as a component of social-cultural and leisure centres. It is not only the size and the building configuration, fixed and movable features, lighting and installations that are of interest in connection with pedestrian zones but above all the location as well. Indoor squares can form the natural focal point of pedestrian systems.[5] ■

In his book *A Tramp Abroad*, Mark Twain wrote of his visit to Milan's famed galleria in the year 1867 when it opened:

> We spent most of our time in the vast and beautiful Arcade or Gallery, or whatever it is called. Blocks of new buildings of the most sumptuous sort, rich with decoration and graced with statues, the streets between these blocks roofed over with glass at a great height, the pavements all of smooth and variegated marble, arranged in tasteful patterns—little tables all over these marble streets, people sitting at them eating, drinking or smoking—crowds of other people strolling by—such is the Arcade. I should like to live in it all my life. The windows of the sumptuous restaurants stand open, and one breakfasts and enjoys the passing show.[6]

Since its inception, the Galleria Vittorio Emanuele II (figure 1.8) has been the center of Milan's public social life and the place to see and be seen—the city's covered public forum. It is the locus for the Italian ritual of the *passeggiata*, or stroll—the time to meet and greet friends in a public setting. The Galleria's success lies not only in its superb design but also in its role as a connecting passage between Milan's two most significant structures: the Duomo, or the cathedral, and La Scala, the opera house. Owned by the municipal government, the Galleria is truly a public street. It remains open twenty-four hours a day and allows freedom of access to the full spectrum of society—from beggars to noblemen. In his superb social critique of urban streets, Bernard Rudofsky offers the following assessment of the Galleria:

> Evenings, when the place was bathed, as the newspapers put it, in an ocean of gaslight; when row upon row of marble tables appeared on the tessellated pavement, and the sound of orchestra music merged with the drone of people's voices, the Galleria achieved a near-apotheosis of the Italian street: a theater where actors and spectators merged and became indistinguishable from each other.[7]

The arcade and its related family of interior places have had a significant social role since their inception. Some recent examples, such as the Ford Foundation in New York City; the East Building of the National Gallery of Art in Washington, D.C.; San Francisco's Hyatt Hotel; and The Gallery in Philadelphia, have become valuable as urban gathering places. In 1980 William Whyte wrote that "the Crystal Court of the IDS Center is the best indoor space in the country, and it is used by a very wide mix of people. In mid-morning, the majority of the people sitting and talking are older people, and many of them are obviously of limited means."[8] Yet, the social functioning of many interior places is problematic. In many, there is a false, contrived sense of how people should gather or meet in a public setting—causing urban residents to long for the genuine experience. In his critique of the State of Illinois Center, Donlyn Lyndon writes:

> Watching people mill past objects they might buy, commit themselves to environments and foods of diverse origins, stand in line at the banking machine, or stare blankly at other people is not a way of learning much especially if what we see mirrors ourselves. What we wish to know and learn, what we wish to encounter, are qualities of mind and sympathy, to observe how others deal with each other, to learn of their works, to recognize lineage and invention, to be made aware of qualities that we might emulate or recommend to our children. We wish, in fact, to find through our encounters with the public some form of ethical thought.[9]

Fig. 1.8. Interior view, Galleria Vittorio Emanuele II. Milan.

One problem is accessibility. Doors that are necessary for climate control also provide the means for access control. Security guards at entrances can prohibit entry by those persons who do not fit a profile of acceptable dress or demeanor. Doors can also discourage entry by those persons who are self-conscious. The psychological barrier of a fixed, visually conspicuous entrance—whether guarded or not—can be a significant deterrent to access. Lockable entrances also enable the controlling authority to limit hours of opening. In New York City, public spaces created through zoning bonuses are mandated to remain open from 8 A.M. to 10 P.M., seven days a week. Privately controlled places usually are open eight to ten hours a day and often are closed on weekends.

Another critical problem is the lack of connection to the surrounding context of pedestrian places. Streets and squares work well as social places because they both connect to other pedestrian places and serve as locations for given purposes. Thus, they are places for people to pass through as well as places to go to. James Sanders observes that "it is this combination of conscious and casual use of the street that makes for its complex web of interactions and possibilities. With no casual use, is it any wonder that a mall, despite its fountains, trees and cafés, might somehow feel 'artificial.' "[10]

To be socially successful in terms of providing opportunities for encounters, interior pedestrian places must be directly linked to both the surrounding exterior and interior places. This design-and-location characteristic gives some assurance that there will be enough people passing through to make the area both lively and interesting. Comparing the new pedestrian places to their historic counterparts, we find that virtually all of the nineteenth-century arcades served as shortcuts—as midblock connectors between busy streets. They were successful in attracting people to pass through both purposefully and casually. This in turn provided opportunities for meeting, which enabled the arcades to become successful as social places.

When interior places are truly connecting, they attract a wide variety of people. They then retain a greater sense of publicness, since a public place must be equally available to everyone. Moreover, the impetus to assure public access is maintained. Having an interior place utilized by a wide variety of people is an important indicator of its social success. Critic Paul Goldberger, in his critique of the IBM Plaza Garden, (see figure 1.9) observes that "the mix of users of this spaces proves its success: the IBM Plaza, like the Tuileries, is able to absorb, at once, a flock of schoolchildren, bag-toting shoppers, museum-goers, tourists, businesspeople and a homeless man who sits quietly, at a corner table with all his gear piled beside him."[11] Interior places can also be successful in promoting encounters without having a wide variety of users; an example is the atrium in Trump Tower, which primarily attracts upper-class shoppers. However, these places cannot be considered truly public because of the restrictions on free access.

A critical spatial problem for many interior places is their detachment from the surrounding urban fabric. Conceptually, they are treated as destinations— as culs-de-sac where the pedestrian enters and leaves by the same door. After the initial period of attraction, such places may lose pedestrian traffic. When an interior place is designed as an end in itself, an opportunity to reinforce the pedestrian network is lost. By being connected, however, every element can contribute to the city's vitality. Effective, efficient, and enlivening pedestrian circulation that maintains exterior-to-interior continuity should be the goal of urban designers.

In his critique of modern architecture, *Complexity and Contradiction in Architecture*, Robert Venturi writes:

Another crutch of Modern architecture is the piazza compulsion derived from our justifiable love of Ital-

Fig. 1.9. Interior view, IBM Plaza Garden. New York City.

ian towns. But the open piazza is seldom appropriate for an American city today except as a convenience for pedestrians for diagonal short-cuts. The piazza, in fact, is "un-American." Americans feel uncomfortable sitting in a square: they should be working at the office or home with the family looking at television. Chores around the house or the weekend drive have replaced the *passeggiate*.[12]

Venturi's dismissal of the open piazza as un-American, although overstated, does have an element of truth. Spending time in a piazza has, in the American mind, always been considered somewhat akin to loitering. Americans need to be purposefully occupied while in public places. This is a subtle but pervasive reason for the high utilization of interior places in the United States. It is somehow more justifiable to spend time in a place where one can be shopping, having lunch, or listening to a concert. It is not the same as lingering aimlessly at a street corner where there is no control over the kinds of social encounters possible. The street, and by extension the plaza, have developed a negative connotation in the American psyche—as illustrated by the terms *streetwise*, *street life*, *street crime*, *streetwalker*, and *street people*.

The social role of public space in America at the end of the twentieth century is undergoing a serious reexamination. Is a public square a space "which makes a community a community and not merely an aggregate of individuals . . . a gathering place for the people, humanizing them by mutual contact," as Paul Zucker writes?[13] Or, is it "a manifestation of the local social order, of the relationship between citizens and between citizens and the authority of the state," as J. B. Jackson states?[14] Surely, the contemporary public space represents a significant departure from Aristotle's ideal public square where nothing could be bought or sold—only discussion and the exchange of ideas could take place.[15] Contemporary public spaces are used less for significant political or social activities than they are for commercial and entertainment activities. The recognition of this reality leads to an even more fundamental question about the nature of public life. Richard Sennett claims that American culture has lost a commitment to public life and has substituted the private life such that it now is an end in itself.[16] The public life that remains has become a matter of formal obligation. As Nathan Glazer states in the introduction to *The Public Face of Architecture*, "we are also in the grip of a deep intellectual confusion about the nature of public life that has paralyzed attempts to cope with those conditions."[17]

Western culture has changed. Public places today do not serve the same social role that they did in the European or American cities of past eras. Within this changing order, interior places are developing a significant role as new kinds of gathering places for varied segments of the population: Enclosed suburban shopping malls provide places for teen-agers to hang-out on a Friday night and places for mothers with small children to meet during the day. Hotel atria serve as meeting places for conventioneers and for people out on the town. Downtown retail centers provide opportunities for business people to have lunch during the week and for tourists and visitors to engage in recreational shopping on the weekend. Atria in office buildings are spaces where employees can meet during breaks from work and where social occasions can occur. These interior places serve vital social roles, albeit different ones from traditional expectations. These roles in conjunction with the evolving roles of exterior places must complement each other to provide a locus for our future public social life. ■

In 1950 Buckminster Fuller developed a futuristic proposal to cover midtown Manhattan with a geodesic dome sheathed with polarizing glass. Underneath this vast structure, weather would no longer be an issue in influencing people's activities—all precipitation, wind, dust, and changes in air temperature would be eliminated. Daylight would illuminate the domed city; but direct sun would be controlled by the polarized surface, thus reducing heat gain. The earth's diurnal cycles of dark and light would remain. In addition to saving energy, Fuller stated that "controlling the environment through domes offers the enormous advantages of the extraversion of privacy and the introversion of the community."[18] Although Fuller's dome was but a futuristic dream, a smaller dome (300 feet [91 meters] in diameter) was designed and built as the United States Pavilion at Expo '67 in Montreal (figure 1.10). The dome's space-frame structure of steel pipe, joined by cast-steel hubs, was covered with a transparent acrylic skin. A vast network of triangular, motorized interior shades were computer controlled to keep out the direct sun. The dome had a monorail running through it and featured the world's highest escalator.

Domes have been used for climate control in many circumstances. For example, professional baseball and football in the United States are played for the enjoyment of the television audience and the spectators. Since these games were invented, they have been played outdoors on natural turf. But inclement or uncomfortable weather discourages attendance and can distort the quality of the television presentation. Thus, in 1964 in Houston, the first domed stadium—642 feet (196 meters) in diameter and 213 feet (65 meters) high with a roof of steel ribs

Fig. 1.10. Exterior view, United States Pavilion, Expo '67. Montreal.

and skylights—was built. The gigantic Astrodome, which seats 66,000 spectators, is artificially air-conditioned and features an artificial playing surface—dubbed *Astro-turf*. Unfortunately, the original dark-and-light ceiling pattern made it difficult for baseball players to catch fly balls—requiring the glare from the skylights to be reduced by painting over them. Not to be outdone, the city of New Orleans decided to build an even larger domed stadium—the Superdome. This 680-foot-diameter (207-meter-diameter) colossus seats 82,000 spectators under one roof—for America's greatest sports event, the Super Bowl (figure 1.11). Other domed stadiums have been built in Pontiac, Michigan; Seattle; Indianapolis; and Minneapolis. Others are planned in San Antonio and Atlanta. Many sports fans decry the playing of baseball and football on artificial turf in controlled environments, claiming that these condi-

tions change the very nature of the games. But the eternal quest to eliminate weather as an activity deterrent continues to be a strong motivation.

One of mankind's longstanding architectural ambitions has been to create structures for public gathering and use that include the positive aspects of the natural environment but eliminate the negative aspects. Daylighting and views are the positive aspects. Changes in air temperature, wind, dust, and precipitation in all forms are the negative aspects. Once these were controlled, a man-made climate could be substituted that provides the constant characteristics of air quality amenable to mankind's activities.

The creation of vast public buildings with controlled interior climates was first made possible in the nineteenth century with the invention of steel structures combined with glazing technology. Great conservatories, such as the Palm House

Fig. 1.11. Interior view, Superdome. New Orleans.

at Kew Gardens in London (1845–48), designed by Richard Turner, allowed exotic trees and plants to be grown in harsh northern climates. Railroad stations—such as King's Cross Station in London, designed by Lewis Cubitt and built in 1851, with its two semicircular shed roofs (each 105 feet wide and 280 feet long [32 meters by 85 meters])—permitted passengers to get on and off trains undercover (figure 1.12). Exhibition halls, such

as the Galerie des Machines (1889) in Paris, designed by C.-L.-F. Dutert, enabled throngs of people to view collections of new machinery within a controlled setting. Markets, such as Paris's Les Halles Centrales (1853–58), designed by Victor Baltard, provided large systems of food stalls protected from the rain and wind. The greatest example was Joseph Paxton's Crystal Palace in London (1851), an international exhibition hall of unprecedented scale (1,848 feet long, 456 feet wide, and 108 feet high [563 by 139 by 33 meters]) made of prefabricated iron members and sheathed in glass (figure 1.13)[19].

An interior pedestrian place can be completely or partially enclosed so as to separate it from the external environment. Most are completely weatherproof, with controlled access through doors. Others are partially covered with a roof, leaving the sides open. Such a design is used for historic fish-and-produce markets. Many of the early shopping arcades were actually covered streets, either without doors or with folding gates. An

Fig. 1.12. Interior view of train shed, King's Cross Station. London.

Fig. 1.13. Exterior view, Crystal Palace. London.

Fig. 1.14. Street view, Leadenhall Market. London.

interesting example of a market and an arcade combined is Leadenhall Market in London (1881), which is a system of covered public streets accommodating both pedestrians and vehicles (figure 1.14). Pedestrian places are traditionally external; therefore, interior places must strongly relate to them in both physical and perceptual access in order to induce use. Thus, the need for large areas of transparency in the roof and/or the walls to admit daylight and to create reciprocal visual access.

In recent decades, there has been a resurgence of interest in creating enclosed public places. Shopping malls—both suburban and urban—are the most ubiquitous example, with public circulation space joining constellations of department stores and shops, allowing freedom of access in a leisurely setting. Outdoor courtyards of hotels, office buildings, museums, and hospitals have been covered to create weather-controlled atria. In some cities, public spaces have been covered to create enclosed public plazas that unite several buildings, such as the Crystal Court at IDS Center in Minneapolis. These places are then con-

nected to other buildings by a system of pedestrian bridges or underground concourses. The result is that the pedestrian can conduct an entire day of business or shopping activities inside.

Weather protection is one of the primary motivations behind the contemporary trend to create interior places. People prefer not to struggle with the climate if it is not necessary. It is no accident that Disneyland is in southern California and Disneyworld is in northern Florida. These are climates that offer a minimum of human discomfort and a constancy that allows activities to take place with freedom. Comfort and convenience are important pedestrian objectives, and those places that offer them have an advantage over those that do not. This is one of the primary reasons the enclosed shopping center has been such a pervasive commercial success in the United States.

For pedestrians, comfort and convenience are the most important benefits of weather control. Comfort is the result of a constant air temperature, a lack of wind, and the elimination of precipitation. Dust and fumes from outdoor sources along with noise from traffic or construction are also eliminated. Convenience results from the ability to schedule activities without depending on the weather. There are, however, other considerations: Safety from falling or slipping due to ice and snow or rain are important factors for children, the elderly, and the handicapped. Events such as concerts, exhibitions, and public occasions can be conducted with certainty. A wider range of amenities is possible in the form of artworks, water features, gardens, and aviaries. There is also a psychological benefit to be derived from being in a protected environment. The freedom from stress enables the pedestrian to concentrate on participating in and enjoying the activity of the moment. This yields a positive experience, making these places memorable so as to induce return visits.

In an evaluation of the public spaces associated with the AT&T Building and the IBM Building, Paul Goldberger deems the IBM Plaza Garden to be "one of the finest urban spaces in New York." The Plaza Garden "is remarkably serene" with the city's "activity visible but its sounds unheard." The multitude of movable chairs within a forest of bamboo trees attracts "a mix of users which proves its success." Goldberger continues:

> On the same recent sunny autumn morning that this range of people were observed at IBM, the public seating areas that are set into the base of the AT&T Building, which is just across 56th Street from IBM, were virtually empty. It is no mystery—the high, open granite arcades at the base of this tower are noisy and windy, and they get only moderate sun.

Indoor pedestrian places are simply more user friendly; and, as Goldberger admits, "it is much harder to do successful outdoor space than indoor."[20]

If weather protection is the primary reason for the proliferation of interior urban places, one would expect the most extensive systems in locations with the most unaccommodating climates. The evidence of actual geographic locations generally supports this proposition. The enclosed-mall shopping center was first created by Victor Gruen at Southdale Center near Minneapolis. The northern cities of Minneapolis, St. Paul, Milwaukee, Toronto, and Montreal have the most extensive interior pedestrian systems. In terms of hot and humid climates, Atlanta and Houston have equivalent interior pedestrian networks. However, there are many examples of these kinds of places in locations where the climate is not as inhospitable, such as Washington, D.C., and San Francisco. Indeed, there are reasons other than the weather for creating interior pedestrian places.

From both the merchant's and the owner's points of view, there is a marketing benefit derived from having a captive audience. Shoppers in hospitable, enclosed environments are put at ease; therefore, they can enjoy the place and engage in shopping as a leisure-time activity. Entertainment, exhibitions, and events are provided as attractions to induce participation. In addition, the ambience creates an overall image for the shopping center that can be used for marketing. The kinds of shops, their quality level, the appearance of the shop fronts, and their placement within the center are carefully considered to achieve the maximum sales potential. The ability of the shopping center as a whole to attract shoppers is much greater than the sum of the individual shops, and the design of the public indoor space with its amenities is an intrinsic part of this attraction.

Yet, the trend to interiorize pedestrian places as a means of escaping the vagaries of the weather can negate some of the joys of life. Who among us has not enjoyed a balmy spring afternoon or a sunny, brisk fall morning? Some pedestrians enjoy the romance of walking in the rain or strolling in the snow. Many people welcome the change of seasons, for it is a profound way of acknowledging the passing of time. Some of these life experiences are being lost or gradually reduced in number. The proliferation of interior places and their connection into vast systems has made it possible for the urban dweller to spend days in artificially controlled environments without venturing outdoors. The nature of urban pedestrian life has changed, and many regard this change as qualitatively negative. For them and all others, the options should remain to traverse and experience both indoor and outdoor pedestrian spaces without constraint. ■

Most of the exterior and interior pedestrian places recently created in the United States have been financed, constructed, owned, and managed privately. This is a significant departure from previous eras when the public sector was responsible for creating parks, squares, and boulevards. Both the political and financial support for this activity have been displaced to education, public safety, public works, and social programs.

One significant motivation for the privatization of pedestrian space is the rapid increase during the last two decades in street crime. In the centers of some cities, street crime is, in fact, a threat to the safety of pedestrians. However, the fear of street crime, although sometimes irrational, can be an even stronger deterrent to pedestrian activity than its actual presence—especially at night. The media tend to give extensive coverage to criminal events and/or to feature crime stories, thereby exaggerating the real threat. Enclosed pedestrian places are safe havens from street crime, particularly if they can be reached directly from adjacent parking garages. Within, there are the ever-present guards who give a sense of security. Since these are usually private places, the guards can

screen the individuals at the entrances, thereby restricting suspicious persons.

Laws of private property rights give owners considerable control over both the access to and the use of interior places, as long as they conform to zoning and building codes. Although individuals cannot absolutely be denied access, they can be scrutinized and evicted if they violate any of the laws of use—such as loitering, sleeping, or littering. Individuals also may be encouraged to leave or move by security personnel. At Eaton Centre in Toronto, police give trespassing tickets to people for "undesirable" behaviors. In 1985 alone, they removed thirty thousand so-called undesirables.[21] Other managements, such as Citicorp in New York City (figure 1.15), are more tolerant of customers and noncustomers in their retail atrium—granting them equal privilege to use the space and its facilities. The IBM Plaza Garden is another interior place where security guards, through the management's direction, tolerate the presence of well-behaved street people.

The United States Constitution guarantees the rights of free assembly and free speech in public places owned by governmental entities. Whether these same rights are extended to privately owned areas provided as places for public use has been the subject of changing interpretation. The Supreme Court initially extended these constitutional protections to private land that assumes a public role or function. However, the court later reinterpreted this decision to mean that this form of freedom of speech could be guaranteed by state constitutions. Thus, the courts of California and four other states have interpreted their constitution in the following manner:

These state courts have recognized the necessity to adjust old definitions in order to maintain the central value of a liberal city. The courts have identified shopping malls,

Fig. 1.15. Social activity, Citicorp. New York City.

corporate office parks, and campuses of private universities as new public places in the American metropolis and they have endeavored to maintain them as the open and essential communications nodes which they in fact are.[22]

Although most commercial development is indeed private, it is usually undertaken with some form of direct or indirect public support. Indirect support might take the form of publicly constructed parking, roads, or transit systems. Direct support might take the form of tax abatements, land-cost write-downs, land leases, or zoning bonuses. Many of the new arcades, retail malls, and atria in New York City are a direct result of a zoning bonus system that permits developers to add up to 20 percent more area to their projects if they include pedestrian spaces. These places must be open from 8 A.M. to 10 P.M. They must be available for all users and must include a performance or exhibition program. In these cases of public support, there should remain legal assurances of public access and free speech.

There are means other than legal or financial for forging public-private partnerships in the creation and operation of interior pedestrian places. Although the buildings surrounding Milan's Galleria Vittorio Emanuele II are privately owned, the glass-covered arcade itself is owned by the municipal government; thus assuring the arcade's perpetuity as a public pedestrian street. At Greenville Commons in Greenville, South Carolina, an eight-story atrium spatially unites a hotel, an office building, and a convention center. In an agreement between the city, which owns it, and Hyatt Hotels, which manages it, the atrium serves as part of the hotel's lobby and as a public place. These examples are the exception rather than the rule. Arrangements such as these need to be encouraged because pub-lic-private partnerships allow the public greater leverage in controlling the use of and access to these places.

Until the 1970s, most central-business districts were declining in environmental quality. The districts' inhospitable exterior environments were characteristically dilapidated, unsafe, noisy, polluted, and littered. The institutions and corporations building in these areas often developed a defensive posture, turning inward to control their settings. This situation was similar to the circumstances that led to introversion in design in some cities at the end of the nineteenth century. In his book *Pride of Place*, Robert A. M. Stern points to this factor:

The Auditorium Building insulated Chicagoans from the packed street of the business district, from the screeching trains of its elevated Loop, from the vast railyards that lined the shore of lake Michigan. The loggia, originally designed as a grand porch open to the lakefront, almost immediately had to be enclosed in glass to protect the guests from the sooty exhaust of the coal-burning trains thundering along the shore and to further sustain its function as a cultural oasis. The Auditorium was a city within a city that offered the environmental and social control unattainable in the real metropolis outside.[23]

From a developer's point of view, there can be great financial risk in the uncertainty of the surrounding context. In an area that is redeveloping or changing, where the context is unstable, it is safer to become introverted—that is, to create your own context. An interior public space can serve as a reliable internal context that provides a controlled setting for arrival, circulation, and views.

In summary, interior places can be private, semi-public, or public in terms of

Fig. 1.16. Atrium view, State of Illinois Center. Chicago.

their ownership and concomitant access rights. Private entities may own buildings that include these kinds of spaces exclusively for the use of employees or guests; they may also choose to make these spaces available for conditional public use, such as a hotel atrium. Privately owned shopping centers may be completely available for public use. In mixed-use projects, only the public portions may generally be accessible, with a security check at the entry to the private portion. Finally, public entities can and do own and operate interior places that are open to the public on a continuous or regular basis. The most notable recent example is the State of Illinois Center in Chicago, which combines retail activities, eating facilities, public functions, and public offices in one building designed around an awesome rotunda-atrium (figure 1.16).

There are significant concerns with the trend toward the privatization of interior pedestrian places; overcommercialization is the most apparent. The motives to sell retail goods to the public and/or extract high rental rates from the tenants are obvious in many cases. Amenities may be provided only in token form to act as inducements or as civil authorities or laws require. As James Sanders states in his critique of recent public places:

> Notwithstanding their lack of civic grandeur, these new spaces are solving many of the stubborn, pragmatic problems of security, climate control, and maintenance that have previously driven a wedge between economic and real-estate practicality and urban graciousness. This crop of spaces may be on the edge of a new generation that will reinforce the strides made in turning our conception of public space inside-out: creating civic places at the inside of buildings.[24] ∎

The critique and evaluation of contemporary interior pedestrian places that follows is based on several well-considered criteria of what constitutes successful design: First, the spaces should be readily accessible from existing exterior places. This can be accomplished through direct physical linkage and/or visual transparency. Entrances and exits are the critical points whether at street level or above, or whether related to a sidewalk or urban square. Second, successful interior places should be legible and imageable for purposes of circulation and orientation. Coherent spatial form and simple plan geometry will aid in achieving comprehensible circulation patterns. A strong spatial concept executed with consistent structural and architectural expression will aid in orientation. Third, the interior places should serve a public pedestrian purpose. They should contain pedestrian amenities and provide opportunities for socializing and public occasion.

Successful urban design and development is the by-product of an integration between the old and the new, between the exterior and the interior, and between the public and the private. In several cities, new private interior places in the form of galleries, atria, skyways, and concourses have been related by design to each other to form integrated networks. These, in turn, have been linked to existing exterior public streets, plazas, and parks—resulting in enjoyable and vital urban centers. The future design and planning of urban pedestrian systems must follow these positive examples, which foster the integration of urban architecture and urban spaces. ■

CHAPTER 2

COMMERCIAL PLACES

More interior pedestrian places are devoted to commercial use—usually retail sales—than to any other purpose. Interior places lend themselves naturally to shopping, since they provide sheltered environments conducive to purchasing goods, foods, and services. In actuality, the purchases do not occur in the pedestrian place but rather in the establishments associated with it. The interior place functions as an integrator of shops. It gives them a visible location to present themselves to the public.

The predominantly commercial use of interior places follows the historical precedent set by the arcades and gallerias constructed at the beginning of the nineteenth century. These successful prototypes were viewed as protected pedestrian adjuncts to the shopping street.

The commercial use of the street was brought inside, thus providing the genesis of a place type that has evolved to the present day. In *Arcades*, Johann Friedrich Geist explains that

> the illusory element of the arcade is the space within its confines: an intended exterior is made interior; the facade with exterior architecture is drawn into the enclosed space. The space of the arcade differs from the street only in its glass roof, symmetrical facades, and exclusively pedestrian walkway.[1]

Interior pedestrian places serve as commercial spaces in many varied forms, including commercial arcades and gallerias, urban shopping centers, festival marketplaces, and multiuse centers. ■

ARCADES AND GALLERIAS

The *arcade*, a covered passage contiguous with the street but devoted to the use of pedestrians, is a design concept appropriate to its context—the urban center. When the pedestrian encounters this spatial phenomenon, he or she understands it intuitively—for the arcade works with the pedestrian's experience of the city as a series of continuous, flowing spaces. The continuity of facades, natural light, shop fronts, and pavement draws the pedestrian into the arcade; and the discovery that the arcade is free from traffic and inclement weather encourages the pedestrian to return. What a wonderful environment for shopping, strolling, and socializing—for enjoying the pleasures of urban life (see plate 1).

The arcade was invented in Paris in the early part of the nineteenth century as the solution to two particular problems: First, the streets were inhospitable to pedestrians; sidewalks did not exist; and the volume of horse-drawn traffic created dirty, chaotic streets. Second, burgeoning industrial development had produced large quantities of consumer luxury goods, which necessitated new means for marketing and selling them. The traditional market places could not satisfy the new demand for better distribution, faster sales, and better promotion. Moreover, the new technology of roof glazing supported by ironwork afforded a new design opportunity. The arcade was designed as a glass-covered passage, lined with shops on both sides. (The interior arcade is distinct from the street arcade, which runs parallel to the street and is open on one side.) The French use the term *galerie*, which derives from the gallery of a palace, or the more prosaic term *passage*. *Galleria*, the term used by the Italians, today connotes a larger scale and a more elegant shopping arcade.

Johann Friedrich Geist enumerated the arcade's characteristics in his book *Arcades* (1983) as summarized below:

1. Access to the interior of a block. The arcade system allowed building speculators to build more densely by providing pedestrian access to commercial space behind street frontages.

2. Public space on private property. This covered space provided public pedestrian access. It derived from earlier street-side pedestrian spaces such as loggias, porticoes, and colonnades.

3. Symmetrical street space. Since both sides had the same facades, the space between was better defined. Arcade facades had the character of urban street facades, although the repetitive opposition made the arcade formally different from a typical commercial street.

4. Skylit space. Either a glass roof or clerestories simultaneously provided adequate natural lighting and weather protection. The transparent glass roof fostered the perceptual relationship with the exterior street.

5. A system of access. The arcade resembled a street in that the space provided access to the building units that defined its sides. Each party wall unit had its own address and entry on this interior street, with internal stairs providing access to upper floors. Later forms of shopping arcades had public stairs between units and street-level entrances to provide access to upper-level galleries.

6. A form of organizing retail trade. The arcade as an association of independent shops was the precursor for the department store and shopping center, subsequent forms of centralized commercial development.

7. A space of transition. The arcade was always a passageway for pedestrian promenade between commercial streets. The design of street entrances was of great importance to invite or discourage appropriate patrons.[2]

Geist's list of characteristics is useful, for it provides a ready basis for understanding the evolution of the arcade.

The architectural evolution of the arcade spanned the nineteenth century. They were built initially in the two great urban centers of Paris and London, and their popularity expanded first to many other European cities and then to a few cities in the United States. The earliest examples at the beginning of the nineteenth century were narrow in width (less than 3 meters [ten feet]), had poor daylighting, and were made of humble materials—usually wood and plaster. These early arcades were composed of independently accessible building units, usually with an apartment located above

Fig. 2.1. Interior view, Passage du Caire. Paris.

Fig. 2.2. Entrance, Passage du Caire. Paris.

a shop. A good example is the Passage du Caire, built in 1799 in Paris, which, although modest in section, is the longest of the Parisian arcades—with a total developed length of 370 meters, (1,214 feet) served by six entrances (figure 2.1). Located in a bustling but economically modest business area of the city, this unpretentious arcade has direct gated entries from the streets (figure 2.2). The small shops facing onto the 2.7-meter-wide (9-foot-wide) arcade have been altered innumerable times, thus forming a collage of facades of different eras.

Also from this early period is the Burlington Arcade, built in 1819 in the Mayfair section of London. This particular arcade influenced the development of many of the subsequent arcades in England because of its pedestrian scale and the clarity of its design expression. The main entrance on Picadilly Street has been redesigned several times, with the present version being in vulgar contrast to the arcade's refined Regency interior. The Burlington Arcade is a simple, straight, narrow passage. It is 180 meters (591 feet) long, 3.7 meters (12 feet) wide, two stories high and is lined with shallow-depth shops with apartments above. In order to ameliorate the effect of the long, narrow, sloping space, architect Samuel Ware divided it into seventeen sections, with firewalls and archways across the arcade. The shops, of varying widths, are articulated with bay-front shop windows, which modulate the facades and perceptually shorten the length (see plate 2). The overall effect is one of intimate scale, created by mahogany shop fronts located below white-painted bay windows and a central row of hanging lanterns and planters. The Burlington Arcade remains in high use as a location for fashionable shops that attract upper-class patrons and as a place for leisurely strolling.

During the years 1820 to 1840, many new arcades were built by real-estate speculators in Paris and in other mercantile cities of Europe. For example, fifteen new arcades were built in Paris in which the architectural possibilities in plan geometry, sectional profile, facade articulation, and skylight structure were explored and developed. By designing variations on the fundamental linear form, the architects of that time contributed to the sophisticated evolution of this building type. The structural possibilities of iron-and-glass roofs with skylights were exploited in the form of wider arcades with interesting roof profiles, which often included domes and rotundas. Geist recounts that by the year 1830

the arcade was complete; all its parts were fully developed. Longitudinal space, central space, frontal house, inner and exterior facades, continuous glass vault, and glass

dome were established as the characteristics of a building type which itself became an indispensable means of opening up public space.[3]

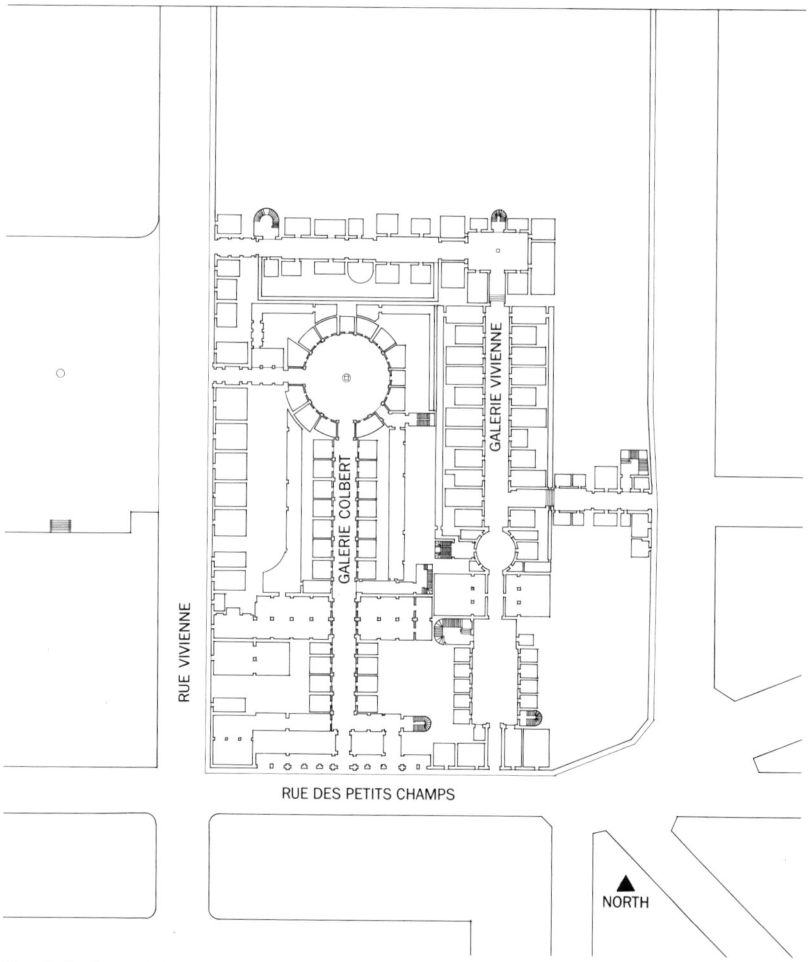

Two of the best examples from this high era of the arcade are located in the same block near the Parisian Palais Royal. The Galerie Vivienne and the Galerie Colbert were built as competitors in the years 1825 and 1826. Both incorporate existing buildings, have principal entrances on the rue des Petits Champs, are L-shaped in plan, and include nodal spaces. The Galerie Vivienne, designed by François Jacques Delannoy, unites three existing buildings in a linked sequence of defined spaces of different proportions and forms (figure 2.3). The arcade was carefully designed with facades defined by a series of arched, wooden shop fronts and a roof spanned by transverse buttresses supporting thinly gridded skylights. The composition is everywhere enriched with moldings, ornaments, and reliefs—with the whole resting on a mosaic floor (see plate 3).

The Galerie Colbert, built in the following year by architect Jean Billaud, has a main entrance off a recessed street arcade—a transitional space between the sidewalk and the enclosed space. The arcade contains two linear sections that lead to the rotunda at the bend in the plan. This dramatic space dominates the composition with its scale (17 meters [56 feet] in diameter) and its conical, radial-ribbed, glazed roof (see plate 4). The arched-facade bays of the arcade continue around the rotunda with a rhythm of yellow marble columns and Corinthian capitals. The simple gridding of the marble floors and the wooden shop fronts stand in contrast to the rich decoration of surfaces and the fanciful bronze candelabra of globe lamps. Fortunately, both of these arcades have been handsomely restored and are worthy of a visit by those who want to experience this historic building type in active use.

Fig. 2.3. Ground-level plans, Galerie Vivienne and Galerie Colbert. Paris.

Fig. 2.4. Interior view, Weybosset Arcade. Providence, Rhode Island.

During this period, many arcades also were built in England; and a few were built in the United States. Since most were not used for housing, each floor had to have gallery access for separate commercial uses. This was the scheme for the arcade built in Philadelphia on Chestnut Street in 1826–27 (demolished in 1863) and designed by John Haviland and for the Weybosset Arcade in Providence, Rhode Island, built in 1828 and designed by Russell Warren and James Bucklin (figure 2.4). The latter had street entrances disguised by temple-front facades on Weybosset and Westminster streets. The linear interior of the Weybosset Arcade is 13 feet (4 meters) wide on the ground floor, increasing in width at the second-floor gallery and again at the third-floor gallery. Thus, all galleries and shop fronts are directly illuminated by the continuous gabled skylight. (The original wood-framed skylight was replaced with steel when the arcade was renovated in 1979.) This historic arcade continues to serve as a thriving urban shopping center, thus illustrating the contemporary viability of this building type.

From about 1840 on, the design and construction of arcades in Paris began to diminish. Poor locations had caused some financial failures, and the creation of sidewalks no longer justified their need as safe pedestrian passages. The era of the grand Parisian boulevard came into being, and arcades could no longer be built without permission. One other interesting Parisian urban design development was the construction in 1846 of the Passage Verdeau. This *passage* links up with the Passage Jouffroy, constructed in 1845–46, which extended the earlier, 1800 system of the Passage des Panoramas to the north across the boulevard Montmartre. The total 350-meter (1,148 foot) length of these three arcades, with entrances opposite each other across major streets, was developed over half a century. They form a portion of a system of independent public pedestrian passages that some urban designers have envisioned in idealized city plans (figure 2.5).

The arcade concept continued to develop in other European cities, most notably in Brussels where several arcades were built. In 1846–47 the Galeries St.-Hubert was designed and constructed by Jean Pierre Cluysenaar—the first of the monumental arcades to be built with public support. Historian Margaret MacKeith, in *The History and Conservation of Shopping Arcades*, writes:

> During the arcade's early years it was open to the public from 8:00 A.M. to 8:00 P.M. with an entrance fee of 25 cents on Sundays and Thursdays and 10 cents on the other five days. There were shops, a theatre, a casino, houses and apartments. Clubs and newspaper offices were opened and artistic and literary meetings attracted intellectuals including such refugees as Victor Hugo and Alexandre Dumas. During its first thirty years it was the centre of city life.[4]

The Galeries St.-Hubert was the precursor for what most historians and critics consider to be the high point of arcade design—the Galleria Vittorio Emanuele II, built in 1865–77 in Milan. Its architect, Giuseppe Mengoni, did indeed meet with Cluysenaar in Brussels in the 1860s. The relationship between the two arcades is based more on concept and scale rather than on direct design. In Mengoni's design, which employs the monumental scale of imperial Rome, the concept of the arcade as a nineteenth-century building type reached its zenith of development. This arcade building was built as much for civic and commercial purposes as it was to serve as a symbol of Italy's emergence as a unified nation (thus, its naming after King Vittorio Emanuele II). The city of Milan owned the project, which was financed by a Brit-

ish development company and was built by Italian craftsmen. The completion of the Galleria in Milan resulted in a competition with the other Italian cities of Genoa, Turin, and Naples to build equal, if not grander, arcades. MacKeith observes that "it is this series of great Italian arcades, each striving for monumentality on a Roman scale, which has become permanently connected in our minds with the concept of the arcade."[5]

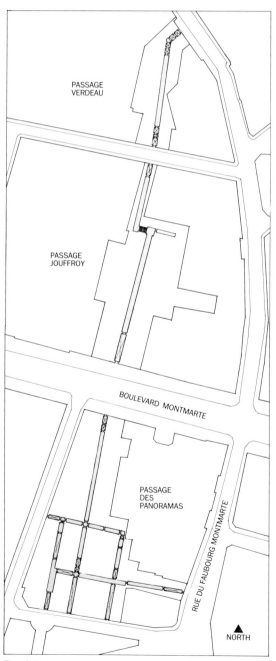

Fig. 2.5. Urban site plan, Passage des Panoramas, Passage Jouffroy, and Passage Verdeau. Paris.

One reason for the success of the Galleria Vittorio Emanuele II was its fulfillment of an important civic-design role: it created a covered passage connecting the two most important places in the city—the Piazza del Duomo and the Piazza della Scala, the locations of the cathedral and the opera house. This location assured a constant flow of pedestrians who would utilize the restaurants and shops along the arcade's length. But it was intended to be more than a passage, for the octagonal rotunda at the juncture made this galleria also a place unto itself (figure 2.6). This central space—being a place for people to meet and gather—was analogous to the piazzas at either entrance. The ambience and vitality of the Galleria has been celebrated by numerous distinguished visitors, and to this day it remains the public social center of Milan. (See pages 18–21).

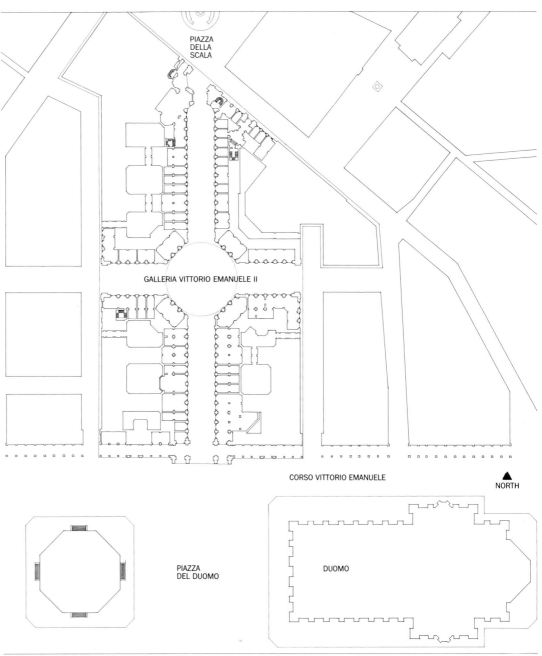

Fig. 2.6. Ground-level plan, Galleria Vittorio Emanuele II. Milan.

The Galleria Vittorio Emanuele II is also a significant architectural achievement. The entrance from the Piazza del Duomo is through a heroic, three-part triumphal arch that forms part of a street arcade (figure 2.7). The interior facades are composed of highly articulated narrow bays—with an arcade motif at the lower floor, a continuous balcony at the top of the third floor, and sculptural figures at each column line above. The seven floors of this arcade are disguised by the facade design to achieve larger scale proportions. The perforated, arched beams support a glazed roof that spans the 48-foot-wide, 96-foot-high (14.6 by 29 meters) concourse with great lightness and transparency. In total, the Galleria contains 1,260 rooms. The shops and restaurants are located on the ground floor and mezzanine; clubs and studios are located on the taller third floor; and the residences, located on the upper four floors, are accessed via stairs reached from courtyards within the block. Among the more striking features is the marble mosaic floor—a richly patterned walking surface of noble quality devoted to the urban pedestrian. MacKeith offers the following assessment of the Galleria:

Fig. 2.7. Exterior view, Galleria Vittorio Emanuele II. Milan.

There are no advertisements to distract the eye but restaurants and superior pavement cafés spill out into the arcade. At night the effect is extraordinary, with light from table lamps and the simple globes suspended from wrought iron brackets on each pilaster. The whole is so far removed from the early Parisian arcades in scale and architecture, that only the retail uses of the building, the free movement of pedestrians and glass in the roof are common to both. The arcade was the high point in the development of the building type.[6]

After completion of the Galleria, the arcade as a building type changed from a place of civic purpose to one of commercial venture. The catalyst was the rapid industrial growth at the turn of the century, which required even higher levels of commercial access by the expanding working classes. The arcades built in the industrial cities of England are smaller in scale and shorter in length than the previous examples, and they are integrated with the pattern of exterior shopping streets. The system of arcades in Leeds is a particularly good example because of the contiguity of the individual arcades. Queen's Arcade (1889), Thornton's Arcade (1878), County Arcade (1900), and Cross Arcade (1900) are pleasant interior shopping streets. They are generally two stories high, are lined with small shops, and connect major exterior shopping streets. The lengthy County Arcade (120 meters [394 feet] long), with its barrel-vaulted skylight, wrought-iron galleries, glazed central dome, and inviting lattice-work entrance arches, has the most Victorian design elaboration (figure 2.8).

The Cleveland Arcade is one of the last great nineteenth-century examples of this building type. It both represents the culmination of the Victorian commercial arcade and establishes a model for the

Fig. 2.8. Interior view, County Arcade. Leeds, England.

twentieth century. Built between two of Cleveland's main shopping streets (Euclid and Superior avenues, which are 4 meters (13 feet) apart in topographic level), the arcade is fronted by the nine-story office buildings located on these streets (figure 2.9) The entry to the arcade is through these buildings, which, by their presence, create an indirect relationship between the arcade and the streets. This gigantic arcade (390 feet [119 meters] long, 103 feet [31.4 meters] wide, and 104 feet [31.7 meters] high) has five levels—each with continuous galleries that step outward in three places so that the 60-foot-wide [18.3 meter-wide] skylight roof provides an abundance of direct daylight (see plate 5). The elaborate roof structure consists of girders supported on arches that rest on columns with griffin-headed brackets. The details are neither bland nor overdone and display a certain turn-of-the-century charm. Following its complete restoration, the arcade today is used much as it was in 1890: the bottom two floors are filled with shops and restaurants, and the upper three floors are reserved for small offices. As MacKeith writes, "Tables and chairs have been placed around the first floor balcony and loitering is encouraged. The visitor can eat, read, listen to music or just watch. The largest arcade in the world is not full of phrenetic activity, it is an extraordinarily beautiful, calm and peaceful arcade, an interior to be experienced."[7] Being born and raised in Cleveland, I came to know this remarkable place as a youth, and it is indeed gratifying to observe its sustained vitality and continuing role in the life of this city.

In some respects, the Cleveland Arcade is a precursor for many of the latter-twentieth-century urban shopping malls and gallerias. It anticipates the need for a high degree of access to all shops via continuous multi-leveled galleries and vertical circulation at both ends. The arcade's proportions and apsoidal ends cause it to be perceived neither as a linear covered street nor as a centroidal covered court, but as something in between. (Similarly, most contemporary shopping malls contain a combination of linear and centroidal spaces.) Finally, the insular quality of the Cleveland Arcade, surrounded as it is by buildings on all sides, anticipates the shopping-center design trend of a century later.

The contemporary project that comes closest to the precedent of the Cleveland Arcade is the Galleria at Crocker Center in San Francisco, designed by Charles Bassett, FAIA, at the San Francisco office of Skidmore, Owings & Merrill. Completed in 1982, this three-level shopping

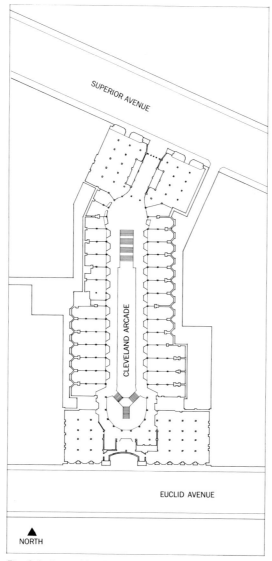

Fig. 2.9. Ground-level plan, Cleveland Arcade. Cleveland.

arcade, located midblock, extends 275 feet (84 meters) in a straight line between Post and Sutter streets (figure 2.10). The center's sixty-two shops and restaurants open off of continuous galleries located on three levels, which are served by escalators obtrusively positioned in the center. The arcade space is covered by a glazed, barrel-vaulted skylight. (Unfortunately, the skylight admits more daylight on sunny days than is visually comfortable.) The smooth, white ceiling and wall surfaces, tempered-glass guard rails, and red-quarry tile floors give the space a neutral, modern appearance—in contrast to nineteenth-century precedents (see plate 6). In the words of architectural critic Donald Canty:

> It is not quite the festive place it might be, however. Aside from the benches, palms, and clocks, the architects have assiduously avoided historicist decor or appurtenances. . . . The detailing is unswervingly

modern, which is to say plain. This has saved the Galleria from cuteness. But it also has kept it from taking on the kind of timeless quality of Baltimore's Harborplace.[8]

The most significant aspect of the Galleria at Crocker Center is the way in which it knits together the buildings and streets of this dense urban block by providing a generous system of pedestrian access. The entrances at both Post and Sutter streets are strongly arched forms of granite and glass. They are recessed from the street and lead down to the arcade level via a few steps, thus giving modest emphasis to the act of entering (see plate 7). From inside, each glazed entrance frames a view that at the Sutter Street end is the elegant curtain-wall facade of the 1917 Hallidie Building, designed by Willis Polk. The lobby of the new thirty-eight-story Crocker Bank tower at the corner of Kearny and Post streets ties directly into the galleria. There is also a rather unappealing side

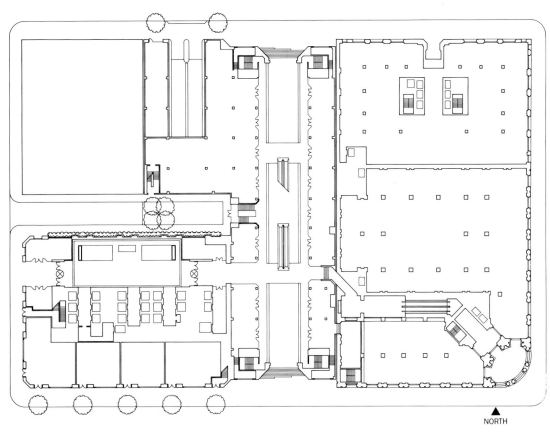

Fig. 2.10. Ground-floor plan, Crocker Center. San Francisco.

entrance from an alley. Along Sutter Street, the Garden Terrace Hotel has a roof terrace above the galleria's shops. At the corner of Post and Montgomery streets, the top eleven floors of the 1908 Crocker Bank Building have been removed to create a wonderful roof terrace overlooking Market Street. Although access from the third level of the Galleria at Crocker Center is somewhat obscure, once there the roof garden is an appealing respite from the bustling streets below. And although the pedestrian cannot enter the galleria from the primary streets, the small detour to reach this vibrant pedestrian place is well worthwhile.

In England, the historic concept of the arcade is more readily adapted to contemporary retail centers due to its presence as a precedent and the tradition of smaller retailers. Although most English urban shopping centers have adopted an organizational model based on anchor department stores, the centers often include certain design aspects of the Victorian arcade—such as linear geometry, fully glazed roofs, bay-window shop fronts, and nineteenth-century color schemes. Royal Priors, a recently built center in Leamington Spa (an eighteenth-century resort in the Midlands), is based clearly on the historic concept of an arcade. The central mall space is located over the existing Satchwell Street, with two transverse arcades (actually, passages) from the Parade leading into it. Designed by Chapman Taylor Part-

ners, the central mall features a combination of Victorian and neoclassical characteristics, such as a fully glazed, barrel-vaulted skylight; a patterned tile floor; and articulated spandrels.

In the United States, an example of a project that was conceived as a commercial pedestrian passage is the Sixth Street Marketplace in Richmond, Virginia, completed in 1985. By occupying the right-of-way of Sixth Street, this project spatially unites existing buildings on both sides, while creating a north-south pedestrian connection from East Grace Street to the Richmond Coliseum (figure 2.11). This is an innovative urban-design concept, for it utilizes an existing public right-of-way to create a private pedestrian passage. The plan also provides additional space for eighty-five shops within its own structure and by borrowing space from the bordering department stores. As an urban-design scheme, it provides pedestrian linkage between several important Richmond enterprises, such as the Virginia Center for the Performing Arts, Miller & Rhoads, Thalhimer's, a new Marriott hotel, a new office tower, a remodeled armory, a new convention center, and the Richmond Coliseum. The intention of this Enterprise Development Company project was to bring a measure of economic revitalization to downtown Richmond; that goal, however, has been realized with mixed success.[9] The shopping center's greatest success has been to infuse this part of Richmond with new pedestrian spirit and vitality.

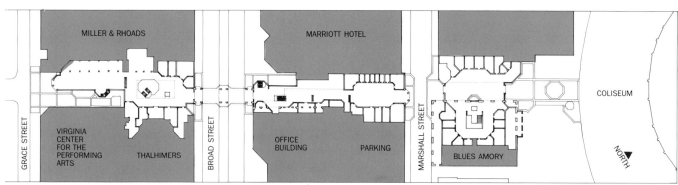

Fig. 2.11. Urban site plan, Sixth Street Marketplace. Richmond, Virginia.

Had the Sixth Street Marketplace been more directly conceived as an urban passage by architects Wallace Roberts & Todd, it would have greater design integrity. The sequence of spaces beginning at East Grace Street is as follows: entry link, Palm Court, Broad Street bridge, shopping link, Renaissance Court, Marshall Street crossing, Crystal Palace, and festival park. The plan alignments change from space to space, as do the sectional properties. The result is an uncoordinated sequence of spaces lacking in perceptual coherence. The quality of these spaces is also lacking because of their unfinished, ad-hoc character—with all of the duct work, wiring, and structure exposed. Although this approach has been successfully used in other recently completed shopping places, here the resulting image is visually chaotic (figure 2.12).

The bridge over Broad Street is the most interesting part of the Sixth Street Marketplace. Symbolically, the bridge links the northern side of Richmond to the southern side—a cultural division with its roots in Richmond's history that is emphasized by the width and extent of this major street. Physically, the bridge links the two parts of the shopping center, a necessity for its functional operation. The bridge is a unique moment in this design scheme. It is a place where the pedestrian can pause to rest while poised above this corridor of commerce (figure 2.13).

The historic concept of the arcade as both a path and a place has been difficult to achieve within the contemporary urban context, formed as it is by zoning laws, land-ownership patterns, and real-estate economics. There are few site conditions where the need for a pedestrian passage is such that an arcade building is the inevitable solution. Current real-estate economics dictates higher-intensity usage, which calls for multilevel buildings of compact form. Thus, the design integrity of the early arcades had been unachievable. Instead, the commercial projects of the contemporary era are much larger in scale and much more complex in their spatial realization.

One such project that draws a direct association between the nineteenth-century arcade and its twentieth-century counterpart is The Grand Avenue complex in Milwaukee, designed by the ELS Design Group and developed by the Rouse Company in 1983. The inspirational genesis for this scheme was the block-long Plankington Arcade of 1915, designed by Holabird & Roche, which paralleled Wisconsin Avenue and is linked to the Gimbel's department store

Fig. 2.12. Interior view, Sixth Street Marketplace. Richmond, Virginia.

Fig. 2.13. Exterior view of bridge, Sixth Street Marketplace. Richmond, Virginia.

via a bridge at the arcade's eastern end. The first step was to restore the three levels of this linear Italian-Gothic space by reglazing the skylight; refurbishing the terrazzo floors; and restoring the ornamental plasterwork, the brass handrails, and the chandeliers (see plate 8). New shops were then brought into the refurbished arcade. At its center is the restored rotunda, in which stands a sculpture of John Plankington surrounded by a unique spiral stair that leads down to the cellar level where offices are located.

On the adjoining two blocks, architect Barry Elbasani designed a new arcade and 160 shops behind four existing buildings. His design extends the passage of the Plankington Arcade to the Boston Store, which anchors the western end of the complex. The new and old arcades link via an awkward diagonal pedestrian bridge over Second Street—a result of difficult contextual circumstances. Paralleling both arcades along Michigan Avenue are two parking garages that can accommodate two-thousand cars. These garages have direct connections into the shopping space. Third Street was closed, which allowed the new shopping center to extend across the street easily. This

also created a location for the main entry to the complex—a 100-foot-wide (30-meter-wide) glazed form that steps back in both plan and section from a small plaza (figure 2.14). This architectural event activates Wisconsin Avenue (as do the existing building entrances along the street) such that the complex does not present a blank outer wall to the city.

The design of the new interior pedestrian spaces was intended to be both sympathetic to the old Plankington Arcade and genuinely contemporary. For example, the width of the new arcade and the bay size were kept the same as in the old arcade, as was the shape of the continuous skylights. The same brass railings and light fixtures were used in both the old and new arcades. Other design aspects of the new arcade are boldly contemporary, such as the steel-frame structure and roofing panels. The earth-toned quarry-tile floor and hanging plants give the new space a distinctly less-elegant look. The details are modern; and the cool color scheme fits well with the historic colors, except for the floor. The Grand Court, which is adjacent to the main entrance, is rather expansive and soaring with large skylights. The irregularity of the court's plan is another mod-

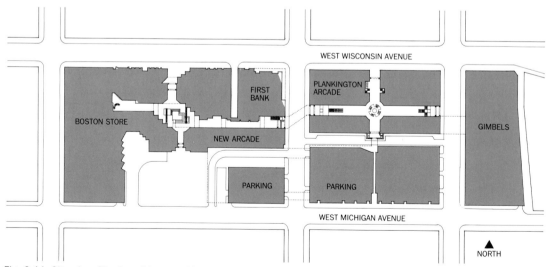

Fig. 2.14. Site plan, The Grand Avenue. Milwaukee.

Fig. 2.15. Exterior view, Galleria at Erieview. Cleveland.

ern trait in contrast to the figural rotunda. Escalators, a fountain, the ubiquitous glass elevator, and street furniture are the featured elements of this space, which is surrounded by eating places on the third level (see plate 9). These new spaces are more visually complex than are the old ones; yet, they are less formal. The result is an intriguing example of new meets old—without the compromise of either.

The critical spatial characteristic of an arcade that distinguishes it from other interior places is that it acts as a place of transition; it connects two or more pedestrian routes or destinations. Traditionally, an arcade connected two major streets through the interior of a block; however, the connection of any pedestrian spaces satisfies this criterion. This connection also implies linearity: an arcade is usually more a path than it is a place; it is more a space of transition than it is a destination. Most successfully designed arcades incorporate both spatial characteristics and balance their presence.

Two recent projects in Cleveland and Milwaukee embody the character of a linear pedestrian passage—with the em-

phasis on its transitional quality. In 1964 a twenty-two-story office tower was constructed in Cleveland on East Ninth Street as part of a downtown urban-renewal project—known as Erieview due to its presence near Lake Erie. A vacuous, 500-foot-deep (152-meter-deep) plaza fronted the tower until 1987, when the Galleria at Erieview was completed to connect the street to the tower (figure 2.15). Designed by Kober/Belluschi Associates, the 85-foot-tall (26-meter-tall), barrel-vaulted arcade acts as the two-story pedestrian spine for seventy shops on two levels and a branch of the Museum for Contemporary Art. Off of East Ninth Street is a food court, surrounded by fast-food restaurants and covered by an angled, glass rotunda roof, which opens onto an outdoor terrace and connects to the galleria. This project, adjacent to the government and civic center of downtown Cleveland, has certainly infused the surrounding area with renewed pedestrian activity. Architecturally, the massing and roof forms result in a somewhat fragmented complex that is contextually awkward. Colonnaded passages and an alley have been provided along St. Clair Avenue, but there are no shop windows and only one small entrance. The main street entry is an imposing arched form, and the direct link to the tower is well resolved. Horizontal shifts in the barrel vaults reflect plan offsets in the galleria itself, with transitional spaces marked by decorative columns topped by palms. The pleasant interior features a soothing pastel palette, modern details, and carefully crafted shop fronts (see plate 10).

In Milwaukee, Plaza East occupies a block near city hall on which are located two polygonal office towers at two corners and two plazas joined by an arcade at the other two corners. Although the arcade of this project designed by Murphy/Jahn Architects physically joins the two towers at its sides, it is primarily a linear space connecting two street corners. Lined by shops on two levels, this short arcade is handsomely detailed with steel-truss roof arches, a barrel-vaulted skylight, and glass-block balcony floors all painted in rose and aqua (figure 2.16). The only design difficulty is the distance of the arcade entrances from the street corners and the banal treatment of these plazas. Although the ingredients are here for an appropriate pedestrian scheme, the dissociation from the street makes the pedestrian passage less vital.

Another use of the term *arcade* is in reference to a pedestrian passage through a building and between streets that may or may not provide access to activities along its course. A good example is the Republic Bank Center (now called First Republic Bank), in Houston, designed by Johnson/Burgee Architects in 1983. This project has a major east-

west arcade that bisects the office-tower lobby, while relating it to the banking hall. As a 75-foot-tall (23-meter-tall) barrel-vaulted passage with crossing bridges, the arcade is spatially dramatic. The project also has a minor north-south arcade. The only toplighting is at the intersection. These so-called arcades really only provide access to the banking hall and the building's lobby. Although they can be used by the public as pass-throughs, there isn't much justification for taking this route.

In Manhattan, where the blocks between the north-south avenues are quite long, urban designers proposed that a system of midblock passages be developed. These could be either open-air or enclosed pedestrian routes for which developers would receive building-area

Fig. 2.16. Interior view, Plaza East arcade. Milwaukee.

bonuses. Many of these covered passages have been constructed, but their use is minimal—primarily because they have few activities or amenities along their course. One well-known example is the passage at the back of the Olympic Tower on Fifth Avenue between East 51st and East 52d streets. This passage was initially quite ordinary but has been redesigned. Now there are some pedestrian services, luxurious landscaping, a skylit fountain, and a café (figure 2.17). Nevertheless, the peak-hour number of pedestrians is four-hundred, whereas it is four-thousand on Fifth Avenue, which parallels the Olympic Tower passage nearby.[10] Pedestrian-passage arcades must be designed as active spaces with amenities and shops if they are to serve as viable alternative routes.

Fig. 2.17. Interior view, Olympic Tower passage. New York City.

The arcade as a system of urban pedestrian access has had a provocative history. It is a captivating concept, cherished by pedestrians for the freedom of movement it allows within a hazard-free, daylit space that is protected from the weather. And yet, the arcade concept cannot be applied indiscriminately to all architectural problems; it must be supported by the surrounding context. Critic Kenneth Frampton comments on the general applicability of the arcade system:

> This city in miniature—the "unreal" counterform of the "real" city—has always gained its substance from being inlaid into the fabric of the city proper. The arcade, or more strictly the galleria, has invariably arisen like a parasitical labyrinth, dependent for its form on the public mass within which it is concealed. Where this context does not exist, the arcade seems to have little capacity for contributing to the continuity of the exterior urban space.[11]

The arcade or galleria as a design concept continues to have a strong following among architects and urban designers. In recent years, the arcade concept has been applied with success in the development of student housing at the University of Alberta in Canada and at the academic facilities at the University of Trondheim in Norway. It has strongly influenced the development of urban shopping centers and continues to be utilized in various ways as the design basis for specialty centers and festival marketplaces. However, due to the changed social and economic conditions of our era, the arcade as a system of pedestrian access and commercial retailing with the complete characteristics of its nineteenth-century predecessors is no longer possible. ∎

Many interior places are closely related to retail activity in the city due to the need for free public access to facilitate sales. Through enclosure, this access space is made more conducive for shopping by creating an environment that is carefree and enjoyable. The commercial success of suburban shopping centers is based on these realizations. Recently, a new urban shopping center has evolved with the interior pedestrian place as its prime attraction and spatial organizer.

THE DEPARTMENT-STORE CONCEPT

In the first half of the nineteenth century, in both Europe and America, there appeared a new form of merchandising known as the department store. It evolved as a concomitant to the profound change in the system of industrial production, whereby factories could produce large quantities of low-cost goods. This change required both the separation of the place of production from the place of sale and a new merchandising means to sell these wares. The department store was an organization of semiindependent units, each devoted to selling a given category of goods, such as clothing, toys, housewares, shoes, and jewelry. The store itself provided the centralized services of administration, publicity, delivery, and accounting. This system related the specialization of individual departments with the economy of centralization, lowering overhead and fostering competition with independent shops.

The greatest merchandising advantage of the department store was the consolidation of all departments in one building. This afforded shoppers the convenience of easy and free access to all available goods. The fixed prices of manufactured products enabled shoppers to compare values among goods at a given store and among different stores. Such comparison shopping generated a great deal of activity that did not necessarily lead to purchasing. Shopping became a social activity and a leisure-time pursuit

rather than simply a necessity. The departments were arranged so as to interact with one another, thus encouraging customers buying in one department to shop in adjacent ones. Impulse goods were placed near the entrances to the floors. The purpose was to stimulate purchases as shoppers passed by on their way to find goods on other floors. This arrangement, along with the methods of display and the attractive lighting of goods, drew customers throughout the building—providing maximum exposure to all departments. All of customers' shopping needs could be satisfied in this new type of store.

The department stores satisfied the shopping needs of the burgeoning population of the nineteenth-century in cities such as Paris, London, New York, and Chicago. The stores were located on large sites near newly developed public-transit stations in the central business districts. The stores' street-level facades were composed of display windows and several large entrances; whereas the upper facades, the cornices, and the roof forms were designed to attract the customers' attention. One favored architectural device was the projecting rounded-corner bay (used by architect Louis Sullivan in his well-known Carson Pirie Scott store in Chicago [1899–1904]), which focused attention on the joining of the two primary facades. Department stores were multistory buildings with deep floors that allowed a flexible arrangement of numerous departments. This vast concentration of merchandising in prime locations was a key factor in the great economic success of the department store. When several department stores were built near each other and competition grew, ancillary activities—such as concerts, exhibitions, fashion shows, and dining—were added to attract customers. Department stores became a new kind of urban institution devoted to consumption. And there were social implications, as Robert A. M. Stern observes:

Merchants like Field and Wanamaker, who orchestrated the transformation of the utilitarian dry goods store into a palace of consumption, were canny enough to realize that labor-saving devices combined with cheap domestic help were enabling affluent women, long relegated to the domestic hearth, to assume a major role in the urban drama. Politicians and lawyers could act out their public roles in the templelike settings of statehouse and courthouse, merchants and bankers could pursue their tasks in equally impressive surroundings, and now, with the department store, women could play their part in a setting that was the equivalent and more.[12]

The Bon Marché in Paris is one of the greatest examples of the department-store building type. Architect Jean-Alexandre Laplanche, aided by Louis Auguste Boileau, his son Louis Charles Boileau, and Gustave Eiffel, administered the store's construction from 1869 to 1887.[13] Occupying most of a block on the rue de Sevres, this vast, five-story structure was a great architectural and technological achievement. To satisfy the essential need of lighting the merchandise within the store, the facades were composed of large, regularly spaced windows; and the plan contained numerous light wells. At the corners were large domed bays that granted prominence to the building and provided entrances and display windows. The structure was constructed entirely of iron, in order to be strong enough to support the considerable weight of the crowds and the merchandise. The widely spaced iron columns provided a free floor plan for display and circulation. Ducts were run throughout the structure to provide heat and ventilation. Artificial gas lighting, later replaced by electrical lighting, supplemented the available natural light.

The interior of the Bon Marché department store was a magnificent spectacle, as here described by architectural historian Meredith Clausen:

> Entering the building, the customer was lured through a labyrinth of display counters into a large, spacious light-filled court: a dazzling four-story skylighted hall surrounded by open galleries piled high with mounds of colorful merchandise. Spilling out into the main floor was a sumptuously decorated, monumental, double-revolution stair, fashioned after the stair of the newly opened Paris Opéra. This was the building's crowning glory: an impressive space destined to overwhelm customers with its sheer magnificence. The huge, skylighted hall full of merchandise was awesome for someone accustomed to the dark, confined quarters and limited displays of the small specialty shop. The grand stair drew customers upstairs, offering them an opportunity to exhibit their newly acquired attire in full view of others. Connecting upper floors across the open court were lightweight, iron footbridges, which served both to facilitate circulation and to provide additional vantage points for spectators. The glazed court was, in short, more than just a practical lighting device—it was a sales ploy to attract customers with an exciting new place to idle away their leisure hours.[14]

The light court, or atrium, and the monumental stair became the two most salient interior features of grand department stores. Printemps and Galeries Lafayette, both built in 1906 in Paris, were designed around large-scaled skylit atria—even though the necessity for natural light had been supplanted by electric lights. Similarly, the monumental stair was a primary design feature within the atrium, even though elevators were then available and were utilized. The four-story, domed rotunda of the Galeries Lafayette—with its grand curving stair, scalloped balconies, polychromed ornamentation, and leaded-glass skylight—remains even today a radiant focal space within this labyrinthian department store (see plate 11).

In the United States, the design features of the Parisian department store were readily adopted. The Marshall Field Store in Chicago, finally completed by Daniel Burnham in 1906, incorporates several light wells within the monumental, block-long building of stone and glass. Architect Robert A. M. Stern comments on the store's grandeur, "Chicago's street grid was raised to three dimensions inside, articulated in piazzalike

Fig. 2.18. Atrium view, Neiman-Marcus. San Francisco.

light wells that were lavish, dizzyingly vertical interior rooms. A mosaic dome of iridescent glass rose five storeys above one galleried piazza; the north well rose thirteen storeys to a skylight."[15] For the Wanamaker's Department Store in Philadelphia, completed in 1910, Burnham designed a twelve-story, grand *palazzo* around a classically formed atrium (see plate 12). This seven-story atrium, reminiscent of a porticoed Renaissance courtyard, is surrounded by balconies, and houses a large pipe organ and the well-known bronze Philadelphia eagle. At Union Square in San Francisco, the turn-of-the-century City of Paris department store had a domed rotunda. In 1976 Philip Johnson rebuilt this salvaged element as a rounded-corner bay in a new Neiman-Marcus department store (figure 2.18). Today, this ornate, four-story, balconied space with its stained-glass skylight acts not only as a historic link between the old and the new, but also as a splendid transition between Union Square and the store's interior.

THE SHOPPING-CENTER CONCEPT

The contemporary enclosed shopping center is an evolutionary merger of the historic department store and the nineteenth-century shopping arcade (see pages 31–47). The simple *dumbbell*-plan shopping center is a literal example of this combination: two department stores serving as anchor tenants that are located at the ends of a covered passage lined with small shops. The numerous design variations on this basic scheme include multiple levels in the arcade, shifts in plan and section geometry, and the inclusion of additional department stores in larger cross-axial centers.

In *Shopping Malls*, Barry Maitland's book on the design evolution of the shopping center, he observes that there has been a constant shifting back and forth between the concept of the shopping center as department store and the shopping center as arcade.[16] This design theory re-

Fig. 2.19. La Vogue, Fashion Square Mall. Charlottesville, Virginia.

Fig. 2.20. Atrium view, The Galleria at Post Oak. Houston.

could now be architecturally and spatially unified through the use of common floor finishes, wall materials, and lighting and environmental systems. The shop front weakened as a design element, and the mall area lost its identity as a defined space (figure 2.19). The use of variegated geometries, in both plan and section, in the shop fronts and the mall area furthered this visual and physical amalgamation. The merging occurred at the mall's sides, which adjoined the shops, and at the malls[1] ends, which adjoined the department stores. The result was a public mall surrounded by shops that was analogous to the atrium of a department store and its free flow of space between and around individual departments.

The design concept of the shopping center as an arcade follows from the historic model of discrete shops lining a linear, skylit street. Such a design strategy is additive: the arcade is first created as a discrete space and then shops are attached to its sides. The important characteristic is the contrast between the two. The arcade is a public space with hard pavement, a distinct roof form, bright daylight, and street furnishings. Distinct storefront facades separate the private shops from the public arcade, thus creating interior spaces for the sale of goods. Energy conservation, an important consideration in the 1970s, fostered higher levels of daylighting and lower levels of cooling and heating in the public areas of shopping centers. This encouraged the adoption of the arcade model. These arcadelike mall spaces grew to grand proportions, similar in concept to the Galleria Vittorio Emanuele II in Milan (see pages 36–38). The Galleria at Post Oak in Houston epitomizes this design evolution, with its three-story-high stepped transverse section generating a linear central space that is 12 meters (39 feet) wide, and 168 meters (551 feet) long—with an ice-skating rink at the center (figure 2.20). The segmented, vaulted

lates to the central mall space and not to the actual department stores connected to it. When shopping centers were enclosed in the 1970s, the absolute need for a discrete separation between the shops and the mall space disappeared; and the mall space began to appear spatially as a department store. The public and private areas (or the landlord and tenant areas)

skylight provides constant contact with the exterior world and gives the mall space an identifiable integrity.

In 1956 architect Victor Gruen designed the first fully enclosed shopping mall in North America, the Southdale Center in Edina, Minnesota, outside of Minneapolis.[17] Due to the severe Minnesota winters, a climate-controlled mall has a competitive advantage over open-air shopping centers. The Southdale Center has a primary, two-story mall space joining the department stores; and short mall spaces extend from it to the exterior. The mall's compact plan reduced the walking distances for the customers and also reduced both the construction and land costs for the developer. The operating costs were reduced by installing a centralized mechanical plant to supply conditioned air to the mall space; from there, the air was drawn into the shops and then exhausted. The lightweight steel-roof structure of the mall space was raised above the stores' roofs to provide daylighting from both clerestories and skylights, thus further reducing energy costs. Parking was arranged so that customers could enter at either level, with truck servicing occurring via ramps to the basement. The mall space, here termed the Garden Court, has its own identity and presence. It became a feature unto itself—a basis for attracting customers and promoting the shopping center (figure 2.21).

The rest, according to Barry Maitland, is history:

> With the opening of the Southdale Center then, all of the components had been assembled which would transform the concept of the shopping center from that of an expedient federation of individual stores into that of a single packaged entity, capable of endless reproduction in a number of set variations under any climatic conditions, and according to a well-defined process which ran from initial merchandising plan and site selection right through to final marketing and promotion.[18]

The enclosed shopping center—with its easy auto access, adjacent parking, and shopper convenience—became the ubiquitous built form for retailing in the suburbs of the countries of the developed world.

In the United States after World War II, the retail functions in the center city began to decline. This change was due to the residential relocation of the middle and upper classes to the suburbs and the subsequent growth of both open and enclosed shopping centers to service the new demand. Many department stores and speciality shops closed their central-city locations in favor of the suburbs. Yet,

Fig. 2.21. Garden Court, Southdale Center. Edina, Minnesota.

the daytime population of downtown had increased greatly, due to the tremendous growth in office employment. After 5:00 P.M., however, the vast majority of these employees returned to the suburbs, leaving behind a desolate area. Politicians, city planners, bankers, and merchants tried to reverse or abate the decline in retail activity by developing improvement programs, including pedestrian malls, streetscape redesigns, and facade renovations. These efforts helped, but they could not by themselves rejuvenate the downtown retail activity of most American cities.

New approaches to urban retailing that would lead to new architectural forms were needed. Could the lessons learned in the suburbs be adapted to the center city? The answer was a resounding Yes! At the time, the suburbs were saturated with shopping centers, and developers were looking for new opportunities. Several of the urban multiuse centers developed in the 1970s had incorporated retail functions with success—notably, the IDS Center in Minneapolis and Water Tower Place in Chicago (see pages 99–109). Moreover, developer James Rouse had demonstrated the potential of the festival-marketplace concept at Faneuil Hall in Boston and at Harborplace in Baltimore (see pages 91–98).

The new urban shopping centers are related directly to their suburban counterparts in their centralized organization, their management, their marketing strategies, and their delivery systems. They are inwardly oriented entities endeavoring to project a unified exterior image. Even when the designs of these centers must be accommodated to the prevalent physical, social, economic, and/or political circumstances of an urban area, they still can be interesting and lively places. If they avoid or subdue these circumstances, they remain much more like their suburban progenitors, with bank facades, meager entrances,

and connections to parking garages. Nevertheless, these centers have encouraged a revival of shopping and entertainment activity in the central city that has supported employment, attracted visitors, and encouraged some people to once again live downtown.

Urban shopping centers can be divided into two broad categories: *anchor centers*, which rely on large department stores to attract customers; and *specialty centers*, which rely on their own ambience to attract shoppers. Both categories can be subdivided further into newly built centers versus centers that are adaptive uses of old buildings or that integrate old and new buildings in a unified plan. Anchor centers generally are designed to attract people who live in the city or those who still come to the city to shop. Specialty centers attract the other constituencies: people who work in the city, tourists, travelers, and conventioneers. The latter groups are especially important to the success of specialty centers.

ANCHOR SHOPPING CENTERS
The most readily available location to build an urban shopping center with the least margin of risk is a site adjacent to an existing department store. This strategy fits the suburban model of the anchor center—whereby the size, scope, and reputation of the department store attracts the customers who then are induced to patronize the adjacent specialty shops. The Gallery at Market Street East in Philadelphia is an example. The new center was built between the existing Strawbridge & Clothier store and a new Stern's store (originally Gimbel's) (see page 208). Likewise, the Grand Avenue complex in Milwaukee stretches between two existing department stores; Gimbel's and the Boston Store. The advantage of this scheme is that the existing landmarks act as the main shopping attractions, while the new center forms a connection among them.

St. Louis Centre is a new, two-block-long, four-story shopping center in downtown St. Louis. It joins the existing Famous-Barr department store to the north and Dillard's department store to the south (figure 2.22). The main entrances are located at the junctures with these two department stores. Two four-story, glass-and-steel greenhouses with arched entries open onto plazas at the street corners (figure 2.23). The bridges to the two department stores are designed as part of these entry elements. Three levels span the street, with the same glazed facade treatment as the entry elements on one side. The center is served by two parking garages that provide four thousand spaces. One garage has a direct bridge linkage to the center across 6th Street; the other is reached by a diagonal bridge through the Dillard's store. Standing above the center on the 7th Street side is a twenty-five-story office tower with a street-level lobby. On the opposite street is the truck-servicing entrance, which leads to an interior loading dock that occupies a significant part of the ground floor. The effort to maintain street activity is particularly successful at the entrance ends where the street-level shops are located. Street-level services and shops are located on all city-block faces, and a pedestrian colonnade runs along 6th Street. Unfortunately, the main shopping level had to be raised above the street to provide for truck loading and mechanical systems. The only incongruous aspect of the exterior design is the green-and-white-paneled facade of the central-building mass and one side of the bridges. This modern, abstract facade does not relate well to the expressive historic buildings on the adjacent blocks.

St. Louis Centre is organized spatially as a linear atrium on three levels above the street. The atrium provides 360,000 square feet (33,444 square meters) of retail area. The escalators, which are located near the entrances, are adjacent to the inviting, sunlit bridges that lead to the department stores. At the atrium's

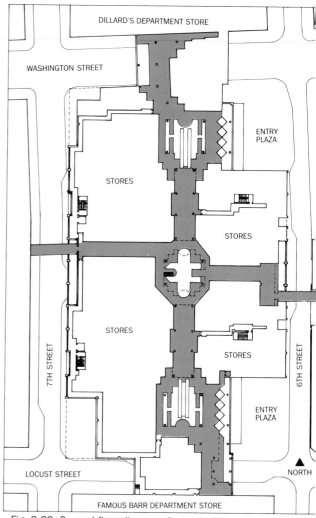

Fig. 2.22. Second-floor diagram, St. Louis Centre. St. Louis.

Fig. 2.23. Entrance view, St. Louis Centre. St. Louis.

center is a feature elevator within a white gridded enclosure near an attractive cantilevered stair. Each level features shops of varying sizes and is organized according to a merchandising theme: the first level is devoted to services and impulse goods; the second level to ready-to-wear clothing and accessories; the third level to better apparel, shoes, and gifts; and the fourth level to leisure-time merchandise and specialty foods grouped around a 750-seat food court. The center is open seven days a week; and there is a regular schedule of entertainment, special events, seminars, and meetings. On a beautiful Saturday afternoon in April, when the streets were only sparsely populated, the center was throbbing with activity and was crowded with residents and tourists of all ages and origins.

Completed in 1985 as designed by RTKL Associates, the interior of St. Louis Centre is one of the most elegantly designed of its genre. The design is based on the concept of the shopping center as arcade—with a strongly defined linear atrium. Pedestrian circulation is well handled with generous spaces at both ends of the atrium for arrival and bridges for crossing in the center. The spatial form is articulated by round, disengaged, three-story columns. These columns, with their unique capitals, support the galleries and the barrel-vaulted skylight (see plate 13). Additional sloped skylights over the galleries provide an abundance of daylight. One of the most refreshing aspects of this design is the planar white treatment of all structural members and surfaces. This allows daylight to distribute evenly throughout the space. As a result, the colors of the merchandise, the greenery, and the people themselves relate well to the neutral color scheme. The plantings are located judiciously: hanging terra-cotta pots on balconies, ficus trees on the top floor, and potted palms on the ground floor. Granite benches surround the central water feature, giving it an urbane quality. The guard rails are elegantly transparent, and the floors are tiled in off-white with lavender and green borders. The white light fixtures, recessed in the spandrels and ceilings and attached to columns or suspended from tracks, are integrated well into the overall design. The whole scheme has a refined, studied quality without garish or visually provoking details. Suspended high within this space is a mobile of oversized red cardinals, a brilliant if not startling feature within this controlled milieu (figure 2.24).

The grandest version to date of an urban shopping center based on the anchor-store concept is Eaton Centre in Toronto, designed by Bregman & Hamann and the Zeidler Partnership (now Zeidler

Fig. 2.24. Atrium view, St. Louis Centre. St. Louis.

Roberts Partnership). This five-block, fifteen-acre site is adjacent to the old city hall on the west side of Yonge Street, a major north-south street under which the subway runs (figure 2.25). Phases one and two of the project, which were completed in 1978 and 1979 (totaling 3.2 million square feet), include two office towers, Eaton's department store, a five-story atrium, 302 shops, two parking garages for sixteen hundred cars, and the connection to the existing Simpson's department store. In phase three, an additional office tower and a hotel are planned. Developed jointly by the Cadillac Fairview Corporation and the Eaton Company (which owned the site), this project has had a tremendous impact on the growth of the northeast quadrant of the center city.

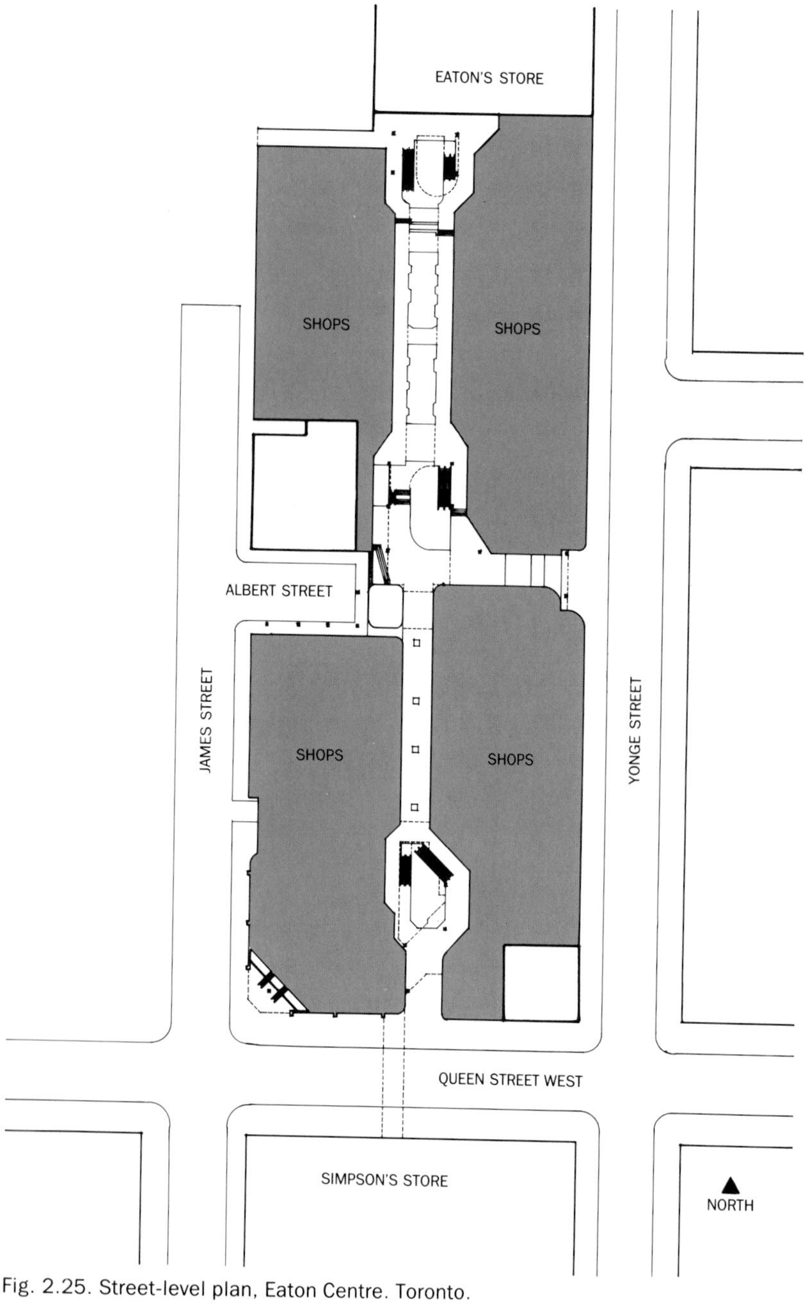

Eaton Centre is appropriately conceived in its integration with the surrounding context. The south entrance is located under the bridge to Simpson's; it connects to the lobby of the Cadillac Fairview Tower and relates to the Queen Station subway stop. At the north end, an awkward lean-to atrium (figure 2.26) was built at the corner of Dundas and Yonge streets to serve as a common entrance to an office tower, Eaton's department store, the subway station, and the concourse of the Atrium on Bay (see pages 201–6). One of the Yonge Street entrances crosses the atrium to Albert Street and the new Bell Canada tower. The other Yonge Street entrance crosses the atrium to Trinity Square—the site of the historic Holy Trinity Church. By designing the new department store in an L-shape, the church was saved. The long facade on Yonge Street was the most challenging design problem. The four-level parking garage above the shops is hidden by a constructivist steel screen that has a recessed, second-level walkway (figure 2.27). In order not to reduce pedestrian activity, seventeen shallow shops open directly onto Yonge Street; however, the opposite side of the street has not yet been renovated.

The central pedestrian area is colossal in scale—stretching 860 feet (262 meters) between the two department stores, rising 90 feet (27.4 meters) to the skylight, and varying in width between shop fronts from 28 to 56 feet (8.5 to 17 meters). These dimensions give the space a strong linearity that is reinforced by

Fig. 2.25. Street-level plan, Eaton Centre. Toronto.

Fig. 2.26. North-entrance view, Eaton Centre. Toronto.

Fig. 2.27. Yonge Street facade, Eaton Centre. Toronto.

Fig. 2.28. Atrium view, Eaton Centre. Toronto.

the continuity of the barrel-vaulted skylight, which serves as a visual horizontal datum (figure 2.28). This space is reminiscent of a Victorian arcade, being a long, covered street defined by parallel building facades. The round concrete columns spaced 40 feet (12 meters) on center throughout the arcade's length add a vertical emphasis. Although Eaton Centre lacks the spatial aura of Milan's Galleria Vittorio Emanuele II, it is, in fact, some 20 percent larger in every one of its dimensions.[19] The pedestrian levels are not continuous, which gives the space sectional vitality not usually found in a shopping center. The street levels, which slope 18 feet (5.5 meters) from north to south, required these internal level adjustments at the center of the atrium. In fact, there are two below-street levels at the south end but only one at the north end, with truck docks occupying the center. Because these lower levels are narrow in width, the view up and out is restricted. The two primary levels, with their wide floor areas and unrestricted views, are horizontally expansive. On the upper levels are galleries, balconies, and bridges—some with access to shops and some that provide useful vantage points for surveying the scene (see plate 14).

In terms of pedestrian vitality, Eaton Centre can be compared to the Galleria in Milan (see page 37). On a Monday afternoon in August, the center was overflowing with people shopping, walking, watching, eating, or just being there. A favorite pedestrian activity was standing around the railing at the central court and watching the automated fountain and the throngs of shoppers. Moving through and around the place and discovering and experiencing it is an intrinsic aspect of Eaton Centre's compelling nature. This vitality is generated by the excellent system of linkages to the surrounding streets and office buildings. The underground concourse system and the subway stops generate additional foot traffic, and the city requires the central space to remain open during subway operating hours to provide public access. On Sunday, when only the restaurants are open, people stroll and window-shop (figure 2.29). To be alone in this awesome place on a Sunday is like being alone in a sports stadium with the din of the crowds but an echo in one's memory.

The dominant architectural expression of the great atrium can be characterized as structurally deterministic. The facade of the upper four floors on the east side disguises the parking garage with a system of blank, white panels and narrow mirrors mimicking windows. On the opposite side, the glazed offices are more appropriate in their role as interior facades. The modular rhythm of the

Fig. 2.29. Atrium view, Eaton Centre. Toronto.

skylight lends continuity to the central space, whereas the exposed vertical air ducts are incongruous visual features. On the lower floors, the design execution is weakened due to the number of special shop fronts and kiosks that project into the main space and weaken its integrity. The modifications in the last decade to storefronts, signage, and furnishings—as evidenced by comparing old and new photographs—have further compromised the original design intentions. There is noticeable aging due to significant maintenance problems—the most significant of which is the cleaning of the huge skylight.

An architectural comparison of the central space at Eaton Centre and the Galleria in Milan is probably unfair but is difficult to avoid. In sectional form, the two central spaces are similar: Both have lower floors used for commercial purposes with residential or office uses above topped by a vaulted skylight. Although the Galleria has a cruciform plan and Eaton Centre has a linear plan, both have central spaces composed of structural bays and regularized facades. However, there the comparison ends—for Eaton Centre has exposed street frontages, a parking garage, and subterranean concourse connections. The Galleria's facades are richer in their developed articulation and ornamentation—in large part, they express the aesthetic of a different architectural era. The most ques-

tionable aspect of the Eaton Centre scheme is the design variety of the lower commercial floors—in the form of floor cutouts, stair shapes, sloped shop fronts, and recessed floor levels. Does this amount of spatial articulation positively contribute to the vitality of the place, or would a more coherent scheme—as represented by the Galleria—work as well?

Place Montreal Trust is a new, more unique form of urban shopping center with only one anchor store. Occupying a full block along McGill College Avenue in central Montreal, the center is linked directly to the existing Simpson's department store to the west (figure 2.30). To the east is the mazelike Les Terraces, an earlier built center that connects to an Eaton's department store which, in turn, links to 2020 University, Galeries 2001, and the future Place de la Cathédrale—all of which relate to the McGill Métro station (see page 183). Les Terraces and Place Montreal Trust are connected through a shop-lined concourse under McGill College Avenue. Place Montreal Trust, designed by the Zeidler Roberts Partnership and opened in 1988, incorporates 120 shops and restaurants on five levels (420,000 square feet [39,000 square meters]), two parking levels, and a corporate office tower at the north end.

Although there is a direct connection to Simpson's department store, Place Montreal Trust is more of a specialty center than an anchor center. The shops are

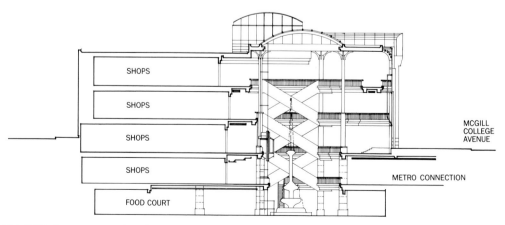

Fig. 2.30. Transverse section, Place Montreal Trust. Montreal.

Fig. 2.31. Food-court view, Place Montreal Trust. Montreal.

Fig. 2.32. Balcony niche, Place Montreal Trust. Montreal.

upscale and feature men's and women's fashions, shoes, jewelry, and accessories. The center also features food consumption as a leisure-time activity and as an incentive for people to remain in the shopping center longer. Place Montreal Trust is the first urban shopping center where the food court and restaurants occupy center stage. This lower-level space—with its splashing fountain, tall greenery, and granite-topped tables—is surrounded by fourteen ethnic or specialty fast-food takeout stands and three food shops (figure 2.31). The restaurant Les Palmes is located on the entry level between the street facade and the atrium, and the Magic Pan restaurant overlooks the atrium from the fifth level. Watching people eat and drink is a significant spectator activity here, and the ambience engendered by this sight gives this center a particularly memorable image. Whereas all new urban shopping centers feature a food court, none place it on display in the center of the plan as does Place Montreal Trust.

Place Montreal Trust is also unique in its architectural design. Instead of the expected facade of shop windows facing the street, the glazed facade of the atrium itself faces McGill College Avenue (see plate 15). This direct relationship between the street and the atrium affords reciprocal views through the atrium's large windows, as well as through a three-story glass wall. The exterior facade of rose granite, blue-painted steel, and glass is boldly figurative—with a certain mannered quality. The central atrium is covered with an arching skylight supported by articulated columns. The atrium's shape changes from level to level, thus creating overhangs and balconies that make it visually intriguing, since the whole space is not revealed at once. These balcony edges step in and out, thus creating niches for benches on which pedestrians can rest and observe the bustling crowds below (figure 2.32).

Fig. 2.33. Entrance view, Plaza Pasadena. Pasadena, California.

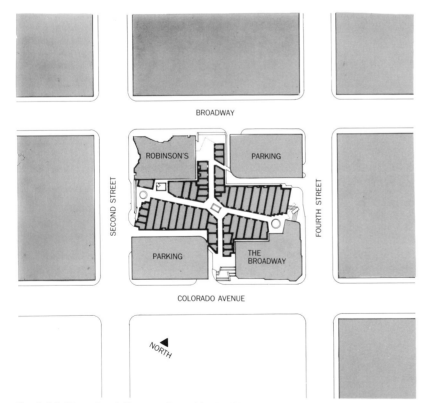

Fig. 2.34. Street-level diagram, Santa Monica Place. Santa Monica, California.

This atrium, with its stepping vertical and horizontal shapes, its cantilevered planters, and the strong blue accent color brought in from the exterior, is visually quite exciting.

In an effort to bolster sagging retail activity, other urban shopping centers with valuable interior pedestrian places have been built in several smaller cities. For example, Plaza Pasadena in California, designed by Charles Kober Associates and completed in 1980, has two worthwhile civic-design gestures within an otherwise ordinary, three-block, dumbbell-plan center. In an effort to enliven the main frontage along Colorado Boulevard, some shops open onto the street. However, without connections to the interior mall, these shops have not succeeded in maintaining street activity.[20] In a bolder design gesture, the axis of Garfield Avenue—extending from the library to the civic auditorium—passes through the mall, creating an entrance and a pedestrian space (figure 2.33). This classically inspired space is enclosed with arched brick walls painted with civic murals.

At nearby Santa Monica Place, completed in 1980, the Rouse Corporation and architect Frank Gehry have succeeded in creating an urban shopping place of distinct quality that draws upon the forces of the surrounding context. On a two-block site located between an existing open-air shopping center and a Sears store and one block from the ocean, Gehry placed two new department stores at the site's diagonal corners and two parking garages at the other two diagonal corners (figure 2.34). This plan enabled him to extend the three-story pedestrian space to the street to create primary entrances with secondary entrances on the cross axis. The east-west, interior, daylit street—ordered by regularly spaced, square, white columns—is slightly rotated, thus joining the two department stores while developing spatial tension.

At the west end, the upper levels of the pedestrian space emerge as decks defined by white stucco frames and blue awnings. This feature distinguishes Santa Monica Place from other shopping centers by establishing a special relationship with the Pacific Ocean.

The small-city shopping center with the most socially useful interior pedestrian place is Courthouse Center in Columbus, Indiana. This center, completed in 1975, was designed by Cesar Pelli for Gruen Associates. Here, the anchors are a Sears store and The Commons—a kind of community center around a large, enclosed civic space. A one-story skylit pedestrian mall joins the two. The Commons is a unique American institution within this unique American community. Donated by the J. Irwin Miller family (the architectural patrons of Columbus, Indiana), the 46,800 square feet (4,348 square meters) of floor area encompass an adventure-playground, cinemas, a cafeteria, and exhibition galleries around the multipurpose space. This "modern American equivalent of the Italian piazza," as Cesar Pelli called it, occupies a full block along the main street. The center is separated from the street by a membrane of bronze-tinted glass that reflects the surrounding buildings during the day but becomes transparent at night.[21] The center's activities are those of a piazza: resting, talking, watching, eating, and strolling. With its own staff, budget, and schedule of events, The Commons is an enormous civic success that is well supported by the citizenry. At the center of the space is a 30-foot-high kinetic sculpture, entitled *Chaos*, by Swiss artist Jean Tinguely, which serves as a captivating visual and symbolic focus (figure 2.35).

Fig. 2.35. Interior view, The Commons. Columbus, Indiana.

Opportunities to build urban shopping centers with anchor department stores are limited. Rarely are new department stores built in downtowns, and many of the old ones have closed their city locations. Where adjacent parcels were available for new centers with parking, the concept has worked well—by drawing upon established urban-retailing patterns and locations. In these cases, the interior pedestrian places have served as the spatial organizers that invest these urban forms with public character and cultural purpose.

SPECIALTY SHOPPING CENTERS

The development of the specialty shopping center as a form of urban retailing is based on the recognition that shopping has become one of America's favorite pastimes. With the increased availability of discretionary income and leisure time, affluent Americans have turned to shopping as a form of spontaneous theatrical entertainment. The success of developer James Rouse's festival marketplaces demonstrates the validity of this cultural trend. Rouse transformed historic urban locations into the urban equivalents of country fairs—replete with entertainers, food stalls, impulse goods, and luxury items (see pages 91–98). The price of the goods or even their utility is not as important as their attractiveness for purchase. Visual merchandising—that is, displaying goods in an appealing setting—is the predominant marketing strategy. In his book *The Malling of America*, journalist William Kowinski caricatures the typical specialty center: "They walk across the cool tiles of the Freight House (which adjoins the refurbished neobaroque train station and, together with it, makes up the center now called Station Square) to shop for fine chocolate, unfinished wood furniture, carpets, and silk; they stop at the Patisserie, where the wife of a former steelworker pauses over the unfamiliar breads while her husband sips French coffee and samples his first brioche. 'I like to try something different,' he explains."[22]

A speciality shopping center is a collection of small stores; each store is devoted to the sale of a particular kind of luxury good, such as leather handbags, custom shirts, fancy sweaters, handmade ties, intimate apparel, exotic chocolates, British teas, and brassware. At Georgetown Park in Washington, D.C., these shops have names like Britches of Georgetown, Colombian Leather, Fit to a Tee, La Sweaterie, Le Sac, Paraphernalia, Victoria's Secret, Chocolate Chocolate, Nom de Plume, and La Bottega. Each specialty center also offers food, either at sit-down restaurants or at fast-food shops from which the food is purchased and then consumed while strolling or sitting in a common café area. Variety of choice is the key—from the ubiquitous giant chocolate-chip cookie to souvlaki. For example, at Union Station in Washington, D.C., the food establishments are named Bun Penny, Delicia Latinas, Dogs Plus, Everything Yogurt, Kabuki Sushi, Larry's Cookies, and Pizzeria Uno.

Since there are no large stores in a specialty shopping center, the environmental character of the public space is the primary attraction. The public areas establish the dominant image of the center. As Barry Maitland states: "The mall is the magnet, which draws shoppers to itself through sheer force of character. . . . The essence of this magnetism is the notion that shopping (at least for nonessential goods and services) can be a pleasurable, social experience, worth indulging for its own sake."[23] The central space as a public social setting is the primary design concern; the elements to be considered include skylights, finishes, materials, furnishings, and special features.

Most of the new speciality centers are parts of larger multiuse projects that combine offices, apartments, hotels, and parking in separate buildings or in one large structure. Multiusage ensures a steady flow of foot traffic—a kind of captive market of office workers, urban dwellers, or conventioneers. One of the earliest projects of this type was Citicorp in Manhattan, completed in 1978. The center consists of seven levels of shops and restaurants formed around an atrium at the base of a corporate office tower. The main attraction is the piazzalike quality of the atrium and its excellent pedestrian connections to a subway station and the surrounding streets. The atrium at Trump Tower features a similar design concept. Its main

Plate 1. Interior view, Passage Jouffroy. Paris.

Plate 2. Interior view, Burlington Arcade. London.

Plate 3. Interior view, Galerie Vivienne. Paris.

Plate 4. Interior view, Galerie Colbert. Paris.

Plate 5. Interior view, Cleveland Arcade. Cleveland.

Plate 6. Interior view, Galleria at Crocker Center. San Francisco.

Plate 7. Exterior view, Galleria at Crocker Center. San Francisco.

Plate 8. Interior view, Plankington Arcade. Milwaukee.

Plate 9. Interior view, The Grand Avenue. Milwaukee.

Plate 11. Atrium view, Galeries Lafayette. Paris.

Plate 10. Interior view,
Galleria at Erieview.
Cleveland.

Plate 12. Atrium view, Wanamaker's Department Store. Philadelphia.

Plate 14. Atrium view, Eaton Centre. Toronto.

Plate 13. Atrium view,
St. Louis Centre. St. Louis.

Plate 15. Atrium view, Place Montreal Trust. Montreal.

Plate 16. Atrium view, Georgetown Park.
Washington, D.C.

Plate 17. West-atrium view, Cour Mont Royal. Montreal.

Plate 18. Southeast-atrium view, Cour Mont Royal. Montreal.

Plate 19. View of the main hall, Union Station. Washington, D.C.

Plate 20. Shopping-concourse view, Union Station. Washington, D.C.

Plate 21. Interior view, Faneuil Hall Marketplace. Boston.

Plate 22. Exterior view, Harborplace. Baltimore.

Plate 23. Interior view of pedestrian mall,
St. Louis Union Station. St. Louis.

Plate 24. Interior view of Crystal Court, IDS Center. Minneapolis.

Plate 25. Atrium view, The Gallery at Harborplace. Baltimore.

Plate 26. Atrium view, Hyatt Regency San Francisco. San Francisco.

Plate 27. Atrium view, Hyatt Regency San Antonio. San Antonio.

Fig. 2.36. Arcade view, Tabor Center. Denver.

Fig. 2.37. M Street facade, Georgetown Park. Washington, D.C.

attraction, however, is the opulence of the setting: surfaces are covered with rose, peach, and orange *breccia perniche* Italian marble; and a trickling water wall dominates one side of the atrium. A more recently completed project, designed by the Urban Design Group, is The Shops at Tabor Center in Denver. This center forms the edge of a complex consisting of two office towers, a hotel, and a 1,900-car underground garage. The two-block-long galleria, with shops along one side, parallels a pedestrian mall and draws pedestrians into the center's nineteenth-century ambience of trees, fountains, sparkle-lights, and steel structure through the visual transparency of its fully glazed facade (figure 2.36).

With ninety shops in phase one, completed in 1980, and forty shops (including a small department store) in phase two, completed in 1987, Georgetown Park in Washington, D.C., is large enough as a specialty center to almost stand alone. It does not, however, for the center's M Street location is within the heart of the tightly knit Georgetown shopping-and-entertainment area, to which the center contextually accommodates by combining parts of old industrial buildings with sympathetic new construction. The center relates to this location with main entrances off of M Street and shop windows on the street. In addition, it has a 600-car, underground parking garage, and 128 condominium apartments on top (figure 2.37). Clyde's restaurant and Garfinkel's store have both exterior and interior entrances. The primary street entrances dramatically bring visitors in at the top of the three-story interior space. From there, the visitor descends on discontinuous escalators or projecting staircases that have been likened to the endless stairs of an M. C. Escher drawing.

At Georgetown Park, the interior public space is once again the most attractive feature. The center is unique among urban shopping centers in that every element has been consciously over-designed according to Victorian concepts of angled space, subdued lighting, subtle colors, ornate decoration, and sculptural furnishings. The interior pedestrian areas are dominated by two sun-filled, octagonal garden courts. These courts are brighter than the linear spaces, making the shop fronts and their interiors stand out in contrast. The color scheme is dominated by the lush green of the metalwork, which is set off by the black-and-white-patterned tile floors and the tan embossed ceilings. The iron edges and railings of the galleries are elaborately ornamented, as are the large, inverted-dome lights, which incorporate planters. The furnishings are reminiscent of a Victorian garden: wrought-iron gates, tiered fountains, pedestals supporting statues of nymphs, and stone planters filled with palms (see plate 16). As a totality, the environment is somewhat preciously self-conscious and not to everyone's liking; but the ambience is indeed sensually evocative. The best aspect is the choice of music—Mozart instead of Muzak.

The public space at Georgetown Park is conceived as a Victorian stage set for social rituals. Domed skylights of decorated steelwork cover two elaborated atrium-courts. One has a three-tiered fountain and a fenced-in sitting area; the other has a raised eating area overlooking a linear landscaped fountain. The incongruity here is that intimate settings for personal behavior are juxtaposed with public settings for informal behavior: Lovers meet over tea at a café. Friends gossip in a private alcove, while shoppers stroll by, tourists gawk, and businesspeople have lunch. Children play in the pool while grandmother watches, and nearby a woman prepares for a business meeting (figure 2.38). As critic Paul Goldberger comments:

> It is not for nothing, then, that Washingtonians are flocking to this place. The profusion of decoration and detail, the colors, the sunlight that floods in through the glass dome, all contribute to a far more relaxed shopping environment than virtually any other large-scale mall has yet been able to provide. Whatever else can be said about it, it is hard to deny that ersatz Victorian is better than an honest suburban mall.[24]

Cour Mont Royal in Montreal is an integrated multiuse center containing a specialty shopping center. Accommodated within the one-block-square structure of the former Mount Royal Hotel, built in 1922, and designed by Ross and McDonald Architects, the center is located one block west of Place Montreal Trust. Simpson's department store is located between the two centers. The H-shaped building plan contained four light courts, which were enclosed with skylights to form four new fourteen-story atria. The structure was converted in 1988 into a multiuse center. It now has a 350-car parking garage, three cinemas, a subway entrance, and a connection to Simpson's—all below ground. Above are 125 shops on four levels, 138 condominiums on ten levels, 270,000 net square feet (25,083 square meters) of offices on eight levels, and a rooftop health

Fig. 2.38. Social activity, Georgetown Park. Washington, D.C.

Fig. 2.39. Rotunda view, Arcade Square. Dayton, Ohio.

club. There are a total of eight exterior entrances from the four streets: four for retail, two for the office towers, and two private entrances for the residences.

The design theme of Cour Mont Royal, executed by Arcop Associates, is to contrast the old with the new. New entrances and shop windows of gray metal have been added to the exterior, and ultramodern shop fronts have been inserted into the old light wells. Great care has been taken with the choice of colors and details, in order to create modern elements that are sympathetic to the restored historic ones. The former hotel lobby, with its crystal chandeliers and richly patterned ceiling, has been restored as an elegant space used for concerts and exhibitions (see plate 17). This space is linked horizontally to the northwest atrium (used for vertical movement) and to the southwest atrium (used as a food court, called Noir et Blanc after its black-and-white color scheme). The northeast atrium, which is designed around a water theme, has a three-story fountain. The southeast atrium features mahogany showcases and honors the former hotel's palm court (see plate 18). All four atria are horizontally joined together with pedestrian spaces that total 145,000 square feet (13,470 square meters) and

feature escalators and curving stairs. With exclusive shops and classical music, Cour Mont Royal has an ambience that adroitly combines an elegance and sumptuousness that is similar in quality to that of Georgetown Park.

Most specialty centers are housed in renovated buildings where the historic character of the spaces, the materials, and the architectural features provide the basis for establishing a design theme. These buildings often are in prime downtown locations that relate well to the surrounding civic spaces and structures. Another incentive for the use of old buildings is that renovation is usually less costly than new construction. The critical design issue is how to convert these buildings to new uses, in accordance with contemporary requirements for servicing and circulation, without destroying their historic architectural character. At Georgetown Park, remnants of the old fabric along M Street were preserved and incorporated. At Cour Mont Royal, the old and the new were effectively combined to create a unique environment.

Those structures that were commercial centers in the past require less intervention to reestablish them as contemporary specialty centers. For example, Arcade Square in Dayton, Ohio, has a turn-of-the-century linear arcade and an entrance opposite Courthouse Square. The arcade connects to a 90-foot-diameter (27.4-meter-diameter) glass-domed rotunda of similar vintage that was used originally as an indoor farmer's market (figure 2.39) The rotunda is surrounded by two floors of shops and restaurants, which have both interior and exterior entrances, and is surmounted by three floors of apartments.[25] Careful restoration and the addition of new, low-key elements successfully combine with the center's multiple entrances and circulation routes to produce a historically sensitive project.

A similar project in Oakland, California, called The Rotunda, involved the renovation and restoration of the 1913 Kahn's Department Store with its uniquely elliptical domed rotunda, measuring 95 feet long and 75 feet wide (29 by 23 meters). A pedestrian concourse gives access to the rotunda space from both Broadway and the future city-hall plaza. The Rotunda combines three floors of retail space and four floors of offices within a building block measuring 350,000 square feet (32,515 square meters). The focal space is indeed spectacular—with its series of two-story, cast-plaster Corinthian columns; a coffered dome with cupola; and gold-leafed ornamentation and elaborate plaster moldings. This conversion of a Parisian-form department store to office space and a specialty shopping center once again demonstrates that projects that are sensitive adaptations of old structures and have interior spaces that are well related to exterior pedestrian spaces can be designed successfully.

A sound design strategy for creating a specialty shopping center is to utilize an existing building with a grand architectural space. Such a structure must have the capacity to attract people by its association with former public uses and its historic and/or present location in the city. The conversion of the Old Post Office, built in 1899 in Washington, D.C., is such a project. The building's public presence on Pennsylvania Avenue allows for instant recognition; and the former mailroom at the building's center afforded the opportunity to create a grand atrium space surrounded by three levels of shops and restaurants, with eight floors of government offices above. In Philadelphia, the Bourse, built in 1895, is another good example. The two-story trading floor at the center of this former Philadelphia stock exchange was converted to a three-story specialty center overlooked by six floors of offices.

Union Station, the grandest specialty shopping center in the world, opened in Washington, D.C. in 1988. It is the grandest because of the new center's intrinsic relationship with the colossal main hall of this Beaux-Arts railroad station designed by Daniel Burnham and completed in 1907. The building was inspired by the monumental scale of the baths of imperial Rome. The station boasts 96-foot-high (29.3-meter-high) vaulted ceilings and coffers decorated with seven pounds of 22-karat gold leaf.[26] Through the station's main hall passed presidents and kings, for it was once the historic gateway into the capital city. One of Washington, D.C.'s greatest interior public places has now been restored and given a new role as the focal space of an extensive specialty center (see plate 19).

The resurrected Union Station is a combination retail specialty center, parking garage, railroad station, and Amtrak headquarters. The federal government, the District of Columbia, and a private development team (La Salle Partners, Williams Jackson Ewing, and Benjamin Thompson & Associates) jointly funded the 160-million-dollar project. The 215,000-square-foot (19,974-square-meter) shopping center alone is larger than either Harborplace in Baltimore or South Street Seaport in New York City. Designed by Benjamin Thompson Associates, the shopping area contains over 100 stores, 5 major restaurants, and a nine-screen cinema located on the street level, the mezzanine, and the lower levels and inserted into the grand concourse behind the main hall (see plate 20). Shoppers enter through the majestic colonnades facing the Capitol; they then cross the main hall—passing by vendors, cafés, and kiosks on the way to the primary shopping area. Parking is at the rear, along with the railroad station and a lower-level connection to a Metro subway station. Great care has been taken to first preserve and restore the existing building and then to make alterations and additions appear contemporary—including the new arched openings cut into the roof of the main hall to visually relate it to the concourse. Other additions are the restaurants overlooking the main hall, two fountains, and a round, central kiosk structure (which preservationists claim is too obtrusive). This example of new retail uses in historic spaces is an eloquent statement of the validity of this design strategy. A dying landmark has been brought back to life, and the surrounding area of Capitol Hill has been energized with renewed urban vitality.

Another effective design strategy for creating a specialty shopping center is to utilize an ordinary, existing building in an excellent commercial location. Interior public spaces are then formed by carving them out of the inside of, for example, old warehouses, factories, and office buildings. Butler Square in Minneapolis, two blocks from Nicollet Mall, is the result of converting a huge warehouse into two floors of shops and seven floors of offices. To provide daylight and orientation within this 200- by 400-foot (61- by 122-meter) building, some of the internal timber structure was literally taken apart to form two atria of constructivist character. Within these orthogonally stepping spaces, the daylight filtering through the old wooden structure creates an optimal location for colorful shops that sell handmade articles. A similar strategy was employed at Jackson Brewery in New Orleans to create sixty shops and restaurants in a superb location at the corner of Jackson Square and the Mississippi River in the Vieux Carré. A glitzy and incongruous atrium has been created within this beautifully restored turn-of-the-century exterior. The atrium emerges on the roof as a volume of black glass with red mullions—a stark juxtaposition of new and old.

In Toronto, on the shores of Lake Ontario, the Zeidler Roberts Partnership skillfully converted the 1926 Terminal Warehouse Building into the Queen's Quay Terminal—an integrated multiuse center with two floors of shops, five floors of offices, and four new floors for seventy-two condominiums grouped around a roof garden. Inside the entry off of Queen's Drive is a small atrium that is connected via parallel passages to the main atrium at the south end and opens onto the lakefront. This focal space, which is surrounded by shops, has a fountain at its center, and four pyramidal skylights, and a theater lobby on the third floor. The atrium was created by removing some of the regularly spaced, concrete, mushroom columns and floor slabs—yielding an intriguing eroded quality that resembles the interior of Butler Square in Minneapolis. At the southeast corner, the atrium opens out splendidly to views of Lake Ontario. A restaurant, terraces, and stairs lead to the surrounding harbor-front promenades and boat docks (figure 2.40). A glass-enclosed arcade along the east and south sides and transparent shop fronts enable the interior and exterior pedestrian spaces to be visually related for orientation and views.

Fig. 2.40. South-atrium view, Queen's Quay Terminal. Toronto.

URBAN SHOPPING CENTERS IN GREAT BRITAIN

Following World War II, Great Britain did not experience rampant suburbanization and its concomitants: dispersed housing, the dominance of the automobile, large roads, and the proliferation of the suburban shopping mall. The retail activity of the town centers remained strong, served as they were by excellent public-transit systems and supported by a population that lived nearby. Following the postwar economic revival, new shopping centers were proposed; their locations were generally in the town center. In this way, the new retail centers both reinforced the existing marketplace and drew upon the tradition of intown shopping.

Two widely held cultural attitudes have shaped the development of Britain's urban retail centers: First, due to a deeply ingrained reverence for history and the physical destruction during World War II, the preservation of worthy old buildings became a cultural ethic. A national system of listing historic structures and the formation of regulations for restoring or modifying them was established and has been adamantly followed. This dedication to careful development was extended to the concept of the *townscape*—the preservation of groups of buildings and the stabilization and improvement of their context. Second, the British dedication to walking influenced their urban-retailing philosophy. The British have always understood the validity of walking as a form of transport, as well as its social, physiological, and recreational potential. When automobiles began threatening the viability of the central shopping districts, they were readily banned; and pedestrian precincts were formed.

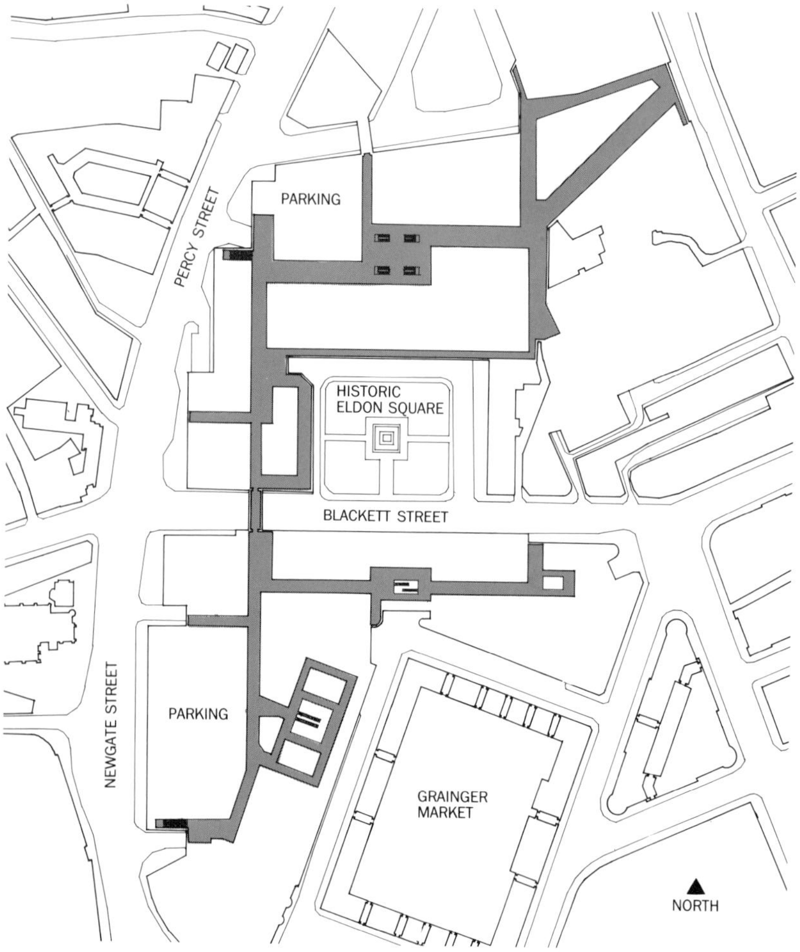

Many urban shopping centers anchored by two or more department stores have been built in British cities, including Manchester (Arndale), Birmingham (The Pavilions), Leeds (Crossgates), Peterborough (Queensgate), Oxford (Westgate). Eldon Square, in the center of Newcastle-upon-Tyne, is a good example of this type of center. Designed by Chapman Taylor Partners and developed by Capital and Counties, it was completed in two phases in 1975 and 1976. The main elements of this 781,700-square-foot (72,620-square-meter) center are Bainbridge's Department Store, four other large stores, 120 shops, a produce market, a recreation center, offices, a bus concourse, and two 750-car parking garages. The F-shaped, ten-acre site surrounds the existing green space of Eldon Square and the historic Grainger Market (figure 2.41). Although attempts were made to provide orientation views out to these landmarks, the mall spaces are quite introverted as well as contorted in geometry and mundane in design. Since most of the two-story mall has been raised above

Fig. 2.41. Second-level diagram, Eldon Square. Newcastle-upon-Tyne. England.

Fig. 2.42. Main-entrance view, Ridings Centre. Wakefield, England.

street level to provide service access and storage space, the pedestrian environment has been severely damaged. Interestingly, the old Grainger Market has shops that open both onto the street and onto the interior arcades. Many of the streets around this market and the older retail center have retained an active street life, despite the presence of the large enclosed shopping center.

A more successful example of urban-design integration is the Ridings Centre in Wakefield, designed and built in 1983 by the same architects and developers of Eldon Square. The design of this 350,000-square-foot (32,515-square-meter) retail center, with eleven hundred parking spaces, is based on the concept of back-land development—that is, buildings are erected on the interiors of blocks so as not to disturb the existing street frontages. This center is, therefore, visible only at the entrances and above the existing stores (three of which were enlarged to allow access from both the street and the mall). The few new facades are sympathetically designed, using pilasters and cornices of red and yellow brick; and the massing is articulated with sloping metal roofs. The parking garages, which are visible only from above and at the back, are disguised as ordinary buildings.

To circumvent the existing buildings and to fit the additions into the oddly shaped site, the plan employs a series of contorted geometric maneuvers—both vertically and horizontally. From the main entrance opposite the cathedral on Kirkgate (figure 2.42), the pedestrian proceeds down two levels through two light wells to the entrance on lower Kirkgate. Surprisingly, the internal pedestrian flow is quite smooth—due to the skillful placement of ramps, escalators, stairs, and continuous skylights that provide spatial orientation. Architecturally, the interior malls are an unhappy mixture of nineteenth-century charm and twentieth-century glitz. The lampposts, some of the railings, the color scheme, the plantings, and the two-toned quarry-tile floors have certain nineteenth-century overtones. The tempered-glass railings, the gridded-plastic ceilings, the fluorescent lights, and the mirrored spandrels are representative of late-twentieth-century commercial design. Together—and along with the glaring storefronts—these details produce a problematic visual cacophony (figure 2.43).

The same design critique can be applied to Waverly Market in Edinburgh,

Scotland: its contextual exterior design is more successful than is its commercial interior design. This newly built specialty center, completed in 1985 as designed by the Building Design Partnership, is located adjacent to the railroad station on the south side of Princes Street. The view across this site to the old town is protected by an act of Parlia-

Fig. 2.43. Interior view, Ridings Centre. Wakefield, England.

ment that restricts the height of buildings to one meter (3.3 feet) above the pavement. In response, the architects developed a subterranean center, which has a flat roof covered with grass, a granite-paved plaza, and two flat, mullionless, armor-plated glass skylights with laminated glass laylights. The entrances are well positioned: two on the street sides

Fig. 2.44. Exterior view, Waverly Market. Edinburgh, Scotland.

Fig. 2.45. West-atrium view, Waverly Market. Edinburgh, Scotland.

and one on a passage to the railroad station (figure 2.44). The market's plaza and lawns are useful urban amenities that provide access to the city's tourist office.

Waverly Market is organized around two irregularly shaped atria: One is a 350-seat food court around a pool, surrounded by nine eating establishments. The other has a landscaped water feature and a wine bar (figure 2.45). Mirror-faced escalators in both atria connect the three levels (consisting of 70,000 square feet [6,503 square meters]) with fifty fashion and gift shops. The design strategy is to make the inside different from the outside by using a 45-degree angle geometry and a multitude of mirrored surfaces. This geometric theme, located as it is on a rectangular site in an orthogonally gridded city, is both disconcerting and disorienting. Multiple reflections from the mirrored spandrels and columns cause the structural members to appear transparent and lead to visual confusion. The shop fronts constructed of elm and glass, are interestingly detailed, as are the innovative skylights. A sophisticated fire-suppression and smoke-exhaust system was installed, along with fire-exit corridors at the rears of the shops. With an excellent location and easy access, Waverly Market attracts many people—making it a lively and active place. The sunlit interiors with their lush plantings are intimate in scale and interesting to explore, despite their visual hyperactivity.

Eldon Square, Ridings Centre, and Waverly Market, along with Grosvenor Centre in Chester (see pages 188–193), illustrate some important lessons regarding urban shopping-center design. Excepting Eldon Square, what the British designers and developers have demonstrated is that an urban shopping center can be a commercial success without having a high degree of exterior building exposure; location in the city and ease of access are more important. The respect for context—demonstrated through design accommodation—makes townscaping the higher priority.

On the other hand, commercial sensationalism in the interior designs is too much of a preoccupation. The British continue to look to the United States for the latest interior-design innovations, instead of looking to their own traditions. The great Victorian shopping arcades and markets were marvelous commercial environments, which were visually provocative with their bold coloring and sculptural detail. Yet, there was spatial order and harmony of composition. Unwarranted geometric manipulation and the use by designers of careless forms and inappropriate materials (such as mirrored surfaces and plastic ceilings) are disturbing in their own right—but also because they do not abide by Britain's rich design traditions.

CONCLUSION

The early urban shopping centers in the United States were suburban in character. They were detached and isolated from their surroundings and, therefore, inwardly focused. Their exteriors were anticontextual in design, and they robbed the streets of their vitality. These tendencies gradually have changed, due to a growing awareness of the important design role of shopping centers in the urban context. New urban shopping centers are more contextually appropriate in that they are located in renovated historic structures or in sensitively designed new buildings. Recently built urban centers are integrated with the surrounding pedestrian systems and contribute to the existing street activity. Barry Maitland likens the transformation to transplant surgery:

It is as if a vital organ had been removed form the ailing patient under which it has been modified and improved according to its own, internal, program. The problem now arises as to how this new part is to be reintegrated into the parent body without incurring disruption and rejection. . . . And if the life support systems seem rather too much in evidence, if the staff maintain an atmosphere of forced cheerfulness, insisting on a sterile environment, rigidly excluding other uses, maintaining cleanliness and discipline with armies of ward orderlies . . . for fear of contamination from the open city outside, we may put this down to the severity of the operation.[27]

Urban shopping centers are not a panacea for saving the city; the problems are too vast and intransigent. Some argue that the gleaming physical and economic success of these centers detracts public officials from facing the real problems—a deteriorating infrastructure, inadequate housing, and neglected neighborhoods. Others argue that the economic clout of the new centers forces private shopkeepers out of business. Even those within these centers complain of stringent rules of operation and inflexible lease arrangements. The market population of the urban centers is composed of the middle and upper-middle classes, white-collar workers, tourists, and conventioneers. Most centers contribute little to the lives of the urban poor.

Although the types of goods have changed and so have the methods of merchandising, the pedestrian has remained a constant factor. Shopping continues to be one of the primary pedestrian activities of the city. External forces, such as traffic, pollution, crime, and congestion, have challenged the pedestrian—yet, the pedestrian sallies forth, undaunted in his or her historic role. As we approach the twenty-first century, shopping is once again an active force in the continued growth and revitalization of our cities. ■

Marketplaces were among the most significant public places of any historic city. They were almost always open-air and were centrally located in squares and plazas. The markets usually were transient in nature—consisting of booths and stalls that were covered and uncovered and brought in or erected by independent merchants on a daily or seasonal basis. Thus, on weekends and holidays, the market space could be used for other purposes. Until the nineteenth century, this was—and in many cities with primarily temperate climates still is—the traditional market for the purchase of vegetables, fruits, and meats.

Some of the physical and economic reasons that led to the creation of the shopping arcade also led to the creation of the indoor market. For the shopper, it was more convenient and comfortable to shop in a place protected from the weather. For the merchant, the indoor market was a more dependable setting in which to offer his or her wares in a collective, competitive atmosphere. The social aspects of the indoor market, however, were not as important as those of the arcade. In fact, only three of the seven defining characteristics of the arcade (as described by Johann Friedrich Geist in *Arcades* [see page 32]) apply to the indoor market: public space on private property, skylit space, and a form of organizing retail trade. Thus, the indoor market is related to the shopping arcade; yet, it is different, for it is primarily a destination rather than a pedestrian passage.

More arcades were built in the nineteenth century than were covered markets. Leadenhall Market, built in 1881 near the financial district in London, is still in active use as a food market (see figure 1.14). In this location, a sheltered precinct was created by covering the existing streets, thus interrelating the market and the city. In Newcastle-upon-Tyne, the Grainger Market also remains in active use as a food market alongside the Eldon Square regional shopping mall. What a contrast in scale, character, and contextual relationship these two centers make. The concourses of Eldon Square are above the street, whereas those at Grainger Market are at street level with shop entrances from both the street and the market interior. The 1904 Kirkgate Market in Leeds, with its polychromed market-hall structure and continuous viewing balcony, is architecturally the most handsome of these three markets (figure 2.46). The Covent Garden Market, built in 1830 in London and designed by Charles Fowler, should also be mentioned here (although it will be discussed in detail later).

The best-known and most extensive covered market of the nineteenth century was Les Halles Centrales in Paris, designed by Victor Baltard in 1853. This market—with its fourteen market halls and a central rotunda utilized for the sale of meats, vegetables, and fruits—virtually created its own city district. The

Fig. 2.46. Interior view, Kirkgate Market. Leeds, England.

arcaded spaces covering the streets provided vehicular and pedestrian access for shopping and deliveries (figure 2.47). This vital, earthy, captivating market—often referred to as "the stomach of Paris"—was demolished in 1971 in order to make way for the Forum des Halles, a shopping center formed around a sunken court. The demolition of this vibrant place is certainly one of the great tragedies of urban renewal.

Fig. 2.47. Interior view, Les Halles Centrales. Paris.

Fig. 2.48. Exterior view, Ghirardelli Square. San Francisco.

A century after the construction of Les Halles Centrales in Paris, a new kind of marketplace was developed in several North American and European cities. Termed the *festival marketplace*, it combines entertainment, socialization, specialty shopping, and recreational eating—usually in a historic setting. Ghirardelli Square in San Francisco, designed by Wurster, Bernardi & Emmons in 1964, generally is regarded as the first example of this market type.[28] The market's unique tenant mix features restaurants and stores selling men's and women's fashions, import goods, and luxury items. Housed in a rehabilitated nineteenth-century chocolate factory near the bay, the location is both historic and captivating (figure 2.48). Since there are no anchor tenants or department stores, the setting itself must be the main attraction. This eclectic group of brick buildings, grouped around a series of terraced courts, possesses an inviting ambience that induces both tourists and residents to enjoy the process of exploring it. Two blocks away, The Cannery, a converted peach-canning plant, adopted the same retail model with equal success.

Several similar projects have been developed in various parts of the United States, but the most significant was the Rouse Company's Faneuil Hall Marketplace in Boston, completed in 1976 (figure 2.49). Faneuil Hall was originally constructed in 1742 as a public market and meeting hall and was enlarged in 1805 by architect Charles Bulfinch. In 1826 Alexander Parris built the 555-foot-long Quincy Market behind Faneuil Hall and added two other granite market buildings. This then became Boston's wholesale market center for seafood and produce. After demolition was threatened in 1964, the city of Boston restored the exteriors and sold the buildings to the Rouse Company, retaining a 99-year ground lease. Following architect Benjamin Thompson's scheme, the area was developed into a festival marketplace, with

Fig. 2.49. Exterior view, Faneuil Hall Marketplace. Boston.

food stalls and eating places in the old Quincy Market building and 150 specialty shops in the north- and south-market buildings (see plate 21). The streets between the three buildings were developed as plazas. An assortment of trees, flowers, benches, and lights were installed; and the area is animated by pushcarts, kiosks, and entertainers. Glass-roofed sheds were added to the side of the Quincy Market building and to the ends of the other buildings so that the shops could open onto these plazas. In 1986 Marketplace Center was built at the east end, adding twenty-two shops and a central arched gateway that leads into the main marketplace.

By any measure, Faneuil Hall Market-place is a great success. Although the development costs were estimated to be 30 percent more than new construction, the unique environment yielded rents three times the national average.[29] Reportedly, over twelve million people a year visit the market, which results in an income of $350 per square foot of rented space.[30] Faneuil Hall has become the single biggest attraction in Boston. In terms of historic preservation, a group of buildings was saved and creatively adapted for re-use. This led to numerous redevelopment projects in Boston's waterfront area—according to an urban-design concept known as "the walk to the sea."

In an article written in 1979, Jane Thompson cited six inherent qualities that generate the attraction of the festival marketplace, as summarized below:

1. People and Activity Are Elemental: Animation attracts people who visibly attract more people.

2. Real Use: Goods and services that relate to daily needs are offered.

3. A True Environment: Use of genuine old buildings avoids pretense and fakery.

4. Elemental Novelty and Change: Intrinsic movement of people evolves with day, night and seasonal changes.

5. Elemental Aesthetic Pleasure and a Sense of Quality: Sensual pleasure from building elements, lights, plants and trees.

6. Authentic Meaning in the Urban Context: Despite private ownership it has public purpose in revitalizing downtown and serving human needs.[31]

In 1980 these six qualities were incorporated by the same development team to produce Harborplace, two new commercial structures on the Inner Harbor in Baltimore. Although the setting was historic, none of the context remained. Architect Benjamin Thompson had to design new buildings that were clearly modern in expression but were inspired by traditional waterfront warehouse and terminal buildings, as well as by nineteenth-century exposition halls and pavilions.[32] The decision not to separate the harbor from the city resulted in buildings that have equal faces and are highly transparent. The entry porticoes break the roof line and draw people in and through the markets. Exterior stairs lead to the second-level galleries, from which visitors can view the harbor-front activities (see plate 22). The most significant design attribute is the fluid relationship of inside to outside pedestrian space. The private commercial space is carefully balanced with the public social space—a visitor can shop for food or watch the boats without being compelled to do either.

Approximately the same size as the Faneuil Hall Marketplace, (250,000 square feet [23,225 square meters]), Harborplace is composed of two buildings set at right angles to each other. The buildings are located at the water's edge and are surrounded by brick-paved plazas. The northern pavilion is the smaller of the two and contains mostly specialty shops along a central corridor (figure 2.50). The western pavilion is devoted to the sale of prepared and fresh foods of all kinds, purveyed from restau-

Fig. 2.50. Interior view, North Pavilion, Harborplace. Baltimore.

Fig. 2.51. Exterior view, South Street Seaport. New York City.

the renovated Schermerhorn Row (figure 2.51). Again, the scheme is based on the sympathetic juxtaposition of the old and new buildings. Fulton Street was converted to a pedestrian spine; it now relates the waterfront and its historic ships to the adjacent business district.[34] The architectural character of the interior-market spaces is unpretentious, with an exposed steel frame structure. The spatial and visual transition from outside to inside is well handled, with broad canopies, large windows, and glazed lean-to sheds. The multitude of uses, in conjunction with the architectural variety of old and new in a fascinating waterfront setting, has yielded a visually rich and vital project.

The formula for creating attractive marketplaces, as developed by the Rouse and Thompson development team, has been carefully thought out and even more judiciously executed. The locations have all been in historically prominent areas of downtown near a harbor. Existing structures with architectural character and tradition have been adapted for new uses through sensitive intervention. Much effort has been expended in the visual control of storefronts, graphics, lighting, and furnishings. These projects depend upon the nearby business districts and tourist attractions to provide a constant flow of people. Two recently completed projects, based on the same concept, in Miami (Bayside Marketplace) and Jacksonville (Jacksonville Landing) have been successful for similar reasons. Waterside, in Norfolk, Virginia, led to the redevelopment of the downtown area, despite the fact that the marketplace itself remains unprofitable. The future of festival marketplaces, however, is not certain. Will they sustain their success once their newness wears off? Will they be permanent places for urban enjoyment, or will they need to be recycled periodically to maintain their attractiveness?

The festival marketplaces in small cities, such as Toledo, Ohio; Flint,

rants, stands, and shops. The floor plan of the western pavilion is informal and open, but the design of storefronts, signage, and furnishings is controlled. Both pavilions consist of two levels and a two-story central space that contains landscaping, seating, amenities, and stairs. As in Boston, Harborplace's commercial success results from the combination of location, design, management, and tenant mix. The project is also a social and civic success, for it gives the Inner Harbor a vital new destination. Here is a place to take visitors and children on the weekend, as well as a place to drink or dine during the week. There is something for everyone in this carefully concocted festive setting. In the first year of operation, Harborplace attracted eighteen million visitors, which is more than the annual number of visitors to Disney World.[33]

The design of South Street Seaport on the East River in Manhattan combines elements from Faneuil Hall and Harborplace. This is not surprising, given that these three projects share the same development team, and all are located on historic waterfronts. This four-block project consists of the restored museum block, a new Fulton Market, the old Fulton Fish Market, a shopping pavilion on a new Pier 17, the new thirty-four-story Seaport Plaza office building, and

Michigan; and Richmond, Virginia, have not been a financial success for Rouse's Enterprise Development Corporation—even though they bolstered downtown revitalization and civic pride. Because the marketplace's operating costs are much higher than for other shopping centers, higher numbers of pedestrians are required who actually buy goods rather than simply stroll and socialize.[35]

A project that demonstrates the temporal continuity of the marketplace concept is Covent Garden Market in London. When it was constructed in 1830 as a produce market, there were three parallel two-story ranges, a central arcade, and a linking colonnade across the east end. In 1880 the courtyards between the ranges were covered with a cast-iron structure that was glazed at the center (figure 2.52). After its abandonment as a fruit, vegetable, and flower market in 1974, there was a great deal of debate about the market's future. The London County Council finally restored the market to its 1880 appearance, except for the creation of two new sunken courts, which significantly increased the leasable area. Today, the food-market theme is no longer dominant. The market is occupied primarily by shops selling luxury goods and a few restaurants (figure 2.53).

As in Boston, the creation of a festival marketplace at Covent Garden has led to the regeneration of an urban district for entertainment and luxury shopping. The restored Covent Garden Market, surrounded by plaza space, continues to give this district its identity. An adjacent transport museum has been created,

Fig. 2.52. Exterior view, Covent Garden Market. London.

Fig. 2.53. North court, Covent Garden Market. London.

Fig. 2.54. South court, Covent Garden Market. London.

along with another markethall and numerous stores, shops, and restaurants. The historic pattern of the structures and streets has not been disturbed, thus leaving the urban fabric intact. The sheds and arcades of the market are always open, allowing the pedestrian space to remain public at all times. Even the old flower sellers' carts remain (figure 2.54).

Important planning and design lessons can be learned from the historic markets and festival marketplaces—regarding interior places as they relate to the character of many urban shopping centers. In one sense, the public's interest in these places can be seen as a negative reaction to the character of many urban centers. With their large, confusing scale; their industrialized character; and the predominance of franchised stores, the urban shopping centers are

the opposites of festival marketplaces. They feature an intimate scale, historic architecture, traditional materials, and unique specialty shops. In the historic markets, the forms of the interior spaces had integrity and clarity; they were defined by sheds of structural purity raised over the bustling activity below.

In contrast to most urban shopping centers, the interior spaces of festival marketplaces are not formal or grandly scaled. They are full of shifts in plan and section geometry, which are intended to form a series of linked spaces. These spaces are modeled on the *souk*, or bazaar, spaces that are revealed through discovery. The architecture alone does not create the ambience. Rather, it is the combination of people, daylight, plants, goods, signs, and architectural elements that creates a memorable character.

Shopping for luxury goods should be an enjoyable experience. In order for people to be in the mood for buying, they must be relaxed and having fun. The settings of festival marketplaces are relaxed, informal, and interesting. The entertainers brought in to provide music, magic acts, and mime create a sense of theater. The chairs and benches amidst the trees and flowers provide places for rest and relaxation. The entire effort is intended to create an ambience that transforms shopping into a form of entertainment.

These are also places for urban socialization. They are popular places to meet and to greet or just to stroll and hang-out. Various areas are designed for these purposes, including promenades, balconies, terraces, indoor gardens, fountains, and plazas. Food and drink are important ingredients in these social processes, making their inclusion essential. A variety of eating opportunities is necessary in order to satisfy the divergent visitor population at different times of the day and night. Thus, a visitor can choose among the terrace restaurants, the indoor cafés, the stand-up counters, and the fast-food takeout stands. The food court—an international array of takeout food places surrounding a large communal area of tables and chairs—has become one of the most successful new food-marketing inventions. Food courts are so popular that they have become an essential part of every new urban shopping center (and some office complexes) in Britain and the United States.

Probably the most important design lesson is the way in which the interior and exterior spaces of festival marketplaces have been related. In all of these projects, the public pedestrian areas have been integrated with the existing street and sidewalk systems. Through the use of multiple, large entrances, these exterior spaces are allowed to flow freely into the buildings and be joined with the interior pedestrian areas. Usually, there are plaza-level connections with subtle level changes. These connections are enhanced by visual transparency (being able to see freely into and out from the buildings). The continuity of pedestrian spaces makes the pedestrian circulation smooth, varied, and effortless. Because there are many different routes to take, each visit is somewhat unique.

The debate continues as to whether festival marketplaces have contributed something genuine and lasting to our cities or something contrived and temporary. Robert Campbell draws an analogy between the festival marketplace and the nineteenth-century urban park, which was seen as an artificial, idealized rural setting brought into the city to remind urban residents of the nature that had been lost. In a similar way, festival marketplaces are idealized settings of an urbanity that has been lost. From them, we can learn something about how to develop a more genuine, vital city:

> It's true, for instance, that the marketplace does not offer an experience of much depth. Not yet. It's a quick fix, an upper of urbanity that lifts your blood sugar and then lets you down, leaving you thirsting for more. Of course it isn't a real city. Then again, no one promised us a real city. We have to make that for ourselves. . . .
>
> The marketplace is an impersonization of a kind of urban life that no longer exists in most of America. It's a theatrical representation of street life. It has to be this, because that is a stage we have to go through as we begin cautiously, self-consciously to re-enact the urban culture we abandoned. No doubt in the future the marketplace will feel real.[36] ■

Multiuse centers are buildings that accommodate more than one of the three main functions of human life: work, recreation, and inhabitation.[37] The definition of recreation has been expanded to include shopping, theater, education, culture, health, and entertainment. The successful multiuse building must not only balance the internal integration of these activities but must also relate them to the external urban context. Placing different activities in one building results in an economical use of land and user efficiency or convenience. Interior pedestrian space is usually the means for achieving this internal integration. Contextual integration is just as important, since multiuse buildings must draw upon a vital context for their existence. The latter issue is important, for the tendency has been to isolate by design—thus causing the surrounding street life to atrophy.

In his book *Multi-Use Architecture in the Urban Context*, Eberhard Zeidler asks some fundamental questions about multiuse buildings:

> Do such buildings make both physical connection and social reference to their surroundings?
> Do they encourage pedestrian use of the street and yet facilitate traffic movement?
> Do they provide public amenities and a better use of urban space?
> Do they create a framework that supports different uses to their common benefit?[38]

These questions form the basis for the analyses of multiuse centers in this section. Although the emphasis here is on the interior pedestrian space, the overall design of a multiuse center should satisfy these criteria. The architect's conceptual approach and the detailed design of the interior pedestrian space are often the keys to a successful design resolution.

One historic precedent for today's multiuse center and its interior pedestrian spaces is the nineteenth-century railroad station. In addition to its basic function, the railroad station usually incorporated a variety of uses—including retail activities, restaurants, offices, exhibition space, and lodging. The main terminal, or concourse, was the central space around which all was organized.

Perhaps the grandest of these stations in the United States is Grand Central Terminal in New York City, designed by Reed & Stern and Warren & Wetmore between 1903 and 1913. More than just a building project, its construction involved placing the tracks in two tiers underground, building Park Avenue above, and enabling thirty blocks of buildings to be built over these tracks north and south of the terminal. The northern and southern sections of Park Avenue were joined together by road ramps that wrapped around the terminal at the second level. At the street level below the ramps, there were shops and terminal entrances leading to waiting rooms and grand staircases leading down to the level of the main concourse. Surrounding this central space and along the concourses leading to it, the traveler could find a multitude of services and shopping.

The Grand Concourse is one of New York City's most celebrated interior pedestrian places. This classically composed, Beaux-Arts space is lit by high arched windows on the east and west and by semicircular windows on the north and south (figure 2.55). The vaulted ceiling, once intended for skylights, spans 125 feet (38.1 meters) and is decorated with constellations of the zodiac. Above the south entry hangs a great sculptural clock—an ever-present reminder of the train schedules to be followed. In the morning and at rush hour, this is the place to sense the pulse of New York City. It is as much a crossroads as Time Square, a place called "New York's Piazza San Marco" by Robert A. M. Stern. As Stern comments, Grand Central Station "seemed to raise the comings and goings

Fig. 2.55. Interior view, Grand Central Station. New York City.

of travelers to the level of romantic rites of passage, luring urbanities to the station to gawk, meet, or simply use it as a covered street, the nexus of the greater theater of New York."[39]

Grand Central Terminal is also an excellent example of how to integrate a multiuse center with its context. The second-level ramps physically link the structure to the surrounding roads. At street level, the vitality of the sidewalks is maintained by the shops and the buildings' entrances. The pedestrian sequence from 42d Street into the terminal, across the concourse, and out the other side and up through the lobby of the Pan Am Building is an integrated series of spaces used by thousands each day. The complex circulation needs of cars, pedestrians, and trains have been adroitly organized and encompassed within a monumental architectural statement.

Several historic railroad stations have been adapted as contemporary multiuse centers—now that their need to serve passengers has waned. The 1901 train shed of Richmond, Virginia's Main Street Station was converted recently into a shopping mall, with the headhouse used as offices and restaurants. The monumental Union Station in Washington, D.C., designed by Daniel Burnham and built from 1905 to 1907, was restored and converted to a shopping and entertainment center—while still functioning as a railroad station (see page 84).

The St. Louis Union Station project is a matter of superlatives: the largest historic rehabilitation project of what was once the world's busiest railroad station with the largest single-span train shed ever built.[40] Designed in 1894 by Theodore C. Link of St. Louis, the station was converted to its present uses in 1985 by Hellmuth, Obata & Kassabaum under the auspices of three developers. The original structure had three components: the headhouse, the Grand Hall, and the Midway (figure 2.56). The 750-foot-long (229-meter-long) Romanesque headhouse on Market Street has been restored to its original functions, which included a hotel, restaurants, shops, and offices. The magnificent Grand Hall (76 feet by 120 feet [23.2 by 36.6 meters] with a 65-foot-high [19.8-meter-high] vaulted ceiling), which was the main waiting room, is now both the main entrance to the complex and the lobby of the new Omni International Hotel. The Midway was a 50-foot-wide (15.2-meter-high) transition zone between the headhouse and the train shed, which now functions as a circulation space—containing stairs, escalators, bridges, and a ground-level esplanade.

The most colossal element of this project is the former five-bay train shed—covering 11.5 acres (4.6 hectares) and

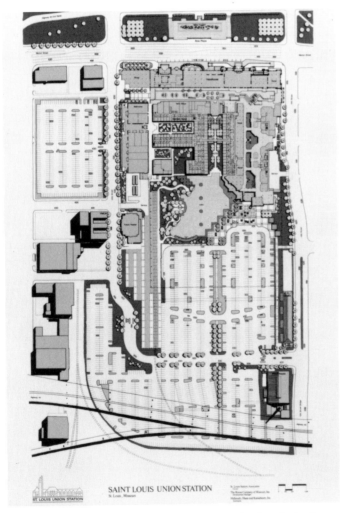

Fig. 2.56. Ground-level site plan, St. Louis Union Station. St. Louis.

measuring 606 feet wide, 810 feet long, and 140 feet high (185 by 247 by 43 meters). The shed has been divided conceptually into discrete zones that provide for 480 hotel rooms, 160,000 square feet (14,864 square meters) of retail space, a lake, a plaza, and covered parking. All new construction has been placed under the shed roof, so as not to detract from its vast soaring quality (figure 2.57). The new hotel, which steps up to six stories, is located in two parallel wings perpendicular to the Midway. The shopping center, with two levels of concourses, and the food court also are located in a wing perpendicular to the Midway. The master stroke is the one-acre, covered lake surrounded by a park containing a beer garden. Portions of the wood roof, supported in five bays by steel butterfly trusses, have been removed to create the unusual spatial effect of partial enclosure, which suggests that the sky is the true roof. These removed roof areas are left open over the plaza and are glazed over the retail areas.

St. Louis Union Station has been brought back to a vital urban role. Neither the hotel nor the shopping mall are

exemplary in themselves, although both are designed in a contemporary character that is sympathetic to their historic context. The way in which these elements relate to the train shed's roof gives them their architectural uniqueness (see plate 23). The shed dominates all—hovering over everything like a colossal umbrella. In summer, the availability of enclosed and partially enclosed space enables expansion of use to the exterior. The station is large enough to be its own island of urban vitality, even though it is removed from the commercial center. And vital it is, bustling on a Saturday night with people young and old. They come to stroll, to eat, and to drink. For them, the station is a safe, secure place in which to undertake our era's favorite amusement—shopping for novelties. The shimmering lake and the music floating on the night air make Union Station St. Louis's equivalent of Copenhagen's Tivoli Gardens.

Many multiuse centers are fraught with problems that result from their conception rather than from their design. Usually, the program is too vast—that is, too many large building elements must be unified. Of necessity, this kind of program requires a large site that can only be found on the periphery of the downtown core. These locations in turn require vast amounts of parking connected to large highways. While these megastructures are promoted for their economic salvation of downtown, they usually weaken its economic vitality by diverting activity.

Much has been written about Detroit's Renaissance Center (or RenCen), which is a textbook case study of the just discussed set of circumstances. This colossal project consists of four thirty-eight-story cylindrical office towers (2.2 million square feet [204,380 square meters]) surrounding a seventy-three-story cylindrical hotel (with fourteen hundred rooms) on top of a podium with a retail mall, restaurants, and parking. The project was completed in 1977 as designed by

Fig. 2.57. View from train shed, St. Louis Union Station. St. Louis.

Fig. 2.58. Atrium view, Omni International. Atlanta.

John Portman & Associates. This bastion, located on the Detroit River and just seven blocks from the heart of downtown, is separated from the city center by a ten-lane road. It is also surrounded by forbidding concrete walls that prevent any pedestrian association with the downtown area. Around the office-tower core is a circular, four-level skylit arcade that was so disorienting that it has already been redesigned. According to an article in the *Washington Post*:

> Shoppers and strollers routinely lose their way on the circular paths and wind up where they started without ever finding the store they wanted. As a result, patronage of the arcade has never come close to projections and numerous stores have opened and closed in rapid succession to disappointing sales.[41]

The disorienting aspect of RenCen is also a by-product of its dissociation from its surroundings; once inside, the pedestrian loses his or her bearings. The largest privately financed real-estate project in the country has unfortunately done little for the economic rejuvenation of downtown Detroit.[42]

The Omni International in Atlanta is similarly separated form the city center. Built over railroad tracks in the rundown western part of downtown, it was intended to compete with Atlanta's outlying regional shopping centers. It does not have the same pedestrian problems as Renaissance Center since it is organized around a huge atrium—called The Great Space. This vast atrium integrates the many elements of this multiuse center which consists of two eleven-story office buildings; a 500-room hotel; an indoor amusement park; and 230,000 square feet (21,367 square meters) of retail shops, restaurants, and cinemas. In 1976, the year of its completion, this was the largest atrium space yet constructed. The atrium is fifteen stories tall and contains eleven million cubic feet (311,700 cubic meters). Four floors of galleries surround an Olympic-size ice-skating rink located on the main level. As a result, this great public space can only be occupied by skaters, and pedestrians are forced to the periphery. Nevertheless, the atrium does serve to spatially integrate the project and provides pedestrian orientation (figure 2.58).

The most successful multiuse centers, in terms of pedestrian use, are those that have been integrated with the urban context they serve and which serves them. This integration is primarily the result of the interior-exterior continuity of the pedestrian systems. Most of the exterior pedestrian areas and routes are established—unless there is a plan to change them. The entrances to the multiuse centers and the internal pedestrian circulation must relate to these areas and enhance them. The spaces themselves should provide public-use amenities as a means for drawing pedestrians in.

Where healthy sidewalk activity already exists, it should be respected and enhanced with building facades that add shop windows, entrances, arcades, and/or exhibition spaces. In many cities, the zoning laws have been changed to prevent the construction of street-facing blank walls. As a result, developers have begun to enliven the facades by providing visual interest or areas for pedestrian activity. Some developers have done this voluntarily. An example is International Square in Washington, D.C., which occupies an entire block and consists of two levels of retail space and eleven stories of offices surrounding a twelve-story atrium (figure 2.59). The shops have entrances from both the atrium and street sides. Moreover, the atrium floor below street level is surrounded by retail uses accessible from the Metro subway station. At Eaton Centre in Toronto, in an effort to preserve sidewalk activity, some specialty shops have been given entrances along Yonge Street.

In terms of pedestrian integration with its context, one of the most successful examples of multiuse centers is the IDS Center in Minneapolis, designed by Philip Johnson and John Burgee and completed in 1973. This square-block project in the center of downtown on the Nicollet Mall unites four buildings: the fifty-one-story IDS office tower, a nineteen-story hotel, an eight-story office building, and a two-story Woolworth's. These four elements and the accompanying underground parking surround and form the Crystal Court, a covered plaza-atrium at the center of the block. The atrium in turn is surrounded by two levels of shops (figure 2.60).

The vitality engendered by this project is in large part due to the thorough integration of the pedestrian systems—both newly formed and existing. Minneapolis has an extensive system of second-level pedestrian bridges (see page 146). Four of these bridges lead directly into the Crystal Court—two of them from the department stores located on adjacent blocks. These skyways become second-level walkways, which access to shops, balcony overlooks, and connections down to the street-level plaza. However, the sidewalks have not been forgotten. Under each pedestrian bridge is a recessed entrance to the Crystal Court, with additional separate entrances to each of the buildings surrounding it. The main entrance on Nicollet Mall is from a small plaza, which features a large expanse of

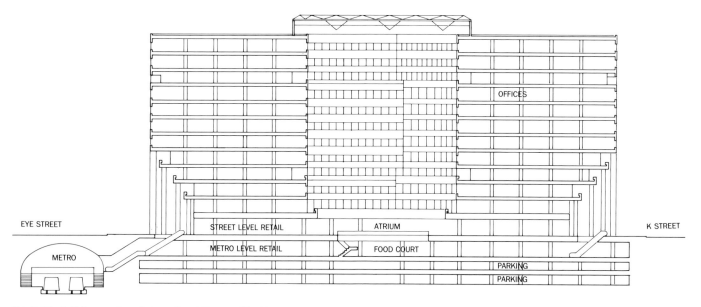

EYE STREET

METRO

STREET LEVEL RETAIL   ATRIUM   OFFICES   K STREET

METRO LEVEL RETAIL   FOOD COURT

PARKING

PARKING

Fig. 2.59. Building section, International Square. Washington, D.C.

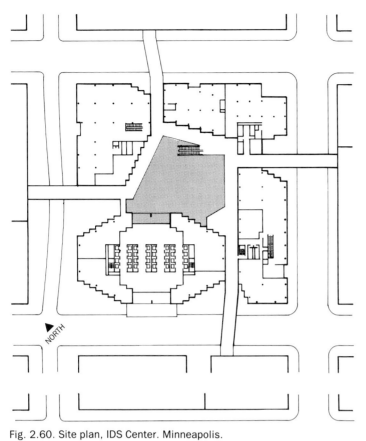

Fig. 2.60. Site plan, IDS Center. Minneapolis.

glass intended to establish a strong visual connection between the interior and exterior pedestrian spaces (figure 2.61).

The Crystal Court itself is unique in both its design and spatial concept. An irregular pentagon in plan, the court encloses 20,000 square feet (1,858 square meters) of pedestrian space. The roof structure is a white-steel space frame rising in steps from two stories to seven stories. The vertical and horizontal interstices are glazed with clear glass and acrylic skylights respectively, and the walkways and balconies of blue-painted steel are suspended from this space frame. The daylight quality in the atrium is always appealing—softly glowing on overcast days and tantalizingly bright on sunny days (see plate 24).

The Crystal Court also represents the invention of a new type of interior pedestrian place. The *plaza-atrium* functions as an outdoor plaza that has been covered

Fig. 2.61. Nicollett Mall entrance, IDS Center. Minneapolis.

and enclosed to become an interior space. It is not the focal space of a given building but rather unites several buildings, as does a traditional outdoor plaza. As such, the plaza-atrium is most successful when it is a well-integrated extension of a city's public pedestrian system. Its use should also be for traditional public purposes, such as strolling, sitting, eating, drinking, and meeting. In all these regards, the Crystal Court is an outstanding example, for its design has been poetically achieved. It has become a place to be sought out and enjoyed—a nexus of pedestrian activity in downtown Minneapolis. (It was maturing well in the variety of activities taking place until a new management policy called for the removal of the seating and restrictions on the court's use.)

Multiuse centers that rely on interior pedestrian spaces as integrators can be divided into two categories: those that are organized around plaza-atria and those that are organized around retail elements. No centers known to this author rely totally upon arcades or linear spaces (although the second category often includes these spatial forms). Multiuse centers organized around plaza-atria may include retail functions, but the public pedestrian space is usually set apart. In multiuse centers organized around retail elements, the pedestrian spaces have no discrete identity (with the usual attendant consequence of weaker design integration among the various elements of the center).

In addition to the IDS Center, several other multiuse centers formed around plaza-atria have been designed and constructed. One Market Plaza in San Francisco is a one-block complex of offices and retail space that incorporates the 1916 Southern Pacific Building on Market Street. A through-block concourse related to two six-story plaza-atria serves to unite this scheme spatially and to infuse it with a moderate level of pedestrian activity.[43] A much more dramatic plaza-atrium is the one at First Source Center in South Bend, Indiana, designed by Murphy/Jahn Architects. This 27,000-square-foot (2,508-square-meter) space relates an office building to a hotel and includes a parking garage underneath and a terraced restaurant at one end. As a connecting space between a parking-plaza and a park, it does not function as well as One Market Plaza. The trapezoidal plan and the inverted gable roof, sheathed in alternating bands of clear and silver-reflective glass, create a visually compelling space with fascinating daylight patterns.[44]

Greenville Commons in Greenville, South Carolina, is a plaza-atrium formed by an L-shaped Hyatt hotel and a parallelogram-shaped office building, which has retail space on its ground floor (figure 2.62). This eight-story space diagonally joins two primary streets, and the entrances access from small plazas located at both ends. Inside, a series of terraced levels used for seating and eating are enhanced by a cascading fountain, waterfalls, pools, and extensive landscaping. The northern and western facades are glazed, which allows visual access to the

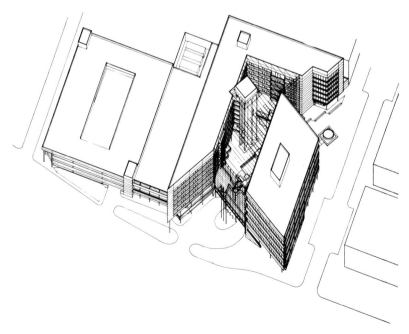

Fig. 2.62. Axonometric drawing, Greenville Commons. Greenville, South Carolina.

Fig. 2.63. Interior view, Greenville Commons. Greenville, South Carolina.

atrium from the exterior plazas and streets (figure 2.63). Because the atrium is owned by the city and managed by the hotel, it functions as both a lobby and a public commons. This cooperative arrangement, which ensures public control over the plaza-atrium's use, serves as a model for similar ventures in other cities.

Tower City Center in Cleveland is a proposed multiuse project that integrates existing office buildings, hotels, and department stores while creating

new elements. These include two new office buildings, a hotel, a retail concourse, and the Rock-and-Roll Hall of Fame. Interestingly, the unifying element will be a plaza-atrium called the Skylight Concourse. This barrel-vaulted, skylit pedestrian space will be surrounded by three levels of shops—comprising 350,000 square feet (32,515 square meters). It will connect directly to Riverview Marketplace—two levels of cafés, restaurants, pubs, food shops, cinemas, and clubs overlooking the Cuyahoga River. The plaza-atrium will be built first, as a linking element for future phases and as a means for generating project momentum (figure 2.64).

Several multiuse centers are organized around retail elements. For example, Water Tower Place on North Michigan Avenue in Chicago houses multiple functions in its ten-story base and its seventy-three-story tower located on one corner of a small block. The seven floors of shopping in the base building (totaling 597,000 square feet [55,461 square meters]) are organized into a compact dumbbell plan, with the Marshall Field and Lord & Taylor department stores at the ends and smaller shops in between.[45] This plan arrangement begins at the second floor requiring a high landscaped escalator lobby at the main Michigan Avenue entrance. At the center of the dumbbell plan is an octagonal atrium

containing three glass-and-steel elevators. Although this space does provide some orientation, it is not a gathering space nor does it have daylight. Connection to the tower lobby is possible only at the second floor. Because Water Tower Place lacks a significant organizing space to relate all of its elements, it is difficult for the pedestrian to comprehend the organization of this multiuse center.

Copley Place in Boston has similar problems. The interior pedestrian spaces are not coherent enough to integrate the elements of this multiuse center. This problem stems from the location of off-ramps to the Massachusetts Turnpike and railroad tracks on the site. These elements required the primary pedestrian level to be located 30 feet (9.1 meters) above the street-level entrances.[46] This retail level is joined to the Westin Hotel by a bridge across Stuart Street and to the Prudential Center by

Fig. 2.64. Rendering of Tower City Center. Cleveland.

Fig. 2.65. Atrium view, Copley Place. Boston.

another diagonal bridge across Huntington Avenue. This scheme forms a complicated but workable pedestrian loop that is, however, not experientially rewarding. There is a strong central-atrium space that reaches up through the office floors to a generous skylight, but the adjacent linear mall spaces are not of a memorable architectural character. Once again, the spaces are too introverted, which causes the pedestrian to be unaware of external references—such as the office and hotel towers (figure 2.65).

One of the best-designed multiuse centers that relies on a retail element as the integrator is Baltimore's Gallery at Harborplace, across the street from the well-known festival marketplace (see page 94). Designed by the Zeidler Roberts Partnership and developed by the Rouse Company in 1988, this compact building block incorporates four levels of shops, the Legg Mason office tower, the Stouffer Hotel, and 1,150 parking spaces. The streetside entry to the center at the corner of Pratt and Calvert streets opens onto a dynamic interior pedestrian place. This space extends diagonally into the block and then widens and rises in height, eventually leading to a café terrace at the back with adjacent access to the hotel's lobby. There is additional café seating on bridges and galleries on the third level in a glazed corner overlooking Harborplace.

Architect Eberhard Zeidler relates his design of this space to the Spanish Steps in Rome—but with escalators instead of stairs. This space has a strong geometric order derived form the imposition of diagonal form onto an orthogonal structural grid. The rhythmic white structure and the continuous skylight create a modulated series of spaces that step in plan and section but yet are legible as a unified grand space. The dynamics of space and light draw the visitor up and through the atrium to the many vantage points that are visually oriented to it and to the street corner. As people move through this space on the white bridges and galleries with their glass guard rails, they appear to be floating. All is suffused in beautiful daylight. The uniqueness of this place is in its dynamic diagonal form, which strongly relates to a prominent street corner through a great window (see plate 25). There are many other kinds of projects that could be termed multiuse centers. Virtually all galleries, specialty shopping centers, and many anchor shopping centers are directly related to office, hotel, or residential uses. Likewise, many pedestrian systems include both office and retail uses.

Developers have progressed from an era of single-use projects to an era of flexible multiuse projects. The hallmark of a multiuse project is a retail element at the base organized around an interior pedestrian place that serves both the project population (employees, residents, or guests) and the public at large. The retail element serves as the functional integrator, and the pedestrian place serves as the spatial integrator that gives these projects their focus and identity. ■

The architecture of retail activity has had an interesting and dynamic history during the last century. The nineteenth-century shopping arcade and department store led to the twentieth-century suburban shopping mall and urban specialty center. Markets were transformed into festival marketplaces, and railroad stations were the precursors of multiuse centers.

In the nineteenth-century precedents, the buildings were designed to be frameworks for retail activity, with clearly articulated structures and well-defined pedestrian spaces. The shops, kiosks, stalls, and counters were destined to change as merchandising changed, while the building's structures remained permanent. Thus, there was an architectonic integrity to these permanent structures—a quality of daylight and a character of space that made these buildings memorable.

The twentieth-century counterparts have not always been true to their nineteenth-century precedents in terms of architectural integrity and quality. For example, there has been considerable vacillation in the definition of the pedestrian space relative to the shops. In some cases, the shop fronts disappeared altogether; in others, the pedestrian space was treated as residual—as a space between shops that did not need a character of its own. The design of twentieth-century commercial places has also suffered because of the increased horizontal and vertical size of shopping centers, which renders them overscaled for pedestrian use and orientation. Perhaps the greatest single change in architectural character has been caused by the influx of numerous mechanical and electrical systems such as artificial lighting, fire-prevention equipment, heating and air-conditioning units, smoke-exhaust systems, and elevators and escalators. This plethora of technical requirements either has been concealed behind surfacing materials or left exposed and painted.

A direct and open relationship between pedestrian space and retail use is critical for the success of both. Buildings intended for other uses in the city can have many kinds of facades, with selected penetrations for light and access depending upon the need to maintain privacy. But retail activity must maintain frontage—that is, an open and permeable boundary between the public way and the private space. The shop front, with its display window and entrance, is an age-old device for the presentation of and access to goods. Ultimately, the public venue for certain kinds of shopping will remain vital, for it serves other social and psychological purposes. For the vast majority of us, shopping—and its ancillaries of window-shopping and people watching—is still one of our favorite urban activities (figure 2.66). ■

Fig. 2.66. Shop front, Burlington Arcade. London.

CHAPTER 3

PUBLIC ATRIA

As a living room serves the house so does a public atrium serve the city. Traditionally, urban squares served the purposes of public gathering and socialization. Now, the public atrium has become an enclosed equivalent. These are spaces of arrival, orientation, meeting, relating, and debating. Public atria are adjunct spaces to the exterior public realm, associated to it but yet distinct, and are characterized primarily by their interiorness.

An *atrium* is a centroidal, interior, daylit space that organizes a building.[1] The atrium subtypes, examples of which are included in this chapter, include closed, open, linear, multiple lateral, and partial. The partial atrium is not a true atrium, in that it is not centroidal and does not serve as a focal space for the building as a whole. Autonomous winter gardens (discussed in this chapter) are not true atria either, since they do not spatially organize a given building.

The public atrium is a space that meets certain conditions of access for pedestrian use. As such, it cannot stand alone and must relate directly to the exterior streets and squares of the city. Accessibility is important because it determines the extent of use. The critical issue is the way in which public atria are connected to the exterior pedestrian system of the city. To be considered public, atria must be freely accessible; yet, by being enclosed, access can be easily controlled. The design of entrances that are welcoming and transitional is, therefore, a significant design consideration.

The crucial sociological issue is the degree of public availability: To what extent is this space open to all of the people all of the time? The degree of availability can be thought of as a bipolar concept—with truly public at one end and truly private at the other. There are many atria that are truly public spaces. Usually, they are located within public buildings—buildings owned and operated by governmental entities. There are also private philanthropic institutions that include public atria in their buildings, such as museums and hospitals. Most public atria fall in the middle of this range of public availability, with use conditioned by the nature of the sponsoring organization. Private entities also increasingly include semipublic atria within their buildings for reasons of goodwill and image enhancement.

In this chapter, public atria as interior pedestrian places are explored by building-type category. Grand hotels often incorporate atria that approach the ideal of urban living rooms. In office buildings, atria serve the greatest gamut of functions—from pedestrian passage to employee lounge, depending upon the corporate entity or tenant mix. The atria of government buildings often serve ceremonial purposes in addition to other uses. Cultural institutions include atria to serve a variety of functions, depending upon their programmatic role. Winter gardens are public greenhouses—social spaces in which to enjoy exotic flowers, plants, and trees. ■

The historic grand hotel served as a social center for the city, as Robert A. M. Stern points out in his book *Pride of Place*:

> More than a resting place for travelers, they have traditionally served as the preeminent social meeting ground of American cities. The great suites of rooms are the sites of the balls, receptions, and dinners of the local populace. Quite frequently in nascent urban areas, with municipal government too weak, poor, or disinclined to invest in monuments to the town's dream of its future, it was the hotel that came to shelter and symbolize a growing city.[2]

To serve this role, the grand hotels were designed to include a series of grand social spaces, such as lobbies, ballrooms, dining rooms, and courts. Two notable historic examples of the grand hotel, both located in the burgeoning western frontier of America, were designed around glass-roofed atria. The Palace Hotel (now the Sheraton Palace Hotel), built in San Francisco in 1875, was an extravagant structure covering two and one-half acres and containing 875 luxury rooms. At its center was a great court, 150 feet by 50 feet (45.7 by 15.2 meters) and seven stories tall, which was planted with palm trees and fitted with fountains. Stern describes the grandeur of this court:

> It provided a setting for twice daily band concerts, skylit by day and illuminated by multicolored gas lights at night. San Francisco's Champagne Society could drive their carriages directly into the court; as they alighted, it was as if on a stage with tiers of spectators gazing from behind the gilt and marble-columned galleries above.[3]

After the 1906 earthquake and fire, the hotel was rebuilt in 1908 with a one story, glass-roofed, garden court. It remains today as a magnificently elegant dining room that veritably glows with sunlight during the day and sparkles from the glow of chandeliers at night. (figure 3.1).

Architect Frank E. Edbrooke's design for the Brown Palace Hotel in Denver, built in 1889–92, is based on an Italian Renaissance *palazzo*. It, too, incorporated an atrium, which was surrounded by six floors of galleries and was topped with a colored-glass skylight. The ground floor of the atrium was lavishly appointed with marble floors, oriental rugs, onyx walls, and fine residential furniture. The atrium was a living room for the hotel's guests but also served symbolically as the living room for Denver—the place where debutantes would make their appearances, and ranchers would celebrate their business deals. It was the social center of this rich city of the Wild West.

The contemporary equivalent of the grand hotel is the atrium hotel—a large (800–1,000-room) hotel primarily designed to accommodate conventions and large meetings. The function rooms are located either below or above the atrium floor, which is surrounded by bars, restaurants, and shops for the leisure time of the guests. In a double-loaded corridor scheme, the windows of the guest rooms overlook the atrium; whereas in a gallery scheme, the doors of the guest rooms face the atrium. The great space formed by walls of rooms symbolizes the gathering of individuals in a communal social setting. In these design schemes, the choreography of movement and the ambience of social activity are favored over the virtues of privacy and seclusion.

When architect-developer John Portman sought in 1967 to bring new life to the grand hotel, he turned to the nineteenth-century atrium model. However, he reinterpreted this model from a twentieth-century perspective of spatial scale and technological invention. The atrium of the Hyatt Regency Atlanta is twenty-three stories high and 120 feet (36.6 meters) square in plan and is covered by a translucent skylight surrounded by a

Fig. 3.1. Garden court, Sheraton Palace Hotel. San Francisco.

clerestory. The eight hundred guest rooms open onto galleries surrounding this awesome space. The Plexiglas-enclosed elevator cabs, located in the atrium, give the appearance of an amusement ride. The atrium's floor is designed as a piazza covered with white pavers, and furnishings include a fountain, shade trees, flowers, and numerous benches (figure 3.2).

Here, the atrium serves as a social center for both the hotel's guests and the residents of Atlanta. It is a kind of grand community living room. In the years after it opened, it was the place to be on a Saturday night or the place to have dinner or drop by for a drink. In this way, the guests, conventioneers, and local residents met and interacted. The scale of the space is large enough to accommodate crowds during meetings and conventions but was also designed with intimate settings for smaller groups and couples.

If you want to see a large gathering of people enjoying themselves in a grand interior place, go to the atrium of the Hyatt Regency San Francisco on a late Friday afternoon. There, in a huge Piranesian space, can be found a great throng of people—dancing, drinking, listening to music, strolling, and conversing. William Marlin, writing in *Architectural Forum*, refers to the atrium as "the perfect place for a Zamzummim romp—assuming those mischievous giants, mentioned in the Old Testament, were up to it." The hotel

has lots to be up to—most dramatically, a lobby space of Zamzummim proportions, hosting a bacchanal barrage of things to do, sights to see, sounds to hear. The senses are all but compelled to measure up to its dimensions: a triangular prism of space 300 feet long, 170 feet wide, and 170 feet (17 stories) high [91.5 by 51.8 by 51.8 meters].[4]

The atrium is the terminating space for the four blocks of Embarcadero Center, with its pedestrian datum three levels above the street. The floor of the atrium at this level is treated with the same gray pavers as the Embarcadero's walkways.

Fig. 3.2. Atrium view, Hyatt Regency Atlanta. Atlanta.

The atrium itself is furnished with trees, flowers, fountains, benches, and birds—all bathed in daylight from a strip skylight (see plate 26). Surrounding the atrium are public amenities, such as restaurants, bars, shops, and lounges. Although the floor of the atrium is located above the street, a continuous colonnade along Drum Street coupled with escalators make the transition less difficult.

Following the precedent of the Hyatt Regency hotels in Atlanta and San Francisco, the atrium-hotel has become the standard for new luxury hotels. The Hyatt hotel chain has adopted the atrium as its marketing image and has constructed over thirty hotels of this type. Recently, the atrium design has been adopted in nonluxury hotels and motels built by chains such as Holiday Inn and Embassy Suites. In virtually all of these, the atrium is treated as an image enhancer or as an activity space. Most of these hotels and motels are located along highways away from the city center. The atrium serves as a means for closing out the negative exterior environment and for turning inward to create a self-contained world. However, the original concept of the atrium as an urban living room shared by the guests and the community has been lost because these hotels are removed from the community.

In several hotels, the atrium concept as an interior urban place failed because of the designer's inclination to isolate the focal space from the city's pedestrian system. At the Peachtree Hotel in Atlanta, designed by John Portman, a seven-story podium located on a prominent corner site has planar concrete walls with narrow slits. The Peachtree Street entry via a long, narrow passage—presumably designed for drama—leads to the five-story terraced atrium, above which the seventy-story hotel rises. Until a 1987 remodeling, most of the atrium floor was covered with a reflecting pool with floating island lounges. At that time the water was removed, and the public space was reconfigured with a series of "temples." In a sense, this space was the antithesis of the original Hyatt atrium up the street. With the tower's structural columns and elevator core occupying the center and the floor covered with water, the space could not be visually comprehended or easily experienced. Its detachment from the street made it difficult to reach and even more difficult to understand as a semipublic space. The separation of the guest rooms into a tower removed the sense of communality and vitality that guests bring to an atrium.

The Bonaventure Hotel in Los Angeles, also designed by John Portman, has virtually the same design problems as the Peachtree Hotel. Here, the problems are exaggerated because of the hotel's size. Five cylindrical guest towers, containing 1,318 rooms and 150 suites, rise from a four-story fortresslike podium containing the atrium. The space is exciting, but it is also extremely disorienting. As social critic Calvin Trillin once remarked, "one way to lure a convention to the downtown of a large American city is to make sure they will never have to go out into it."[5] At the Bonaventure Hotel, guests cannot find their way out nor in.

Except for the Hyatt Regency Atlanta, all of John Portman's atrium—hotels are designed with their main levels above the street—including the colossal Mariott Marquis on Times Square in New York City and his own Portman Hotel near Union Square in San Francisco. Although such an arrangement enables the architect to locate certain service spaces and meeting rooms on the ground floor, the real reason for its prevalence is a preferred arrival sequence. Portman wants visitors to ascend the atrium, where they will be surprised by the space's scale and verticality. Although this introduction to the space is awe-inspiring, it does not provide a welcoming entry sequence for the street-bound pedestrian. Moreover, the exterior facades of Portman's hotels do not clearly reveal the presence of a grand semipublic space inside. In order to be valuable additions to the repertoire of pedestrian spaces in the city, the atria of hotels must directly relate in a spatial sense to exterior spaces; and their presence must be suggested by the facades' design.

The Hyatt Regency San Antonio, designed by Thompson, Ventulett, Stainback and Associates (with Ford, Powell & Carson) in 1981, exemplifies this design approach. A branch of San Antonio's Paseo del Rio (landscaped river walk) flows through the main floor of the hotel's atrium, which is located one level below the street. Hotel functions begin at the street-entry level—with three floors of terraces for public activities surmounted by nine floors of hotel rooms. Interior-facing guest rooms, a guest terrace, lounges, bars, and restaurants all relate to the fourteen-story, U-shaped atrium, which is poised over the juncture of the main river walk and its branch. The elevator system's five observation cabs at the atrium's center provide vertical animation. A separate one-story public elevator connects the river walk to the hotel's lobby (figure 3.3).

The Hyatt Regency San Antonio achieves a rare symbiosis of architecture and urban design by spatially engaging the hotel and the river walk. This is achieved in and through the atrium, which vertically coalesces the levels of the hotel and the city. The fully glazed western facade of the atrium allows views to and from the river walk—a level of literal transparency seldom achieved in atrium design. Pedestrians are encouraged to proceed on their river-walk excursions through the hotel and along a series of pools, waterfalls, and rapids to the historic Alamo. The terraced public levels of the atrium give it a fragmented spatial character, which is overshadowed, however, by the unique pedestrian experience of this building (see plate 27).

At the present time, there appears to be a hiatus in the design development of atrium-hotels. Many were built in the last two decades, and many more continue to be built. However, these schemes are either insipid versions of past design triumphs or are attempts to be more dramatic in the use of geometry, scale, form, ornament, or internal features. A recent example is the 907-room Grand Hyatt Hotel in Washington, D.C., designed by RTKL Associates. The hotel's thirteen-story, rectangular atrium, with its clear-glazed gable skylight, is coherently defined by the walls of room windows. One-half of the main level below the street is water covered, and the other half is paved in a diagonal, geometric pattern that contradicts the axial clarity above. Three circular features are the main attractions: a domed gazebo, an arrival space on axis with the gazebo, and a circular island they both overlook, on which stands a white grand piano (figure 3.4).

There is a fundamental appropriateness in designing a hotel with a central atrium that can be shared as a social space by guests and visitors alike. To

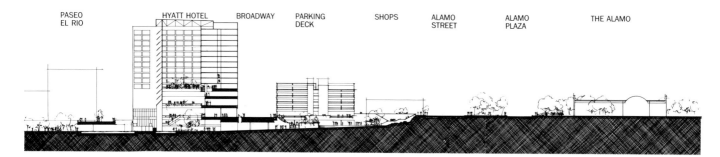

Fig. 3.3. Site section, Hyatt Regency San Antonio. San Antonio.

Fig. 3.4. Atrium view, Grand Hyatt Hotel. Washington, D.C.

create such a space successfully, designers must return to the basics and must look once again to the historic models. There, they will find the following design criteria: First, the atria should be correctly proportioned and well daylit, unlike many of the newer hotel atria that are tall and narrow and resemble light shafts in sectional proportion. Second, the atria must have surrounding rooms and/or galleries to animate them with the presence and movement of people. Third, the ground floor should access public-use activities, such as restaurants and bars. Fourth, the atria should provide pedestrian amenities—the same ones necessary to make a useful plaza or court, such as generous seating, sculptures, plants, trees, water features, and handsome paving. Finally, these spaces must be visually and physically connected to the urban pedestrian system in order to provide an invitation to use. In this way, the atrium-hotel can simultaneously become a lasting urban amenity and enhance its own prestige. ∎

Based on their spatial properties, atria in office buildings can be categorized into four types: *destinations*, or centroidal spaces of buildings that are sought out as ends of sequences; *passages*, or spaces that serve as pedestrian passages at the street level; *place/path atria*, or spaces that are a combination of the destination and passage types; and *partial atria*, or spaces that are associated with a part of a building and provide an amenity for that building.

There are fundamental differences in the roles of atria in multiple-tenant office buildings versus those located in single-tenant or corporate office buildings. Atria in buildings with multiple tenants serve as extensions of the entries and lobbies, as marketing devices to attract tenants, and as public or employee lounges. Atria in single-tenant buildings can be private spaces for exclusive use or can provide a public amenity as a philanthropic gesture. All of the spatial types defined above appear in examples serving both multiple- and single-tenant buildings. (Since this book addresses interior pedestrian places open to the public, exclusive-use atria in corporate office buildings will not be considered.)

The 1893 Bradbury Building in Los Angeles, designed by George Wyman as a destination-type building, is an early precedent for the multiple-tenant office structure. The atrium of this masonry structure, with its Mexican-tile floors, elaborate wrought-iron railings, and handsome brick interior facades, serves as a magnificent interior lobby (see plate 28). This relatively small atrium (47 feet wide by 119 feet long [14.3 by 36.3 meters] at its base) is stepped in section—being wider at the top to allow direct sunlight to the surrounding galleries. The roof is a clear-glazed, hip-shaped skylight with windows at its perimeter that provide natural ventilation via door transoms for the atrium and the offices.

The design concept of this atrium is to consolidate and make visible all circulation—from building entry to office door. The two elaborate open stairs at either end of the focal space make vertical movement a gracious experience. These stairs lead to the continuous galleries, which can be likened in character to interior streets. In the center are two open-cage, counterweighted traction elevators, in which all of the working elements are exposed. The elevators provide a fascinating mechanical animation in contrast to the human animation of people moving throughout the space. Indeed, circulation is celebrated and is made an intrinsic part of this atrium's captivating architectural character.

At the turn of the century, architect Daniel Burnham designed at least nine major single- and multiple-tenant office buildings based on the concept of a combined light court and atrium.[6] The place/path atria in these buildings were usually only two stories high and featured elaborate, exposed structural steel roofs that supported skylights. These partial atria provided pedestrian access to the adjacent commercial functions and to the vertical circulation core. The light court above was open to the sky and brought light and air into the surrounding offices. The seventeen-story Railway Exchange Building, built in 1903–5 on Michigan Avenue in Chicago, is an example of this concept. The building's two-story atrium serves as an elegant entry court. There is one gallery level, which accommodates shops, restaurants, and services (figure 3.5). The vertical circulation to the office levels is not evident in this classically composed space. During a recent restoration and remodeling, a second skylight was installed at the roof level; and the original exterior windows were removed to create an upper atrium surrounded by galleries.

Since the 1970s, there have been a plethora of office buildings designed and built around atria. The vast majority have been treated as enlarged lobbies not designed for pedestrian activities (other

Fig. 3.5. Atrium view, Railway Exchange Building. Chicago.

than circulation) or public amenity. These gratuitous atria contribute little to the enhancement of urban pedestrian life and, therefore, are not considered here. Fortunately, many new office buildings do include atria that serve a public purpose. These include public gardens, exhibition spaces, indoor courts, pedestrian passages, and retail centers. These atria have been incorporated in both multiple-tenant speculative buildings and in single-tenant corporate buildings.

The destination-type atrium in 1300 New York Avenue in Washington, D.C., designed by Skidmore, Owings & Merrill in 1984, was inspired by the *cortile* (courtyard) of an Italian *palazzo* (palace). An exedra-shaped lobby joins the arched, recessed entrance to the square-plan atrium. Surrounding the atrium is a colonnade that leads to the elevator lobbies on the cross axis. On the main axis is a

six-story waterfall that begins its descent from a private upper terrace (see plate 29). Originally, the ground floor was to include commercial enterprises that would be entered from both the street and the atrium. Now that the building is occupied fully by the Inter-American Development Bank, a security-conscious tenant, the internal commercial space is used as a library. Otherwise, this is a strictly formal space with no specific purpose other than pedestrian procession.

In contrast, the handsome atrium of the BP America building (formerly Sohio Tower), fronting on Public Square in Cleveland, is a pedestrian destination that offers shops, exhibitions, and restaurants. Designed by Hellmuth, Obata & Kassabaum the 8-story atrium is a structural appendage to the front of a 46-story tower with connections under and through the tower's lobby. The space is a splayed quadrilateral in plan and has four gallery levels, a sloping skylight roof, and a fully glazed facade facing the square (figure 3.6). Shops surround the ground floor, and at the back is an exhibition space. With its fountains and planters, this is a rather formal space. However, as an elegant extension of the tower's lobby, the atrium successfully forges a spatial relationship with downtown Cleveland's primary public square.

The Ford Foundation Headquarters in New York City remains after two decades one of the most profound urban versions of the atrium-based office building. By locating the atrium at the corner of the building, architect Kevin Roche was able to interlock the realm of the city with the space of the office worker. One ten-story

Fig. 3.6. Atrium view, BP America. Cleveland.

glass facade faces 42d Street; the other faces an adjacent park. The atrium's other two sides are surrounded by offices, and the roof is a ridge-and-furrow skylight. The atrium is an ethereal space poised between the inside and the outside, with visual transparencies across it from both the public and private directions (see plate 30). Thus the atrium exists in balanced tension between the realm of the institution and the realm of the city. James T. Burns and C. Ray Smith in an article in *Progressive Architecture* describe the distinctiveness of the building in this way:

> The building is an epitome of our age's awareness of and involvement in multiple levels of experience, and it suggests a comprehensive level of perception that measures architecture by a huge scale—one based on the cityscape rather than on images of single buildings.[7]

This atrium also exists in its own right as a terraced indoor park of 8,500 square feet (790 square meters), shared as a destination by both office workers and the public. The brick surfaces of the city outside have been brought inside, and landscape architect Dan Kiley's planting scheme has matured into lush growth. With its seasonal plantings and a sunken pool, this is truly an urban oasis. It is a place of respite and refreshment from the tensions of work and the city. The Ford Foundation, in keeping with its philanthropic mission, has indeed made a lasting gift to the people of New York City.

Hercules Plaza in Wilmington, Delaware, is an example of an office building that contains an atrium with an indoor garden but was conceived primarily as an urban passage. This thirteen-story corporate-headquarters building, containing two levels of shops and pedestrian amenities, was designed by Kohn Pedersen Fox Associates in 1983. Shoppers, employees, and the public are gathered

Fig. 3.7. Atrium view, Hercules Plaza. Wilmington, Delaware.

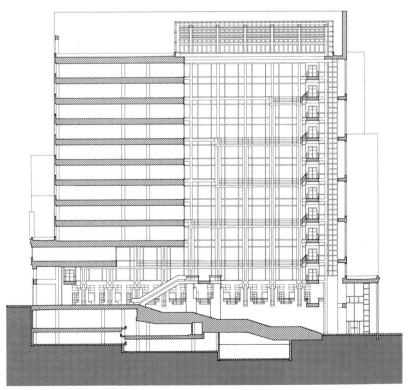

Fig. 3.8. Longitudinal building section, Hercules Plaza. Wilmington, Delaware.

at a small plaza in front of the building before entering the lobby. There, they take separate paths—one of the reasons for the design success of this project. The shoppers proceed along arcades on both sides of the atrium, which has a bridge at the far end that forms a circulation loop. The employees take the escalator to a mezzanine security point and proceed to elevator lobbies on both sides of the U-shaped office floors (figure 3.7).

The most enticing procession is reserved for the public—via terraced steps down through the garden to a plaza and park overlooking Brandywine Creek (figure 3.8). A watercourse cascades down the atrium's axis to make a symbolic association with the creek beyond. Like the atrium of the Ford Foundation Headquarters, this atrium is an overlapping space between the interior private world and the exterior public context. Bridges located at the northern facade, which is entirely glazed, allow the visitor or employee to be suspended between the interior garden and the exterior park. This design scheme successfully connects the space of the city to its larger natural context. The corporation has given a part of its superb new building to the citizens as a gesture of good will.

An atrium that combines attributes of destination with those of pedestrian passage is located in the Philadelphia Stock Exchange Building. This atrium-park not only provides a communal setting for the building's tenants, employees, and visitors but also provides an amenity for the public. This block-long, eight-story building on Market Street has two vertical cores served by two recessed entrances at each street corner. The atrium contains two feature elevators and numerous balconies and terraces festooned with overhanging vines. It is covered by a clear-glazed, gabled skylight (figure 3.9). This project is notable for the appropriateness of its concept in terms of relating its atrium to the city.

The atrium-park's lushly landscaped space features thirty-six species of trees, shrubs, vines, groundcover, and flowers. A watercourse forms pools, streams, and cascades that run throughout the atrium's ground levels. The space is terraced down 19 feet (5.8 meters) from the entry level to a plaza from which visitors can view the action on the trading floor of the stock exchange. Pedestrians can use the atrium-park as a diversionary passage or as a green oasis in which to rest (figure 3.10).

All of the office buildings discussed thus far (except for the BP America building) have been organized spatially around complete atria that encompass the buildings from top to bottom. Partial atria, on the other hand, spatially organize only one part of a building.[8] Where site circumstances, project budget, or design intentions prohibit a complete-atrium scheme, developers and corporations have opted for partial atria as part of their office facilities. In some cases, these are provided for goodwill; in others, to obtain zoning bonuses. Whatever the reason, these atria can enrich the life of the urban pedestrian.

Several recently completed office buildings have incorporated art galleries or branches of art museums in partial atria as a means of enhancing the corporation's image and providing a public amenity. For example, two corporate structures in New York City incorporate

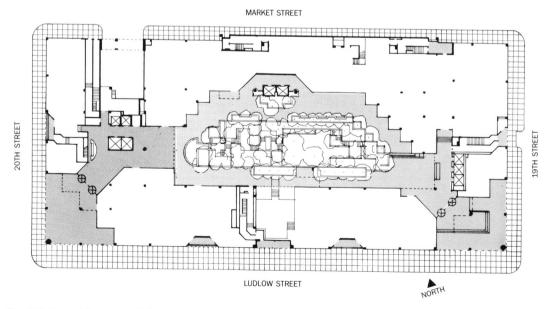

Fig. 3.9. Ground-floor plan, Philadelphia Stock Exchange Building. Philadelphia.

Fig. 3.10. Atrium view, Philadelphia Stock Exchange Building. Philadelphia.

Fig. 3.11. Philip Morris Gallery. New York City.

branches of the Whitney Museum of American Art. At the Philip Morris World Headquarters on 42d Street, architect Ulrich Franzen designed a 6,000-square-foot (557-square-meter) sculpture garden in the base of a twenty-six-story office tower (figure 3.11). Featured are several sculptures by artists George Segal, Alexander Calder, Claes Oldenburg, and Roy Lichtenstein. The sculptures displayed are in a garden setting of trees and seasonal flowers, and the paintings are displayed in an adjacent gallery. What makes this partial atrium interesting is the large expanses of glass that visually relate the interior to the streetscape. From the arcaded passage along Park Avenue, pedestrians can glimpse the sculptures day and night. The entrances from Park Avenue and 42d Street, which are separated from the corporate entrance on 41st Street, allow a free flow of pedestrians. Because it is located across the street from Grand Central Terminal, this space is highly populated by a wide variety of people. Critic Paul Goldberger states that:

> this space surely represents the most significant advance on the idea of the public plaza in some time. The 45-foot-high windowed room fills the building's base; it is both lively and serene, at once involved with the city and a tranquil place apart from the hubbub.[9]

A unique combination of art, public space, and corporate environment was completed in 1986 on Seventh Avenue between 51st and 52d streets in Manhattan. The Equitable Life Assurance Society of the United States invited the Whitney Museum of American Art to install two exhibition spaces. The company also commissioned several major artworks for the variety of public spaces designed by architect Edward Larabee Barnes. The two museum spaces are located on either side of a five-story skylit atrium at the front of this fifty-four-story office tower.

Fig. 3.12. Atrium view, Equitable Life Assurance Headquarters. New York City.

(This is similar to the BP America building design scheme.) Two interior passages lead past the tower's core to a partially covered open-air passage that links the two side streets. The museum spaces are neither memorable in character nor strongly associated with the lobby. The public pedestrian areas are all quite mundane, with their uniformly planar surfaces sheathed in burgundy and gray granite or white plaster. In an article about the building in *Progressive Architecture*, Pilar Viladas observes that "The 72-foot high arched entrance leads into the surprisingly banal lobby, which looks disorientingly like the building's exterior; only the impressive artworks rescue this space from the ranks of the forgettable."[10]

These artworks are, indeed, impressive in both quality and scale. In the lobby is Roy Lichtenstein's 68-foot by 32-foot (20.7 by 9.8-meter) *Mural with Blue Brushstroke*. The painting is fronted by Scott Burton's *Lobby Furnishment*, a 40-foot (12.2 meter) semicircular green marble bench and water table (figure 3.12).

Hanging along one interior passage are Thomas Hart Benton's 1930–31 series of murals entitled *America Today* and large-scale drawings by Sol LeWitt. In another passage is Paul Manship's 1938 sculpture *Day* and Barry Flanagan's 1983 sculpture *Hare on Bell*. In the passage behind the building are more art-furniture pieces by Scott Burton, additional pieces of sculpture, and large-scale abstract wall paintings. Through their scale and color, these artworks bring these stark pedestrian spaces to life.

A completely different approach is to provide an unprogrammed partial atrium in an office building. Such a plan usually is viewed as risky by both developers and corporations because it is difficult to control the number and/or character of the occupants. On what basis can so-called undesirables be kept from entering or using a place made available to the public? If "undesirables" are permitted, will they discourage other people from using the space? If people of all kinds use the space, will the image of the sponsoring entity be adversely affected?

Will the cost of providing guards, maintaining landscaping, and cleaning be excessive? The answers to these questions usually discourage the owners of office buildings from including unprogrammed public space. Certainly, when zoning bonuses were the impetus for providing interior pedestrian areas, owners should be obligated to provide freely accessible spaces, since such projects are subsidized indirectly by the public. Unfortunately, this kind of space—which often brings the greatest enjoyment to pedestrians—is not often provided.

Several owners have been undaunted

by these potential problems and have included unprogrammed pedestrian spaces in their buildings. Often, these take the form of interior gardens or palm courts—places to enjoy plants and people together. The Winter Garden at PPG Place, the IBM Garden Plaza, and the World Financial Center Winter Garden all possess a strong sense of public place (see pages 139–43).

In 1976 architect Philip Johnson, working with developer Gerald Hines, incorporated a slope-roofed partial atrium to join the bases of the twin towers of Pennzoil Place in Houston. This uniquely shaped space serves both as an entrance for those going to the office towers and as a diagonal passage across the block for pedestrians. During the day, the space is actively used as a processional passage; unfortunately, it is closed at night. An escalator and three drumlike elevators access to a below-grade concourse, the parking levels, and Houston's pedestrian tunnel system. The clear-glazed atrium roof, supported by white-painted steel Warren trusses, slopes from the street at an angle of 45 degrees to a height of eight stories (figure 3.13). Peter Papademetriou writes that, "In terms of its scale, related to size, the atrium is at once too small for pure monumentality (as at IDS) and too large for intimacy. It is a bit uneasy, a quality underscored by the presence of principally financial institutions adjacent to it."[11] Nevertheless, this is a unique event in the otherwise limited pedestrian life of downtown Houston.

The fifty-story world headquarters of Chemical Bank, built in 1964 on the east side of Park Avenue in Manhattan between 47th and 48th streets, originally was separated from the street by an open-air plaza. Architects Haines Lundberg Waehler proposed a glazed urban greenhouse to give the building a new entrance and to provide an amenity for pedestrians. Termed ChemCourt, this 12,500-square-foot (1,161-square-meter) partial atrium aligns with the Park Ave-

Fig. 3.13. Atrium view, Pennzoil Place. Houston.

nue sidewalk (as do the older buildings along this block). A shallow, recessed main entry is located midblock, and two deeply recessed entries are located at the corners.[12] The gridded structure of white-painted truss work is covered with 5- by 10-foot (1.5- by 3-meter) insulated glass panels and rises in steps to a height of three stories. This unique space functions as a passthrough for pedestrians, as a lounge for employees, as a waiting area for customers using the branch bank, and as a viewing space for employees using the second-floor cafeteria. The atrium's most interesting feature is the seasonal horticultural display main-

Fig. 3.14. Atrium view, ChemCourt, Chemical Bank. New York City.

tained by the New York Botanical Garden (figure 3.14).

Office buildings are the most ubiquitous building form of the twentieth-century city. Recent planning-and-design trends have led to the provision of pedestrian amenities in the bases of these buildings—often termed *social skyscrapers*. The intention is to humanize these otherwise dull buildings by providing opportunities for social interaction. The formal exterior plazas of recent decades are now being brought inside and enlivened with retail, restaurant, and exhibition activities. As a result, the interior and exterior spaces are integrated, and both are invigorated with renewed public life.

A 1985 research study by the architectural firm Kaplan · McLaughlin · Diaz employs the term *indoor agora* relative to indoor public spaces, in order to make reference to their Greek precedents.[13] A user-questionnaire survey of significant outdoor and indoor public spaces in the San Francisco area revealed that meeting people, private use, and watching people are enjoyed equally as pedestrian activities. According to the survey, indoor spaces were favored for their shopping opportunities, for protection from inclement weather, and for architectural interest. The results of these surveys generated several design principles: First, indoor agoras should be highly visible from the street, thus providing a view of the activity within. Second, they should have ample seating in a variety of forms, be liberally landscaped, including moving water, and be illuminated by natural light of varied levels. Third, they should be at least three stories in height—with at least two stories devoted to public-oriented uses, such as galleries, shops, service and retail areas, entertainment, and restaurants. Finally, and most importantly, they should be linked in a series with other public spaces to form a continuous pedestrian environment composed of shortcuts and alternative routes. ∎

The Rotunda of the United States Capitol in Washington, D.C., is the most symbolically significant interior pedestrian place in this country. This magnificent circular room, with its dome and cupola rising to a height of 285 feet (87 meters), is traversed daily by thousands of citizens and lawmakers. On occasion, it is reserved for national events, such as the lying-in-state of national leaders. Although not included in the original spatial program, the rotunda was incorporated into architect William Thornton's design scheme. Entrance porticoes, legislative chambers, and corridors all converge upon this interior place, which is surrounded with statues and murals. It is the spatial center of the Capitol and the symbolic center of the capital city.

The U.S. Capitol established a design model for state capitol buildings across the country—which included corridors, which can be likened to interior streets, leading to a domed rotunda, which can be likened to a piazza. The state capitols of Illinois, Indiana, Texas, and Rhode Island were all designed according to this model. This concept was also interpreted for the designs of city halls, county courthouses, and numerous other civic and governmental buildings.

Robert A. M. Stern's likening of the rotunda of the U.S. Capitol to an exterior piazza provides an interesting insight:

> Absent the traditional institutions that shaped Europe's public places by framing squares and piazzas with cathedrals and palaces, America inverted the hierarchies of Europe: the public square itself became the glorious room inside the walls, rendering the Capitol's Rotunda at once a pantheon and a piazza—a national village square.[14]

If the streets and squares of a city are public pedestrian places, then the corridors and halls of a public building should be the same. These spatial connotations lead to a desire for an urban character in these interior places—in their proportion, form, materials, and furnishings. The traditional design of interior pedestrian places is to form a spatial continuity with exterior equivalents, while maintaining a transitional relationship with other interior rooms and halls.

Following the neoclassical era of buildings designed with domed rotundas, another spatial form developed—the atrium-based government building. Whereas the domed-rotunda form has its origins in the cathedrals of Europe, the atrium building has its origins in the courtyards of Italian *palazzi*. At the end of the nineteenth century, many post offices, courthouses, and city halls featured atria as a means to accommodate the circulation of large numbers of people. Several of these buildings have since been adapted to other uses. For example, the one-story atrium of the post office and federal building in Buffalo, New York, built in 1900, was converted to a four-story atrium for the Erie County Community College in 1982. The celebrated Old Post Office in Washington, D.C., was converted to a retail center and federal office building formed around a ten-story atrium (see plate 31). In St. Paul, the old Federal Courts Building is now Landmark Center, a cultural center with a four-story atrium. And in Richmond, Virginia, the old Gothic Revival city hall has been restored and is now used as an office building.

The tradition of designing city halls around great enclosed public rooms is evident in several European design schemes. Arne Jacobsen's design for the city hall of Aarhus, Denmark, built in 1936–41, includes a galleried ceremonial atrium that has a fully glazed end wall facing a park. Another five-story, linear atrium in the administration wing of this building serves to facilitate circulation and communication. In neighboring Sweden, Gunnar Asplund designed an addition to the Göteborg City Hall, built in

1934–37. There, a three-story atrium was added as an enclosed complement to the original city hall's courtyard. The new atrium visually relates to the old courtyard through a glazed wall. In Germany, architect Gottfried Böhm's designs for the Bensberg city hall, built in 1964, and the Bergisch-Gladbach citizens' center, built in 1980, incorporate complex and provocative public atrium spaces. Yet to be built is Richard Meier's 1987 scheme (which lost the design competition but was awarded the commission) for the Hague City Hall in the Netherlands. Meier's plan calls for a monumental ten-story atrium contained between two L-shaped building blocks. All of these schemes reflect the validity of incorporating a large, enclosed gathering space in a city hall. Although the *hall* in the term *city hall* initially referred to the council chamber or meeting room, the meaning has now been extended to include the public atrium as an antehall.

An interesting example of an atrium-based American city hall still in active use is the Milwaukee City Hall, built in 1895. The exterior was designed in the Flemish Renaissance style. The interior is organized around a lozenge-shaped, eight-story-high atrium, which is surrounded by galleries and is topped with a patterned-glass skylight. The building's vertical form stands on an oddly shaped narrow site. The arched entry under a tower at the building's narrow end leads to a set of grand stairs on the atrium's side. These stairs lead up to the second-floor Common Council Chamber at the opposite end. This ornately figured space—related through anterooms to the galleried atrium—associates the formal and informal meeting spaces to the organized processional sequence (figure 3.15).

The design for I. M. Pei's Dallas City Hall, built in 1978, bears no formal relationship to the Milwaukee City Hall other than its internal organization around an atrium. This linear building of seven monumental bays, with its perplexing inward-sloping facade, contains a linear atrium five bays long and six stories high, topped by three curved, north-facing monitors. One side of the atrium is vertical with continuous spandrels and glazing, while the other side is composed of a series of stepped galleries, each of which receives direct daylight (figure 3.16). One of the bays contains the entrance lobby, above which is the mayor's office and the council chamber.

The relationship of the internal and external public space is well conceived in the Dallas City Hall scheme. The 550-foot-long (168-meter-long) building fronts

Fig. 3.15. Atrium view, Milwaukee City Hall. Milwaukee.

plaza, and the city beyond.

Although the Dallas City Hall functions well as a complex government building, the character of the atrium more closely resembles the atrium of a modern corporate office building than the hall of a civic monument. As Robert A. M. Stern comments:

> The space and the walls that bound it [the atrium] are wonderful for what they are—clean, well-lighted spaces. But they lack the symbolic dimension that unites the modest county courthouse or town hall of the nineteenth century to the grand places of public administration and enterprise, most notably the Capitol in Washington.[15]

Other government buildings that are primarily administrative in function also reflect the spatial tradition of grand public halls. However, since public meetings and ceremonies do not take place in these buildings, the traditional role of the great hall as a place for formal gathering has been altered. In these cases, the atrium becomes a location for informal gathering, circulation, and public services.

An excellent historic example of a government building with an atrium used for informal gathering is the Pension Building in Washington, D.C. Designed and built between 1882 and 1887 by General Montgomery Meigs, this colossal structure north of Judiciary Square housed the Pension Bureau (the predecessor to the Veteran's Administration). Here, six hundred clerks worked in offices located along four levels of galleries surrounding the atrium. The scale of the ground floor, which is surrounded by a loggia, resembles a civic square with a fountain where pensioners would meet and socialize. Its present use is as a display space for the National Museum of the Building Arts. This atrium, being one of the great interior spaces in the United States capital, has been the site of eleven presidential inaugural balls.

Fig. 3.16. Atrium view, Dallas City Hall. Dallas.

on a seven-acre plaza, with the main atrium floor one level above. Escalators bring the citizen or visitor up to the atrium, which is surrounded by city-government offices. The totality of the city's administration is revealed in one view, thus aiding building comprehension and maintaining orientation. The primary service functions are located on the atrium's floor, along with double-height lounge spaces that visually relate the atrium to the civic plaza. Balconies adjacent to the council chamber on the sixth floor allow an overview of the atrium, the

Fig. 3.17. Atrium view, Pension Building. Washington, D.C.

The Pension Building contains the oldest known atrium in the United States and one of the most monumental—measuring 292 feet long, 92 feet wide, and 159 feet high (89 by 28 by 48 meters). The atrium is contained within a 400-foot-long and 200-foot-wide (122- by 61-meter) brick building block. Daylighting is provided by high-arched clerestory windows. The most dramatic feature is the atrium's high central section, supported by two sets of four gigantic Corinthian columns (figure 3.17). The scale of the atrium is deceiving because of the articulation into three spaces and the richness of the repetitive architectural detailing. The four narrow building entrances make the discovery of this space even more surprising in this city of classical architecture.

A building with an interior public space that fulfills a similar role is the Gregory Bateson Building in Sacramento, California, designed by State Architect Sim Van der Ryn in 1981. Here, the atrium is at once an indoor plaza and an employee lounge. Inviting entrances encourage the public to walk through this common space, which lies between a city park and an urban plaza. Visitors also are encouraged to stop and use the atrium's pedestrian amenities and snack bar. Employees whose work spaces surround the atrium use it for breaks, lunches, and meetings. Thus, employees and the public have the opportunity to meet in a conducive social setting. The four-story space, with its many energy-saving features, has generous skylights, brick paving, and colorful furnishings (figure 3.18).

The Hart Senate Office Building, located near the Pension Building just north of the Capitol, is a recent example of a federal office building designed around a large-scaled atrium used primarily for circulation. This building, designed by John Carl Warnecke & Associates and completed in 1982, appears from the exterior to be four stories but actually contains eight floors of offices (some double height) for fifty senators and their staffs. The 100-foot-high (30.5-meter-high) atrium spaces are intended basically for circulation—with the building's entrances leading to bridge-span-

Fig. 3.18. Atrium view, Gregory Bateson Building. Sacramento, California.

ned passages that join the wings. The vertical circulation, hidden from view, leads to recessed galleries. These public spaces, with their unarticulated surfaces of white Vermont marble and tinted glass, are rather characterless. Paul Goldberger observes that:

> the atrium itself is stark and now gives the impression of emptiness more than anything else; funds set aside for a huge Calder sculpture were cut from the budget, as was money for lobby furnishings and plants. The enormous marble space has neither furnishing nor much human traffic, and it seems mysteriously dead, as if every day were Sunday and no one had come to work.[16]

The funds eventually were found to construct Alexander Calder's last work, a combination stabile and mobile made of black-painted steel and aluminum and entitled *Mountains and Clouds*. Although this huge sculpture fills a portion of the atrium, it remains a grandiose and formal circulation space without the vitality that active human use could bring.

A recently completed city-government building and a state office building were conceived with atria to serve as locations for public services. The Franklin D. Reeves Center of Municipal Affairs, a District of Columbia office building at 14th and U streets, N.W., has a common corner-entry lobby used by both visitors and employees. The employees go up to a mezzanine and then to their offices. The visitors remain on the ground floor, where they have access to shops, health facilities, or the day-care center. A skylit linear atrium visually and spatially unites all the facilities and their users (figure 3.19).

One of the most architecturally provocative state office buildings of recent years is the State of Illinois Center in Chicago, designed by Murphy/Jahn Architects in 1984. This uniquely shaped

structure with its colored curtain-wall exterior has drawn strong reactions from the critics and the public. At the building's center is a huge rotunda-atrium with a sloped roof—a space unlike any other. This gigantic space is 175 feet (53.3 meters) in diameter and 18 stories high and has two freestanding elevator towers located on a radial axis with the entry. Of particular interest is the entry space, which makes a strong transitional statement—visually and spatially—between the corner plaza and the rotunda (figure 3.20). The rose-and-aqua exterior color scheme is restated throughout the interior of the atrium. Even for those without vertigo, use of the interoffice stairs (which are suspended from the roof) is a dizzying experience. The entire space is visually frenetic in stark contrast to the staid rotundas of past architectural eras (see plate 32).

This project is also programmatically provocative, for it is a hybrid of the traditional state capitol and a conventional mixed-use office building.[17] A new kind of public program has been added to the sixteen floors of open-plan offices that surround the rotunda-atrium. The ground floor and one level above and below have been given over to public use, such as shops, restaurants, an auditorium, and an exhibition gallery. Certain public-related state functions, such as taxation, vehicle registration, and driver's licenses, are also located here. The circular, recessed well in the atrium's center is a kind of public forum for meeting, eating, drinking, and talking. The well's paving pattern is reminiscent of the pattern used in Michelangelo's Piazza del Campidoglio in Rome. In a short time, this building has become a public attraction for both citizens and tourists—a rare occurrence in the history of civic architecture.

The enthusiastic public response to the State of Illinois Center has caused officials and architects to reconsider the relationship between government build-

Fig. 3.19. Atrium view, Reeves Building. Washington, D.C.

Fig. 3.20. Atrium view, State of Illinois Center. Chicago.

ings and the public they serve. No longer can these buildings be designed only for administrative functions. The citizens want to have other reasons to go to the buildings that their taxes support. The presence of a shopping center is the most controversial aspect of the program, causing the distinction between a government building and a commercial building to become blurred.

Interior pedestrian spaces—whether programmed, ceremonial, utilitarian, or spontaneous—are important aspects of government buildings, for they make them public in use. But architect Donlyn Lyndon calls for more meaningful uses:

> It would be better to make the public realm in ways that sustain investigation, that accommodate many imaginings; to make settings in which one can attend to the transaction of people on issues that matter. It would be better to give a structure for experiencing individuals in the public realm, for being able to know and understand the works of men and women from dimensions of time that exceed the present. Solidity in time is not easily achieved, and in this building it is hard enough to grasp and difficult to imagine keeping a storehouse of civic memories.[18]

Helmut Jahn's grand rotunda at the State of Illinois Center promotes the historic continuity of such a space in government buildings. The lineage of rotundas—from the United States Capitol to the state capitols, city halls, and courthouses—is a strong architectural tradition that gives these structures symbolic value. The centrality of this circular space can represent the government as the common purpose of the civil servants or the dominant role of government in our culture. Although architectural styles and expressions change, continuity of such a spatial tradition maintains public confidence in the stability of the government. ■

To enter the Isabella Stewart Gardner Museum in Boston is to step into another era, another culture, and another location. Soon after entering the museum, located in what was once a private home, the visitor is confronted by the magnificent garden-atrium—complete with ancient statuary and resplendent with flowers, greenery, and palms. Can this be Boston in midwinter? Or is it Venice, Italy, during the Renaissance? The glass-covered atrium is surrounded by majestic rooms filled with an overwhelming collection of paintings, tapestries, etchings, sculptures, books, and furniture from every part of the world. When Isabella Stewart Gardner set out to build her palace in 1902, she asked architect William T. Sears to re-create a Venetian Renaissance *palazzo* on the Fenway. Although visitors no longer are permitted into the garden, its view from the surrounding balconies and windows is enough to start one dreaming (figure 3.21).

The role of a courtyard in a museum is to provide a place of repose. Viewing numerous works of art for long periods of time can be an emotionally and intellectually intense experience. A place of rest where there is little art is needed as a kind of "antigallery." The atrium of the Isabella Stewart Gardner Museum serves this purpose. Many eighteenth- and nineteenth-century museums incorporated courtyards for the purpose of repose, as well as to bring daylight into the museum and its galleries. When skylight glazing became readily available, these courtyards were covered and converted to enclosed atria. The galleries of John Russell Pope's well-known National Gallery of Art in Washington, D.C., built in 1941, are organized along an interior street with skylit garden courts at both ends.

Architect I. M. Pei's design concept for the East Building of the National Gallery of Art is a late-twentieth-century version of the garden court. This atrium is related to the rotunda and garden courts of the original museum by a below-grade concourse and by an at-grade plaza. An isosceles triangle in plan, it encompasses 16,000 square feet (1,486 square meters). The atrium's floor and wall surfaces are sheathed in the same soft pink Tennessee marble as was used on the original building. The technological tour de force is the stainless-steel-and-aluminum skylight with integral sunscreen louvers. The skylight's structure is a triangular tetrahedron space frame, which rests on the walls surrounding the atrium. The quality of the daylight that suffuses this space changes with the days and seasons. The dynamics of light, people, and a gi-

Fig. 3.21. Garden court, Isabella Stewart Gardner Museum. Boston.

gantic Alexander Calder mobile create changing patterns of subtle richness (see plate 33).

This atrium is one of the great public rooms of the nation's capital. From the Fourth Street plaza, the transitional sequence is gracious and open: a few steps up to the recessed entry, through the lobby, and into the welcoming focal space. The atrium's main role is to organize—if not choreograph—the circulation pattern through a series of stairs, bridges, and escalators. Secondarily, it serves as a place for meeting, resting, gathering, and exhibition. The atrium's use in 1987 for a large-scale exhibition of contemporary sculpture provided an interesting juxtaposition of art and people—all seemed to float above and within the soft-colored marble planes.

The design of the East Building fostered a lively discussion of the nature of its atrium and its relationship to the museum. In 1978 the editors of *Progressive Architecture* debated these issues.[19] Martin Filler wrote:

The interior of the East Building is both a biting critique of the difficulty architects have nowadays in dealing with monumental space and an unintentionally appropriate expression of the art ritual as consumer event. For in resembling nothing quite so much as the poshest of suburban shopping malls, the atrium of the East Building meets its visitors more than half-way in providing an experience that supplants the purported one of the building, much as the Pompidou Center, and not the art within it, has become the real tourist attraction.[20]

James Murphy replied:

Some of these comments vaguely hint that galleries are only for the sober-faced elite, and not for the kind of public that Washington and the Mall attract. I don't feel the need

to imply guilt by association with Portman. He didn't invent grand volumes, and excitement isn't limited to shopping malls. Indeed, art needn't be housed only in monastic surroundings to be appreciated.[21]

Suzanne Stephens concluded:

I sense we are getting away from a valuable part of the museum experience—contemplation and repose. The older building's majestic entrance rotunda and the serenely beautiful garden courts communicate that intention. The East Building, by adopting the kind of spaces associated with shopping and entertainment, says "keep moving to the next event."[22]

Other art museums have incorporated either complete or partial atria in their buildings, but none as grand or as accessible as the one in the National Gallery's East Building. The two skylit atria of the Yale Center for British Art in New Haven, Connecticut, are neither grand nor dynamic: one is an entry court; the other is a picture gallery. These are beautifully proportioned public rooms, surrounded by galleries that bring internal spatial order to this disciplined building block. In contrast, the atriumlike space at the rear of the 1984 addition to the Museum of Modern Art in New York City is devoted entirely to circulation—via escalators, bridges, and walkways. Frank Lloyd Wright's Solomon R. Guggenheim Museum on upper Fifth Avenue in Manhattan contains a circular atrium surrounded by ramped picture galleries. The atrium's direct connection to the street makes it a successful arrival and orientation space, but its use for socialization is lacking. Similarly, the carefully articulated atrium in architect Richard Meier's High Museum of Art in Atlanta is defined by curving ramps and layered galleries. However, here the atrium's primary role is for orientation

Fig. 3.22. Atrium view, High Museum of Art. Atlanta.

and circulation—with no programmed or suggested use for the ground floor (figure 3.22).

An excellent opportunity to create a monumental museum space was available recently in the creation of the Musée d'Orsay on the Seine River in Paris. The central space of this museum is housed in the former main hall of an 1898 Beaux-Arts railroad station that is enclosed by a roof of barrel-vaulted skylights. The 1979 proposal for its adaptive use as a museum treated this hall as an interior street lined with transparent galleries. The 1986 realized scheme compromises the integrity of the grand space by its placement in the hall of "stone temples," which accommodate individual galleries. In the end, the balance in this museum between public space and exhibition space has been significantly shifted in favor of the latter.[23]

In 1970 the Metropolitan Museum of Art in New York City embarked on a master plan, developed by Kevin Roche John Dinkeloo and Associates, that included the addition of exhibition wings with three new, major public spaces. The first addition, completed in 1975, was the Lehman Wing, which is located on axis with the main Fifth Avenue entrance but faces Central Park. These galleries, which house a private collection, are arranged in two bands around a square garden court with a pyramidal skylight that rises to a height of 82 feet (25 meters). The space is defined by limestone wall planes that contain the stairs and is simply appointed with chairs and trees. This bright but quiet space is a welcoming place of repose within this overwhelming museum.

The next addition to be completed was the Sackler Wing, located on the northern side of the museum. This is a space of monumental proportions, designed to provide an appropriate setting for the first-century B.C. Egyptian Temple of Dendur. The 165-foot by 200-foot (50.3- by 61-meter) space—defined by a softly glowing wire-glass-and-aluminum ceiling; limestone end walls; and a 72-foot-high (22-meter-high), sloped-glass curtain wall facing the park—actually overwhelms the sandstone temple and gateway (figure 3.23). A large reflecting pool and podium are intended to suggest the original Nile River site. However, the temple looks forlorn in this starkly modern, scaleless setting—as do the museumgoers. Unfortunately, it is only the colossal space that is monumentalized here—not the object that the space was meant to honor.[24]

As a public space, the most successful of the three wings is the American Wing, located on the northwestern corner of the museum. Its Englehard Courtyard has a glazed wall and roof, an exposed steel-frame structure, and balconies along both sides. On the north-end wall is the 1820 facade of the United States Assay Office, reconstructed here in 1924. The visitor enters through this facade to view the galleries. On the wall at the opposite end is the ornate, reconstructed loggia from Louis Comfort Tiffany's Long Island home. This space is appropriately the scale of a nineteenth-century garden court. The detailing includes brick and stone paving, wood benches and planters, and gridded screens (see plate 34). The visual reciprocity between Central Park and this garden court is more successful than in the other two wings. Design restraint is the hallmark of this court—nothing, including the daylight, vies for attention. Harmony and balance characterize the composition. Fortunately, the pedestrian traffic through this area is light enough not to destroy its tranquility.

Fig. 3.23. Interior view, Sackler Wing, Metropolitan Museum of Art. New York City.

Pedestrian spaces in museums and institutional buildings generally are not as readily available for use as they are in other building types. If these buildings are public, their purpose may prescribe restrictions on entry and hours of use. If they are philanthropic in nature, entry fees, membership, or tickets may be required for entry. Interior pedestrian spaces usually have a prescribed role to play that is related to the building's purpose. In museums, these areas can be places of circulation, exhibition, rest, or a combination of all three. In university buildings, such areas can be meeting rooms, lounges, or exhibition spaces. Interestingly, several recently completed buildings for architecture schools—at the University of Washington, the University of Houston, and the University of Tennessee—have been designed around large atria used for all of these purposes. Likewise, such spaces are used as socializing areas in student-union buildings on university campuses. Examples are the Wilson Commons at the University of Rochester and the Student Union at Cleveland State University (figure 3.24). In hospitals, they serve as combined eating-and-lounge spaces, as at the New Thomas Jefferson University Hospital and the Children's Hospital, both in Philadelphia.

In libraries, pedestrian spaces are places of orientation or are used as reading rooms. The great reading rooms of the Bibliothèque Nationale and the Bibliothèque Genevieve in Paris serve as suitable historic precedents. Two new libraries will contain dramatic public spaces: Colin St. John Wilson's design for the British Library near St. Pancras Station in London is organized around a sequence of pedestrian spaces. Likewise, Hardy Holzman Pfeiffer's design for an addition to Bertram Goodhue's Los Angeles Central Library is organized around a central atrium, which will have escalators for descending to below-grade departments.

When cultural institutions are located in the city and when spaces have been included for the public, they contribute positively to the experience of the urban pedestrian. In some cases, the spaces can be used only conditionally—that is, for specific purposes and at specific times. Nevertheless, they can be used effectively for semipublic activities. Many cultural institutions, even when located in the city, maintain a bastion mentality that separates them physically and socially from their urban milieu. This outlook is unfortunate, for it prevents mutual enhancement. We can, however, be grateful for those institutions that effectively reach out to the public and provide pedestrian places for all to enjoy and experience. ∎

Fig. 3.24. Interior view, Student Union, Cleveland State University. Cleveland.

Georg Kohlmaier and Barna von Sartory have thoroughly documented the intriguing history of winter gardens in their book *Houses of Glass*.[25] In it, they describe the intriguing variety of activities and socialization throughout the day and night in a Berlin winter garden in the year 1840:

> In many of these gardens or orangeries there are also bands of musicians, sometimes also poetry is recited; on Sunday as occasion arises there are little plays. In the evenings the whole is brightly lit. In some of the winter gardens there are separate rooms with billiard tables for ladies who want to escape from the tobacco smoke; also rooms for card playing, and for small societies. If one visits these gardens in the early morning one finds there gentlemen reading the newspapers, drinking chocolate, and discussing politics. After 3 o'clock one sees ladies and gentlemen and people of every sort sitting among the trees, conversing, smoking, with punch, grog, coffee, beer or wine in front of them. . . . In the evening when the theatre is letting out there appear many well-dressed people of both sexes who visit these gardens before their journey home, to enjoy the beauty of the plant kingdom splendidly illuminated with artificial lighting and to talk a little about the play and the players.[26]

At first, these palm houses and orangeries were created for members of the aristocracy and upper class as private places of contemplation and enjoyment related to residences. In time, vast winter gardens were constructed for the public to enjoy. They became places to exhibit the great collections of exotic flora gathered from all over the world. The first large public winter garden was designed by Decimus Burton and Richard Turner and constructed in Regent's Park in London in 1842–46. The garden was used primarily for flower shows and social occasions. It was soon followed by a much larger structure on the Champs Elysées in Paris, the Jardin d'Hiver of 1846–48. In addition to an extensive plant display with fountains and rocks, this winter garden contained a café, a bakery, billiard rooms, music rooms, flower stalls, bird cages, and a picture gallery.[27] These two examples exemplify the two basic historic purposes of public winter gardens: botanical display for education and botanical display for amusement. In these plant museums, specimens from around the world were gathered together, displayed under the best lighting conditions, identified as to genus and species, and preserved for the future. Throughout the nineteenth century, both types of winter gardens were built in urban parks throughout France, England, Germany, Belgium, and Austria.

The creation of winter gardens was motivated by the changing relationship between man and nature in nineteenth-century Europe. Burgeoning urbanization was destroying vast natural areas, and the by-products of expanding industrialization were polluting the air and water. At the same time, scientists were gaining insights into the biological processes, which led to a better understanding of plant growth. Winter gardens preserved the vision of a natural paradise, albeit in a controlled setting and exhibited man's discovery of exotic plants and his ability to control their growth. Another motivation was the enjoyment of nature as an art form—for its beauty and aesthetic appeal. These three motivations—combined with the development of iron structural members and the ability to manufacture large sheets of glass—enabled architects and engineers to create wondrous winter gardens of great variety.

In the United States, winter gardens, or conservatories, were built primarily for educational purposes as botanical museums. Usually, they were located in large urban parks—as was the recently restored Enid A. Haupt Conservatory of The New York Botanical Garden in the Bronx. Architect William R. Cobb designed this large and complex structure in 1899 as a kind of cathedral devoted to nature (figure 3.25). The structure is composed of eleven separate greenhouses joined together in a C-shaped plan, which defines an entry plaza and two courts. Commenting on the successful restoration of the conservatory, Eleni M. Constantine writes that it "preserves the elusive, unquantifiable exhilaration of the architecture, and the shimmering domes retain a younger century's poignant marveling at man's capacity to

fashion a machine-house for making a garden in."[28] Almost every major city in the United States has a nineteenth-century botanical conservatory, and interest in this building type remains strong. Recently, new structures have been built in Chicago, Milwaukee, and San Antonio.

The history of winter gardens as a building type is of interest in that it illustrates the genesis of an important architectural concept relative to interior urban places. The notion of keeping plants and trees in an appropriate enclosed environment where they can be enjoyed year round has had a pervasive influence on architecture since the first half of the nineteenth century. Greenhouse spaces have been incorporated in almost every building type—particularly residences, offices, restaurants, stores, and museums. All of us now enjoy plants, primarily of tropical origin, in these settings. This is especially satisfying in northern climates, where many plants are dormant in the winter, and the climate does not permit their enjoyment outdoors.

The technology of greenhouse architecture has become highly sophisticated in recent decades, thus enabling architects to develop innovative design schemes. The availability of new glass types, gaskets, and sealants in conjunction with refined metal-glazing bars and steel structural members has resulted in elegant, safe, leak-proof, and trouble-free glass buildings. The development of systems for automatic fire suppression, electronic fire detection, and smoke exhaust have made these spaces much safer. There have also been concomitant interior-landscaping developments, such as the propagation of plant materials, watering and fertilizing systems, humidity controls, and artificial lighting that have enabled lush gardens to flourish in these architectonic settings.[29]

Many interior places have been inspired by the winter-garden concept. This greenhouse-inspired architecture

Fig. 3.25. Exterior view, Enid A. Haupt Conservatory. The Bronx, New York.

features rooms with roofs and walls of glass. Like winter gardens, these spaces are infused with natural light, which allows plants and trees to flourish. The projects to follow come closest to the ideal of a landscaped winter garden. These are virtually autonomous structures, interior places in which to enjoy plants, flowers, and trees.

Behind the forty-story Gothic glass tower at PPG Place in Pittsburgh, Philip Johnson has designed a Gothic winter garden. This space is a kind of interior analogue for the formal open plaza that fronts the tower on the opposite side—with the circulation space of the tower's lobby joining the two. The winter garden's roof is constructed of four pointed arches supported by clear-span space trusses.[30] Sheathed in the same reflective glass as the tower, the greenhouse is an informal place for employees and the public to meet and socialize. It is paved in a checkerboard pattern of granite and is landscaped with large ficus trees in square planters. The white structural members and furnishings create a light and airy image (see plate 35).

From the perspective of design integrity and pedestrian use, the most successful of these winter gardens is the IBM Garden Plaza at the back of the IBM Building at 57th Street and Madison Avenue in New York City (see figures 1.6 and 1.9). Spatially, the plaza garden links the forty-three-story tower to Trump Tower on Fifth Avenue and to the Bonwit Teller department store on 57th Street. It also provides pedestrian linkage to the AT&T Building across 56th Street, by means of a through-block passage that remains open during favorable weather. Direct spatial connections to the lobby and gallery of the IBM Building and visual connections from the third-floor employee's cafeteria complete the relationships of this space to its environs.

Architecturally, the IBM Garden Plaza can be compared to a nineteenth-century conservatory—a greenhouse brought into the city. Approximately triangular in plan, it is spanned by 15-foot-deep (4.6-meter-deep) white pipe trusses that form a 68-foot-high (20.7-meter-high) sawtooth roof. The 11,000-square-foot (1,022-square-meter) space is simply paved with light gray granite. A significant aspect of its design integrity is the use of one planting type: 45-foot-high (13.7-meter-high) bamboo trees set in eleven groves. The trees lend mass at the floor and a feathery lightness above and also provide a tranquil, pale green color to the overall scheme (see plate 36).

With clear glass all around, the plaza garden is a highly transparent space of ethereal definition. Paula Deitz, who has chronicled its construction, offers the following description:

> It is an interior world of light and air defined by a structure but not restricted by it from its exterior surroundings—the tracery of its framework creates only a veil-like separation. It is a place to be inside without surrendering the outside; and yet from out-of-doors, the interior appears to have a fixed life, a quiet orderliness that is becoming to good architecture. At night, the structure glows jewel-like on the city street; the roof, facets of light against a dark sky.[31]

The greatest success of the IBM Garden Plaza is from the pedestrian's point of view. Its climate is tempered by the exhaust air from the tower—creating temperatures that are either warmer or cooler than the exterior and free of wind. Although the structure is monumental, the bamboo trees create intimate zones of privacy. The movable chairs and tables are residential in scale, as are the somewhat incongruous nineteenth-century street lamps and benches. But they lend an informal ambience to the space that allows the pedestrian to be in control of his or her activities. Coffee and pastries are available, and there are scheduled musical performances. It is a space freely usable and available to all pedestrians through the policy of an enlightened management. This is as it should be for a space that was created through zoning bonuses. The atmosphere resembles the ambience of a European piazza—where individuals can be alone or in groups in an ennobling public domain.

The Rainbow Center Winter Garden in Niagara Falls, New York, designed by Cesar Pelli while at Gruen Associates, has been termed both a "triumphal arch" and a "city gate."[32] As a triumphal arch, the windows at both ends of the ground-floor and mezzanine levels fold back to create an open-air passage. As a city gate, the structure separates the pedestrian mall on the city side from the park overlooking Niagara Falls. The garden's economic purpose was to spur development of the downtown by providing a focus for the area. The intention was for future structures to attach themselves to the sides of the winter garden so as to directly access this enclosed pedestrian environment during the harsh winters. For the exterior, Pelli's design uses maroon-painted steel lacework glazed with clear-tempered glass for the roof, clear-float glass for the suspended curtain walls, and tempered glass around the ground floor and the mezzanine. The structure is a complex pattern of five transverse trusses and twelve longitudinal trusses—all supported on twenty post-tensioned concrete columns. The sloping, south-facing roof provides passive solar heating, which is supplemented by electric heat in winter (see plate 37).

There is an unresolved tension in this place between the architectonic form and the garden setting. The density of structural elements, the geometric form of the roof, and the heaviness of the concrete columns all tend to overwhelm the space. The structures of nineteenth-century winter gardens were lighter and airier, and they had slender columns. At the

ground level, the Rainbow Center Winter Garden is a true winter garden—having a wide variety of tropical plants and trees that create a lush, green oasis. However, from the two observation towers and the mezzanine, the structure itself dominates. Nevertheless, the space is widely used as a pleasure garden by elderly strollers, conventioneers, tourists, lovers, mothers and children, and concertgoers and artists.

The pièce de résistance of contemporary winter gardens is surely the World Financial Center Winter Garden, designed by Cesar Pelli and completed in 1988 in downtown Manhattan. This structure, with the proportions of a railroad-station concourse, is the gateway to the four office towers of the World Financial Center—through which thousands of pedestrians pass each day. It is located at the end of a pedestrian bridge that runs from the World Trade Center across West Street. This majestic form of stepping steel arches opens outward to a plaza on the Hudson River (figure 3.26). At the center of this vast space is a bosque of sixteen elegant palm trees from California. With discrete shops along both sides, this place is destined to become another crossroads of New York City. (Arguably, this space is more of a covered plaza than a winter garden, due to its role as an urban living room and the paucity of plant material.)

Robert A. M. Stern likens this space to the Grand Concourse of Grand Central Terminal:

> Like it, the Winter Garden is both a place of passage and a place of repose where one can sit down, have a drink or a cup of coffee, or just contemplate the sweeping Hudson River vista. It is also like an Italian piazza, in some ways like San Marco in Venice, covered in glass and air-conditioned to suit the extremes of the American climate.[33]

At the 1988 American Institute of Archi-

Fig. 3.26. Exterior view, World Financial Center Winter Garden. New York City.

tects convention, the host chapter party made splendid use of this great public room (see plate 38). In Robert Stern's words, "Pelli's Winter Garden recalls the glory of nineteenth century urbanism and its recognition that great enclosed places were an essential element of a livable city."[34]

Whether a true winter garden or not, this great glazed room overlooking the Hudson River has a potent sense of place. The curved tiers of steps physically relate the passages along both sides to the patterned marble piazza floor. The steps create a theatrical setting for each pedestrian to pause and process, to view and be viewed across the polished blue, gray, and rose marble surfaces. The structure of dark green painted steel creates a balance between spatial definition and openness. The only incongruous features are the stage and its white fabric bandshell, which partially blocks the Hudson River view.

The concept of the winter garden is important to the development of interior pedestrian places because of its amenity and imagery. An interior garden is a conducive setting for respite and meeting within the context of the frenzied city. To be inside but visually outside has always been an experience of magical appeal. Here one can be in the presence of palm trees on a bitterly cold winter day. Suffused in daylight and filled with strolling people, the winter garden presents a compelling attraction to every urban pedestrian. ∎

DESIGN EVOLUTION

In the last two decades, there has been a remarkable resurgence in interior urban places realized as public atria within various building types. There are many reasons for this occurrence—not the least of which is the value of creating a spatial identity or focus.

The two most salient differences between the nineteenth-century and twentieth-century atrium buildings are the greater scale and extensive mechanical systems of the contemporary examples. Contemporary urban atria are usually about ten stories high but sometimes exceed twenty stories in height for hotels and office buildings. In some cases, the horizontal dimensions are not proportionate, resulting in spaces that are overly vertical in orientation and, lack natural light at the ground level.

The architectural quality of public atria is also directly related to the extensive technical requirements such as heating, ventilating, air conditioning, smoke exhaust, fire suppression, electric lighting, and elevators and escalators. Horizontal and vertical glazing systems have reached new levels of sophistication, resulting in the opportunity for expansive transparent enclosures. These contemporary factors often have led to confused architectural expression that is driven by these technical requirements and innovations rather than transcending them to achieve higher intentions.

The court and the winter garden are the two strongest historic architectural concepts relating to atria. The paved or landscaped court with the addition of a glazed roof is the model for the contemporary atrium. Its interior facades can either be walls or galleries. The proportions are of utmost concern for achieving pedestrian scale and for daylight distribution. The nineteenth-century concept of the winter garden as an interior place for people to enjoy trees and plants has been developed in its contemporary design expression. It has also been combined with the atrium concept to create public atria that are both visually intriguing and fulfill a social purpose. ∎

CHAPTER 4

PEDESTRIAN SYSTEMS

Urban designers should undertake displacement of the ground level as a pedestrian datum only after great deliberation. Humans have always considered the earth's surface as the ultimate basis for vertical orientation—that is, as a reference plane. As creatures of the earth, we walk upon it and value its solidity (*terra firma*). The sidewalks, squares, and parks of the city are built upon the altered earth's plane—the common ground upon which streets lie and buildings stand. When we are above or below the earth's surface, we often experience a disorienting uneasiness. A subterranean tunnel can be a fearful place, and the top of a skyscraper can be exhilarating to some but vertiginous to others.

As the centers of cities intensify in use, the competition for ground-level space increases. The cars, trucks, buses, and taxis usually prevail because they are bigger and pose a threat to the defenseless pedestrian. A design solution increasingly employed in many large cities is the vertical separation of these competing modes of circulation and commerce— as Leonardo da Vinci first suggested in his idealized city scheme of 1490 (see page 16). Such a design creates additional circulation space, allowing each mode to function independently and efficiently. Today, two basic conceptual schemes are being utilized: skyways and concourses.

The skyway system creates a separate pedestrian level above the ground, linking buildings with bridges that cross streets. In the concourse system, below-street tunnels serve as pedestrian passages (which often are related to subway stations). In both cases, pedestrians no longer have to confront street-level vehicles; thus, their safety and convenience are ensured.

The use of these two types of pedestrian systems raises the following questions: In cities that have skyways or concourses what will become of the street? Will it be relegated to cars, buses, and trucks? Or will it become a no man's land of service zones and parking? Do skyways and concourses as privatized pedestrian systems relegate the streets to social outcasts?

In ideal circumstances, street-level pedestrian spaces would continue to prosper and be used in conjunction with the above- and below-ground pedestrian ways. However, the examples discussed here indicate that in many cities the skyways and concourses have caused street-level activity—primarily the retail element—to decline significantly. These pedestrian systems have led to the creation of a virtual "second city"—a result with serious economic, social, political, and aesthetic implications that should cause urban designers to reconsider the validity of this concept.

The design of our urban pedestrian spaces will ultimately need to acknowledge the omnipresence of the street level. As urban designer Jaquelin Robertson states:

> I believe there is only one level in the city. It is grade: where people walk, where trees grow and where one has the best chance of solving almost all design problems. With few exceptions, one assumes a tremendous burden in traditional design terms when taking on a second-level scheme. By traditional, I mean tested, not stylistic.[1]

Many urban designers are espousing a return to the street as the basis for organizing a city's pedestrian space. Access to skyway and concourse systems begins and ends at the street level; and those systems that make these connections will, in the long run, be the successful ones. For example, the long-term viability of Minneapolis's skyway system is rooted in the presence of Nicollet Mall, a grade-level pedestrian space that was built before the skyways. Similarly, the long-term viability of the concourse system in Toronto resides in the availability of the ground-level parks and squares. Interior pedestrian places that relate well to the street level are those that contribute to the tradition of continuity in a city's pedestrian systems. ■

SKYWAYS

In Venice, three pedestrian bridges cross the Grand Canal—the S-shaped central waterway that serves this island city. Ponte di Rialto, the bridge at the center of the three, links the commercial districts on the opposite banks. Lined with small shops on both sides, the bridge maintains the continuity of the adjacent shopping streets. Not until reaching the center of the span does the pedestrian realize that this is a bridge. Here, the shops are disrupted by an overlook—a place to stop and view the myriad of activity up and down the waterway. Ponte di Rialto is both a pedestrian bridge and a pedestrian place; it is truly an urban event that gives meaning to the experience of crossing (figure 4.1). The Ponte di Rialto can be compared to a skyway that crosses a trafficked street, linking two commercial areas and, ideally, creating a place to pause.

A skyway system is a network of enclosed, second-story, pedestrian bridges and interior walkways that crosses streets and joins buildings together. The bridges usually cross the street at midblock, and the walkways pass through the centers of buildings. Within these structures, the network is lined with banks, shops, and services. In office buildings, access via elevators is provided to the offices from both the skyways and the building lobbies. In certain buildings, the network engages public atria of varied size and character. A skyway system can join and/or pass through virtually all kinds of buildings—including department stores, urban shopping centers, hotels, apartment blocks, office buildings, government centers, and parking garages. A vast all-weather network is thus created, which facilitates pedestrian circulation within a dense urban center.

One of the most extensive and best-planned skyway systems is located in Minneapolis. By 1988 a total of thirty contiguous blocks had been linked together, with a crucial thirty-first block on Nicollet Mall soon to be linked to the system (figure 4.2). It all began in 1962, when the late Leslie Park connected the Cargill Building, the Roanoke Building, and the Northwest National Bank with two skyway bridges crossing the intervening streets. Other businessmen, noting the leasing success, built an additional four bridges by 1969.[2] In the meantime, the city's plans for establishing a pedestrian

Fig. 4.1. Ponte di Rialto. Venice.

precinct were implemented in 1967 with the completion of the eight-block Nicollet Mall (which was extended four more blocks in 1981). Designed by Lawrence Halprin, Nicollet Mall features a sine-curve traffic way, heated bus shelters, a snow-melting system, innovative furnishings, and luxurious landscaping.

A significant element of the rejuvenated central district was completed in 1972 with the IDS Center, four buildings around a large plaza-atrium joined to the surrounding blocks by four skyway bridges (see pages 104–6). This project and its interior pedestrian spaces still serve as the center of downtown Minneapolis, and additional commercial projects have since been built to reinforce its nodal presence. Since 1972 the skyway system has grown rapidly, with extensions to and through both new and old buildings. The Minneapolis Metro Cen-

ter Plan for 1990 envisions a total of sixty-four blocks to be served by these interior walkways.

Minneapolis's skyways system is organized into a primary and a secondary network: The primary network has a north-south axis in the blocks east of Marquette Street and an east-west axis crosses at the IDS Center. Wide walkways link the perimeter parking garages and apartment complexes to the core area. These walkways are well policed and stay open longer than the secondary network skyways. The secondary network links additional blocks to each other as well as to the primary network to form a continuous pedestrian system. In 1988 the primary network was substantially in place within the central retail and financial district—with extensions east to the government center and north to the Gateway Center. Extensions west

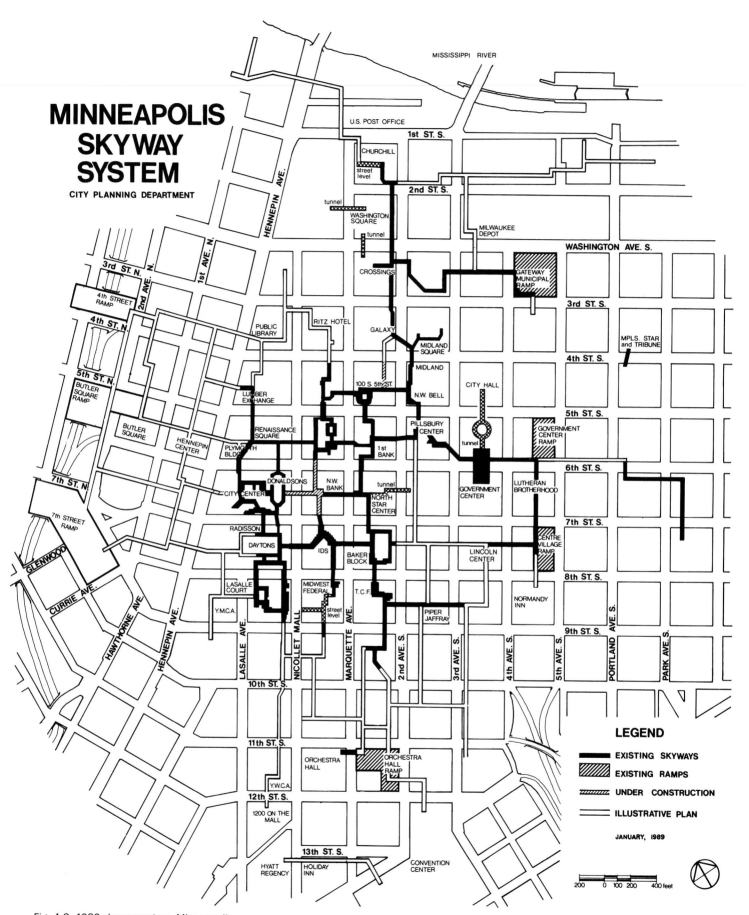

MINNEAPOLIS SKYWAY SYSTEM

CITY PLANNING DEPARTMENT

MISSISSIPPI RIVER

U.S. POST OFFICE

1st ST. S.

CHURCHILL

street level

2nd ST. S.

tunnel

WASHINGTON SQUARE

tunnel

MILWAUKEE DEPOT

WASHINGTON AVE. S.

CROSSINGS

GATEWAY MUNICIPAL RAMP

3rd ST. N.

4th STREET RAMP

4th ST. N.

5th ST. N.

BUTLER SQUARE RAMP

PUBLIC LIBRARY

RITZ HOTEL

GALAXY

MIDLAND SQUARE

MIDLAND

100 S. 5th ST.

N.W. BELL

3rd ST. S.

MPLS. STAR and TRIBUNE

4th ST. S.

CITY HALL

LUMBER EXCHANGE

BUTLER SQUARE

HENNEPIN CENTER

RENAISSANCE SQUARE

PLYMOUTH BLDG

PILLSBURY CENTER

tunnel

5th ST. S.

GOVERNMENT CENTER RAMP

7th ST. N.

1st BANK

6th ST. S.

DONALDSONS

CITY CENTER

N.W. BANK

NORTH STAR CENTER

tunnel

GOVERNMENT CENTER

LUTHERAN BROTHERHOOD

7th STREET RAMP

RADISSON

DAYTONS

IDS

BAKER BLOCK

LINCOLN CENTER

7th ST. S.

CENTRE VILLAGE RAMP

GLENWOOD

8th ST. S.

LASALLE COURT

MIDWEST FEDERAL

street level

T.C.F.

NORMANDY INN

CURRIE AVE.

Y.M.C.A.

PIPER JAFFRAY

9th ST. S.

10th ST. S.

11th ST. S.

ORCHESTRA HALL

ORCHESTRA HALL RAMP

Y.W.C.A.

12th ST. S.

1200 ON THE MALL

13th ST. S.

HYATT REGENCY

HOLIDAY INN

CONVENTION CENTER

HENNEPIN AVE.

1st AVE. N.

2nd AVE. N.

HAWTHORNE AVE.

HENNEPIN AVE.

LASALLE AVE.

NICOLLET MALL

MARQUETTE AVE.

2nd AVE. S.

3rd AVE. S.

4th AVE. S.

5th AVE. S.

PORTLAND AVE. S.

PARK AVE. S.

LEGEND

▬▬▬ EXISTING SKYWAYS

▨▨▨ EXISTING RAMPS

▥▥▥ UNDER CONSTRUCTION

═══ ILLUSTRATIVE PLAN

JANUARY, 1989

200 0 100 200   400 feet

Fig. 4.2. 1989 skyway system. Minneapolis.

to Butler Square and the new basketball arena are planned, whereas extensions south to a lower Nicollet district do not appear to be imminent.

In many respects, Minneapolis's skyway system can be deemed a great success, as evidenced by its continued growth and utilization. Furthermore, its construction and maintenance are privately funded, therefore confirming the financial viability of the system. Buildings located on the skyway system earn an estimated 10 percent more in rental income than do buildings located elsewhere, and many firms seeking prestigious office space choose this location.[3] The creation of a second retail level also greatly increased the available space for leasing.

The skyways function like a giant drawstring tying the stores together so that they function as a shopping center, thus enabling them as a group to compete effectively with regional shopping malls. In a location with only 126 ideal shopping days a year, the protection from the weather afforded by the skyways is a necessity.[4] A dense core of multilevel retail activity has thus been created with the recent construction of City Center, The Conservatory, and Gaviidae Common—shopping complexes with exclusive stores and shops located around IDS Center. The additional growth in office buildings and hotels confirms the financial strength of the downtown core, in large part due to the marketing potential of the skyway system. In some respects, the skyways have been too successful—causing an erosion in grade-level retail leasing and sales. Developers are now virtually forced to extend the system to their projects due to market demand. In fact, a 1979 resolution by the Minneapolis City Council grants to the city the authority to build skyways according to an adopted plan and to assess the benefiting property owners for the costs.[5]

The growth of the skyway system in the retail district has had both positive and negative impacts. When City Center—with its three levels of eighty shops surrounding an atrium—opened in 1983, many shop owners along Nicollet Mall decided to pay the higher rent and moved there. This left vacant storefronts now filled with secondary uses. After Donaldson's Department Store (now Carson Pirie Scott) moved across the mall to City Center, its store burned down. Fortunately, it is being replaced by Saks Fifth Avenue and sixty other shops in a shopping center called Gaviidae Common, designed by Cesar Pelli. Three other stores on Nicollet Mall have also closed; Powers, J. C. Penney, and Young Quïnlan. In the meantime, The Conservatory, located between 8th and 9th streets, has opened. The Conservatory adds fifty-five new exclusive shops and restaurants. This retail district along Nicollet Mall is in a state of economic transition, and many blame the new interior-oriented mall centers and not the skyway system. With the passing of the twentieth anniversary of Nicollet Mall, a plan for its rebuilding has been developed. The plan includes a series of stair towers that will connect the skyways to the sidewalks, in an effort to encourage street-level retail activity (figure 4.3).

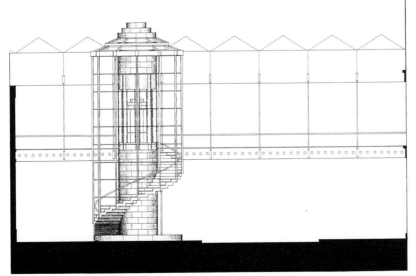

Fig. 4.3. Drawing of proposed skyway stair towers. Minneapolis.

Another new four-block retail project, curiously called The Park, is being proposed at the intersection of Tenth Street and Nicollet Mall. The design concept utilizes this intersection as a spatial node, with towers at each corner connecting the street-level entrances to two-level skyway bridges that cross each of the four intersecting streets.

Complete data on skyway use by pedestrians is not available; even if it were, it would be immediately inaccurate due to the constant changes in the system. Even without data, it is obvious from observation that the greatest use is at lunchtime—with additional peaks of use at the morning and evening rush hours. Only one-third to one-half as many people used the skyways in summer as in winter in 1973 and 1974.[6] Peak daily use of approximately 20,000 pedestrians was recorded on the bridges entering IDS Center in 1980—a growth of over 26 per-

cent in four years.[7] The skyway system is a public right-of-way guarded by the city police department. Most reported personal crime is purse snatching or package theft. Shoplifting is a significant problem, especially where the skyway passes through a store (figure 4.4). In these instances, the access hours conform to the store's hours, thus causing discontinuity in the system's use.

Since the skyway bridges in Minneapolis are privately financed and maintained, they are also individually designed. Although there are published design guidelines and a design-review procedure, the results are quite varied. Some of the older bridges are neutral dark steel trusses infilled with clear glass, such as those leading to the IDS Center (figure 4.5). The interiors of these bridges are bland in character, with skylights and glazed walls (figure 4.6). Other bridges are better integrated in their

Fig. 4.4. Interior view, skyway bridge at Dayton's Store. Minneapolis.

Fig. 4.5. Skyway bridge to IDS Center. Minneapolis.

form, color, and materials with the buildings they join—such as those leading to The Conservatory, to City Center, and to the new Opus Building (figure 4.7). The bridges to the Opus Building have continuous glazing on the walls and roof. The red steel structure is outlined in neon tubing—a design motif that is carried into the building's lobby. This contextual approach is the most prevalent current design trend. It is quite successful, for the bridges have their own identity and yet relate to the buildings they join. This is in contrast to the design approach used in neighboring St. Paul, where the skyway bridges are all brown steel Vierendeel trusses. This uniformity is intended to give a common identity to the skyway system. This is unnecessary because the bridges by definition have a common identity. The bridges to Cesar Pelli's Norwest Center are unique: they are self-supported; they create a skylit place in

Fig. 4.6. Interior view, skyway to IDS Center. Minneapolis.

the center; and they contain stained glass (figure 4.8). Skyway bridges are most successful when designed as Pelli's is—as places poised above the street where pedestrians can obtain a unique view of the city—much as the Ponte di Rialto affords a unique view of Venice.

The spatial quality of the skyway-system design in Minneapolis is a direct by-product of its incremental growth— ranging from excellent integration in the new buildings to the forced accommodation in older structures. In buildings built since the skyway system was initiated, the system has been well integrated with the interior circulation, which gives access to private floors via elevators. The lobbies of these buildings, usually at least two stories high, spatially relate the second level to the street level; and esca-

Fig. 4.7. Exterior view, bridge to City Center. Minneapolis.

Fig. 4.8. Skyway bridge to Norwest Center. Minneapolis.

lators connect the buildings' entrances at both levels. At Norwest Center, the skyway leads into a handsome faceted rotunda that serves as the building's focal space (figure 4.9). Here, the horizontal and vertical circulation are successfully integrated. A similar design approach was employed at the recently built Opus Center, where a recessed street entrance leads to a skylit lobby set between two curvilinear towers. These spatial connections—among the skyway bridges, the elevator lobbies, and the buildings' entrances—are essential for pedestrian orientation and convenience.

The skyway system east of Marquette Street and North of the IDS Center has been placed through existing buildings. It has an ad-hoc quality that is spatially problematic. As the bridges enter the

Fig. 4.9. Lobby view, Norwest Center. Minneapolis.

Fig. 4.10. Typical skyway corridor in an old building. Minneapolis.

buildings, they become interior corridors. These corridors usually are contorted and often are narrow, with variations in widths and geometric distortions. Users become disoriented easily and must rely constantly on directional signs to find the way. Fortunately, these signs are conveniently placed, along with overall system maps, at each skyway bridge. Most of these corridors are lined with shops and services, and adjoining hallways lead to the elevators (figure 4.10). The only value of these parts of the system is continuity—the integrated corridors provide convenient access to banks, copy center, travel bureaus, drug stores, cafés, and gift shops. An important feature of Minneapolis's system is that all of the skyways have been designed to be completely accessible to the handicapped and the elderly.

Fig. 4.11. Atrium of City Center. Minneapolis.

The most rewarding aspect of the skyway system is the arrival atria that are celebratory spatial nodes. The Crystal Court of IDS Center, which directly relates to Nicollet Mall, is the grandest of these atria (see pages 104–6). In contrast, the City Center atrium is isolated from the mall by a department store, the Multifoods Tower lobby on 6th Street, and the Mariott Hotel lobby on 7th Street (figure 4.11). This atrium, with its glazed shed roof, also lacks in the architectural character and appointments required to establish the space as a vital interior public place.

The twin-towered Pillsbury Center, designed by Skidmore, Owings & Merrill and developed by Gerald D. Hines Interests, establishes excellent relationships among its atrium, the skyway system, and the adjacent exterior spaces. Two small corner plazas are joined diagonally through the block by a stepping, skylit atrium that serves both office towers (figure 4.12). The skyway system enters the towers at the other two corners and crosses the atrium. The modern structural character of this space, which is surrounded by shops and restaurants, works well with the angular pedestrian passages to create a significant spatial node in the business district. From the Pillsbury Center, a diagonal bridge across Third Avenue leads to the twenty-three-story atrium of the Hennepin County Government Center, completed in 1974 as designed by John Carl Warnecke. The axial form and relationship of this atrium across a plaza to the 1906 Municipal Building creates an effective interior focal space for this rapidly developing civic center.

Fig. 4.12. Exterior view, Pillsbury Center. Minneapolis.

St. Paul also has a skyway system that has developed contemporaneously with that of its twin city of Minneapolis. The beginning of the system was the twelve-block urban-renewal project planned in the 1960s. In 1967 the first skyway bridge was completed (figure 4.13). In the 1970s, this core area was given a focus with the completion of two contiguous two-block projects, both of which span the intervening street. One of these projects, Northwest Center, is primarily an office development—consisting of a parking garage, a bank, and twenty-five shops spanning Cedar Street. The other project, Town Square, spans Seventh Street and is made up of a three-level podium containing a Donaldson's Department Store, a hotel lobby, a shopping center, and parking. Two office towers and the hotel rise above this podium; on top is an indoor urban park the size of a football field. The park is spanned by trusses supporting skylights and is filled with plants and water features. It is used both for relaxation and cultural events—such as concerts, dances, exhibitions, and lectures (see plate 39). Even with all of its amenities, Town Square lacks a unique identity. Bruce N. Wright observes that "it provides a nice retreat from inclement weather, but fails to produce a sense of

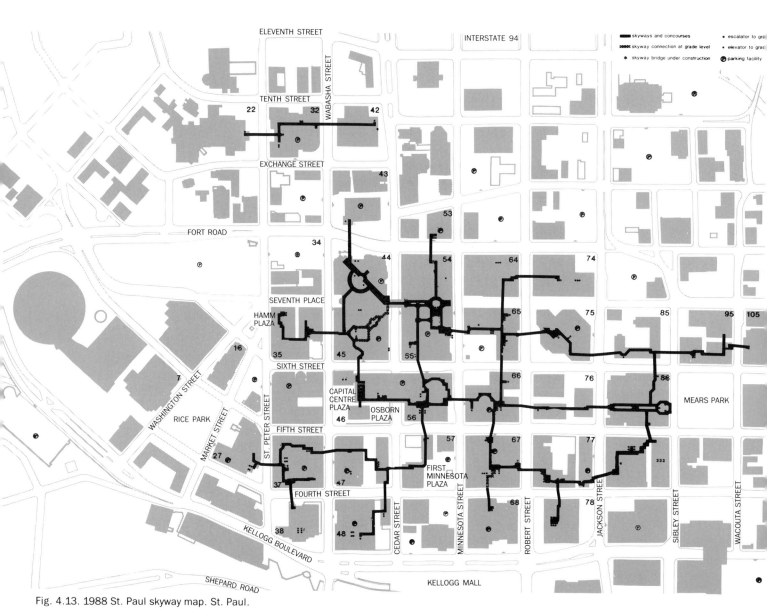

Fig. 4.13. 1988 St. Paul skyway map. St. Paul.

centrality. . . . In Town Square, to borrow from Gertrude Stein, there is no there there; you could be in any of half a dozen suburban shopping centers in the outlying areas."[8]

Recently, another two-block project, called Town Court, was completed on the west side of Cedar Street in an effort to consolidate this core renewal area. Town Court has four levels of shops and restaurants related to an existing Dayton's Department Store and parking garage. Directly linked to the well-designed rotunda-atrium of Town Court is the lobby of the World Trade Center tower at the corner of Seventh and Cedar streets (see plate 40). Town Square and Town Court are now promoted together as St. Paul Center. With their store windows and shopping-center entrances, both projects display a responsible relationship to the street.

In the 1980s St Paul's skyway system began to expand outside of this twelve-block core area. The expansion links existing and new buildings south toward the Mississippi River and east to Lowertown. The Lowertown area, with its splendid collection of late-nineteenth-century wholesaling and manufacturing buildings is the most interesting. At its center is Mears Park, which is fronted by Galtier Plaza—a multiuse project completed in 1984 that incorporates three existing historic facades. Galtier Plaza is the anchor project for this redevelopment area—with 192,000 square feet (17,837 square meters) of commercial space, 100,000 square feet (9,290 square meters) of offices, 121 condominiums, 347 apartments, a YMCA, and a parking ramp. The residential units are located in two towers that rest on a base organized around a seven-story linear atrium (four stories of offices overlooking three levels of retail), which stretches from Jackson Street to Sibley Street. Miller Hanson Westerbeck Bell Architects have designed a splendid interior pedestrian place with interesting features. The central elevator core divides the linear atrium into a downtown-focused space—featuring a theater marquee—and a Lowertown-focused space—featuring a food court and a ground-level seating area. The public spaces of Galtier Plaza are characterized by Victorian-inspired detailing—sculpted spandrels, dark red ceilings, patterned tile floors, and iconographic elevator towers (see plate 41).

By 1988 St Paul's skyway system encompassed a total of thirty-eight contiguous blocks. Within those blocks, a 3.5-mile-long (5.6-kilometer-long) interior pedestrian system connects office buildings, shopping centers, hotels, apartments, banks, federal courts, a science museum, a hospital, and a city hall. In 1982 the average weekday pedestrian trips totaled 70,000. Throughout the year, an average of twice as many people use the skyways rather than the sidewalks.[9] Presently, there are plans to connect the civic-center buildings around Rice Park and eventually to extend the system to the state capitol several blocks to the north.

In many respects, the skyway systems of Minneapolis and St. Paul are similar: They are both about the same length and link a variety of building types. Both function better in new buildings where the skyways can be related to the vertical circulation nodes that connect the skyway to the tower floors and the street entrances. (Atria are particularly important in this regard, for they forge these connections spatially and visually.)

The single most important difference between the two systems derives from their initial funding. The skyway system in Minneapolis was privately funded, whereas St. Paul's was constructed with public funds. Building owners in both cities pay the maintenance and utility costs. In St. Paul, public funding led to bridges built according to a uniform steel Vierendeel truss design. St. Paul's skyways are considered part of the public-transportation system. Because the bridges and easements are publicly owned, the buildings they traverse must be open seven days a week from 6 A.M. to 2 A.M. Security is provided by both private personnel and city police with the aid of video cameras. The use of the skyways and their operation is established by a city ordinance. Recently, the bridge-construction funding has been shared by the city and the developer, with the building owner responsible for interior-concourse and escalator costs.

The other difference between the two cities' skyway systems is in the role of the sidewalks. Minneapolis has had the publicly owned Nicollet Mall throughout the course of its skyway development—thus offering a pedestrian option. Since skyways and sidewalks are both publicly owned or supported in St. Paul, the city tacitly promoted one at the expense of the other. There is little street-level open space in St. Paul, and the streetscape has been allowed to deteriorate. Street-level activity and rentals have suffered, and an estimated 90 percent of all retail activity now is located on the skyways. In addition, the connections between the two systems are inadequate. This is a serious concern for the future of downtown St. Paul, for without attention the sidewalks will become a no-man's-land. Too much success for the skyway system eventually will harm the economic and social vitality of the entire downtown.

Other North American cities, such as Milwaukee, Des Moines, Cincinnati, Atlanta, Houston, Charlotte, and Calgary, have begun to develop significant skyway systems. Part of the justification for these interiorized pedestrian systems is climate protection (understandable in the northern cities, with their harsh winters and in some of the southern cities, with their hot and humid summers). However, the promotion of real-estate development is also a part of the justification for the growth of these systems.

The city of Milwaukee has made a concerted effort to develop a skyway system that links ten contiguous blocks west of the Milwaukee River with a planned extension east of the river. The system focuses on the linked blocks of the Grand Avenue shopping complex along Wisconsin Avenue (see pages 43–45). The skyways then turn north to link the new federal office building and the Hyatt hotel and convention center. Here, the development of landscaped atria as places of arrival within the skyway system is encouraged by floor-area bonuses.

Cincinnati is another city with a growing skyway system. This system was constructed with public funds as a planned network of heated and air-conditioned second-level walkways that would be maintained by the owners of adjacent properties. In 1987 the system included sixteen blocks. One section links the river-front stadium and coliseum across Ft. Washington Way to the city center. The other section focuses on Fountain Square—linking hotels, department stores, the convention center, banks, offices, shops, and parking garages. At Fountain Square Plaza, Cincinnati's splendidly designed five-and-one-half-acre pedestrian piazza, the skyway runs along the northern edge and is designed with a public-stairway connection. This relationship is significant for the views, orientation, and access it affords to pedestrians. A mixed-use project, called Fountain Place, is planned for the block west of Fountain Square. It will include an atrium hotel and an office building located above a four-story retail podium to be linked to three skyway bridges.

As of 1987 the most extensively developed skyway system in the world was located in Calgary, Alberta, Canada. At that time, forty-one bridges and nine kilometers (5.6 miles) of walkways were completed.[10] The plus-15 system (that is, skyways located fifteen feet [4.5 meters] above the street) was achieved through an elaborate system of development control, whereby developers provided the bridges, walkways, and public amenities in exchange for rights to build at a higher density of up to 12 to 15 FAR (building floor area to site area ratio) instead of 8 FAR. These strong incentives induced developer's to construct large segments of the system during the office-building boom of the 1970s. The shift of retail activity from the street to the plus-15 level caused planners to reconsider the bonusing provisions. In 1984 the bonus system was revised, requiring mandatory grade-level open space to achieve a base level of 7 FAR. Bonus rules were reversed, with grade-level amenities obtaining higher square-footage ratios than plus-15 features. Mandatory financial contributions to a plus-15 fund enable the city to build missing links and stairs connecting the bridges to the street (figure 4.14).

A progressive planning policy in Calgary has produced a system that balances pedestrian activity between the skyway and the street levels. The two lower levels of buildings are designed as public areas with shuttle-elevator access and exterior stairs located at the skyway bridges. The access via elevators to the office floors is provided only from the main grade-level entrances to the buildings. Ideally, the system would be open twenty-four hours a day and would be guarded by city police. In reality, the opening hours vary between twelve and eighteen hours, and the buildings' owners provide their own security.

Since its inception, the plus-15 system has been viewed as an alternate pedestrian environment to an enhanced street-level system of malls and plazas. According to a City of Calgary Planning and Building Department user survey:

> For most, the system is used in the trip to and from work as well as over the lunch hour. Users like the weather-protected environment created by the system, but many of them tend to reserve its use to more inclement days. The corresponding surges in pedestrian volumes on the outdoor Stephen Avenue Mall during not only the summer months, but also the January and February chinooks, show that Calgarians have not entirely abandoned their grade-level pedestrian system.[11]

Fig. 4.14. Exterior of skyway bridge. Calgary, Alberta, Canada.

EVALUATION OF SKYWAYS

After two decades, it seems that skyways are not just an urban-design fad but are viable interior pedestrian systems that will continue to function into the future. A critical evaluation is necessary before the next generation of skyways is planned and designed. Skyways have been criticized by many for their negative urbanistic, social, economic, and aesthetic influences upon the development of city centers. These criticisms need to be acknowledged and addressed by the planners and designers of future systems.

Many critics of skyway systems blame them for the deterioration of street-level pedestrian activity. Relocating vital retail and commercial functions to the skyway level changes street life in both quantity and quality. With the development of inward-oriented urban shopping centers—linked together with skyways—shops with street frontage have suffered and have been forced to close or relocate. Offering a possible solution, architect Victor Caliandro observes that:

> this system separates pedestrian and vehicular traffic into two competing orders, establishing a vast—perhaps impossibly vast—interface between public and private. Previous difficulties of sustaining the vitality of the commercial frontage of the city grid are now extended throughout the two systems. A possible response would be conversion of the skyway to include residential use thereby substantially increasing pedestrian use and commercial activity.[12]

Few cities are dense enough to sustain two levels of pedestrian retail activity. Retail activity does, however, propagate; and, in time, there may be enough activity in the central core to sustain both the street and skyway levels. To achieve this, however, the vertical connections (stairs, escalators, and elevators) must be readily available; and signage must be coordinated to enable pedestrians to utilize effectively the bilevel system. Nodal atrium spaces, which visually and spatially link these levels, are important for they encourage balanced use.

In office, governmental, and residential activities, the prospects for balanced use of a bilevel pedestrian system are not as positive. On days with inclement weather, the enclosed skyway system always will be preferable. Even during good weather, the convenience of the skyway system and the force of habit are difficult to overcome. It is just too easy to get around in a dry, warm pedestrian network. In St. Paul and Minneapolis, people who live in apartments on the skyway system can function for days without going outside. The same is true for commuters who arrive at parking garages connected to the skyways. In these situations, the street-level pedestrian system becomes redundant—to be used only by vehicles or the unfortunate pedestrian whose destination is not linked to a skyway.

The most-often-voiced concern at a 1985 conference that focused on the benefits and problems of skyways was "that skyways represent an anti-urbanistic, anti-democratic privatization of the street, the one remaining realm in an American city which has the potential to be a truly heterogeneous public sphere."[13] Skyways tend to cause social stratification: businessmen and support staff use the skyways; street people, teen-agers, and members of the lower classes use the street. In Charlotte, North Carolina, the skyway system has stratified the city's once-active streets—the mostly affluent whites are above, and the mostly poor blacks are below.[14] The higher rents on the skyways attract expensive stores, whereas the less-expensive stores are relegated to street level. People enter the skyways from parking garages to which they drive in cars; people on the street ride the bus. This social stratification is ironic, particularly in cold climates.

Plate 28. Atrium view, Bradbury Building. Los Angeles.

Plate 29. Atrium view, 1300 New York Avenue. Washington, D.C.

Plate 30. Atrium view, Ford Foundation Headquarters. New York City.

Plate 31. Atrium view, Old Post Office. Washington, D.C.

Plate 32. Atrium view,
State of Illinois Center.
Chicago.

Plate 33. Atrium view, East Building, National Gallery of Art. Washington, D.C.

Plate 34. Interior view, American Wing, Metropolitan Museum of Art. New York City.

Plate 35. Interior view, PPG Place Winter Garden. Pittsburgh.

Plate 36. Interior view, IBM
Garden Plaza. New York City.

Plate 37. Exterior view, Rainbow Center Winter Garden. Niagara Falls, New York.

Plate 38. Interior view, World Financial Center Winter Garden. New York City.

Plate 40. Town Court atrium. St. Paul.

Plate 39. Town Square indoor park. St. Paul.

Plate 41. Atrium view,
Galtier Plaza. St. Paul.

Plate 42. The plaza at Rockefeller Center. New York City.

Plate 43. Concourse view, Place Ville Marie. Montreal.

Plate 44. Exterior view of Rows. Chester, England.

Plate 45. Newgate Row, Grosvenor Precinct. Chester, England.

Plate 46. Atrium view, International Square. Washington, D.C.

Plate 47. Atrium view, Columbia Square. Washington, D.C.

Plate 48. Atrium view, Metropolitan Square. Washington, D.C.

Plate 49. Interior view, Mellon Independence Center. Philadelphia.

Plate 50. Arcade view, Strawberry Square. Harrisburg, Pennsylvania.

Those who can afford overcoats are on the skyway in shirt sleeves, while the poor are left out in the cold. Victor Caliandro similarly concludes:

> Internal pedestrian systems limited to commercial facilities . . . are, I believe, ultimately counterproductive in relation to the whole urban fabric. They segregate a range of activities and therefore function for only part of daily and weekly cycles. . . . They do not act as social condensors associating people interested in many different goals and thereby they also diminish the potential for access, interchange and accidental encounter.[15]

The issue of social stratification is a difficult one to address. In spite of their role as public pedestrian systems, skyways vary in their degree of publicness. Those skyways located in high-use retail areas are reasonably public and readily accessible, whereas those near residences or businesses are at best semipublic and are marginally accessible. Different police-patrolling standards are utilized in these areas, leading to differing standards of acceptable public behavior. Only the streets of the city remain truly public because access to skyways can be controlled by guards and limited by owners. The location of public functions on the skyways, as was done in St. Paul with the branch library, science museum, and city hall, increases use by all segments of the population. Exterior stair towers, as proposed in Minneapolis (and in place in Calgary), greatly improve public access between the two pedestrian levels.

Skyways are generally judged to be successful in economically revitalizing downtowns, particularly in terms of retail and convention activity. The remarkable growth of real-estate development in cities with skyways is well documented. (Of course, it is difficult to know whether the same growth and economic success would have been achieved without the skyways.) A possibly temporary shifting of business locations and leasing rates between the two levels is expected.

Skyways have had a positive role to play in the return of retail, convention, and entertainment activity to the city center. On a Sunday afternoon in downtown Minneapolis, it was surprising to find a substantial number of people shopping, especially when there was a professional football game being played a mile away.

The aesthetic critique of skyways is generally severe, for they have detracted from the visual quality of urban architecture in form, color, scale, and material. In cities with large skyway systems, this detraction has been extensive; in fact, many building facades have been defaced by obtrusive bridges. Historic facades do not blend gracefully with contemporary bridges. These visually offensive intrusions have been termed *skewering*. In the historic St. Paul area of Lowertown, the United States Department of the Interior has registered a significant objection to this practice relative to landmark buildings (figure 4.15). Skyway bridges are

Fig. 4.15. Exterior of Lowertown skyway bridge. St. Paul.

easier to connect to contemporary buildings where the bridges can be designed as an integral element of the facade. The positioning of skyway bridges relative to building facades is a difficult problem because there are two different facades to consider on opposite sides of the street, resulting in the need for a design compromise. Some critics believe that if skyway bridges cannot be designed well, they should not be forced into buildings for the sake of the system.

Skyway bridges also seriously damage the streetscape of the city. For example, vistas to landmarks or distant views are blocked. This is critical in a city of high-rise buildings, where distant views are cherished. One skyway bridge visually damages a vista but several virtually destroy it (figure 4.16). A design approach that alleviates this situation is transparency—that is, to use as much glass as possible (as in the bridges to the IDS

Center). Future skyway bridges should be located with much more concern for street views by grouping them or spacing them. They should not be permitted to cross streets that have significant urban vistas.

The interiors of skyway bridges should be designed as places rather than as tubes for movement. A bridge has a beginning, an end, and a middle; it is a place to pause and take in a unique view of the world below. As critic Colin Rowe observes, "great bridges such as the Ponte Vecchio in Florence, Old London Bridge, the Pont Neuf in Paris, and the covered bridges of New England and upstate New York have always been places in themselves."[16] To this list can be added the shop-lined Pulteney Bridge over the River Avon in Bath, England, designed by Robert Adam (figure 4.17).

Skyway systems of the future should be developed as part of an overall city-

Fig. 4.16. Multiple skyway bridges. Minneapolis.

Fig. 4.17. Pulteney Bridge. Bath, England.

land-use and transportation strategy. Minneapolis has just such a development plan, which includes entertainment, retail, office, and residential zones that form a central core. This central core will be surrounded by fringe parking structures to be served by a ring road. Buses and cabs will operate throughout this central area, and a proposed express bus station will be linked to the skyway system. Nicollet Mall is the primary pedestrian space of this plan, and related plazas and side streets will form an integrated system of open space. The goal is an organized, compact downtown in which activities support each other and the interests of the pedestrian are paramount. In this type of plan, the skyway system is viewed as one element of a comprehensive scheme. Without this comprehensive view, a skyway system becomes independent, self-serving, and unrelated to the rest of the city. Today, the tendency is to continue extending the skyway systems at great cost (for example, a 500-foot-long (152-meter-long) bridge in Minneapolis linking a residential project) and not to concentrate on developing an integrated downtown. As a result, the other pedestrian elements of the city eventually suffer through neglect and become run down. ■

During the Great Depression, one of the most significant urban-design projects in the United States was being planned and built in Manhattan. Rockefeller Center occupies three long blocks between Fifth and Sixth avenues and 48th and 51st streets. An intermediate north-south private street was added to create six building sites for office buildings of varying footprints and heights. A below-grade concourse system, lined with services and shops, extends throughout the complex and leads to the subway stations. At the street level, buildings are brought to the street line, with some setbacks to create enhanced sidewalk spaces. At the center of this scheme is a sunken plaza that spatially integrates the complex's two pedestrian levels. The plaza is used as a café in summer and as an ice-skating rink in winter. In his book *Multi-Use Architecture*, Eberhard Zeidler observes that "the sunken plaza is a rather extraordinary piece of urban topography—a lush valley inside the dry, flat New York grid. The juxtaposition of this festive public space with its hard urban surroundings gives it an oasis-like appeal."[17] Rockefeller Center is a useful model of a large-scale development in which the concourse and street levels are effectively related by means of an exterior pedestrian place (see plate 42).

A concourse pedestrian system located below the street level is the counterpart of a skyway pedestrian system raised above the street. Concourses usually develop in cities that have below-ground transit systems. There, they link the street-level entrances to the transit stations. Service-oriented commercial activity is often located along these routes. The system is extended as more entrances are added or as these entrances access department stores, office buildings, government centers, or cultural complexes. In large cities with extensive subway systems—such as New York, Paris, and London—such a pattern of development has yielded a system of tangled subterranean networks that are confusing and disorienting. In cities with more recently developed subway systems, such as Washington, D.C., the concourses are organized more rationally and are related more closely to the stations. In older cities, such as Boston and Philadelphia, the results of concerted redesign and renovation are subway stations with distinct environmental qualities that enhance associations with grade-level locations.

Houston and Oklahoma City, Oklahoma, do not have underground transit systems and yet have subterranean pedestrian networks. The city of Dallas also has embarked on the construction of an extensive combined skyway-and-tunnel system. The existence of these underground pedestrian systems is highly unusual because they have no intrinsic basis of support. They are used solely for pedestrian convenience—as a means for going between buildings without having to go outside. The tunnels are accessed from lobbies, parking levels, or office towers via stairs, escalators, or elevators (figure 4.18). Parts of the system are lined with commercial and service functions, whereas other parts are simply bare-walled tunnels. These systems are disorienting to the average pedestrian, who must rely on the use of maps and signs until memorization of particular routes occurs. The only potential points of orientation are the buildings' lobbies, but usually there is no spatial relationship between the street and tunnel levels even there.

The most extensive of these systems is in Houston. There, the system is approximately 2.8 miles (4.5 kilometers) in length and connects fifty buildings and parking facilities (figure 4.19). Land in Houston is owned to the center of the street, thus allowing owners of buildings on opposite sides to cooperate in constructing tunnels that cross or run parallel to the streets above. The city's only control is an annual building-code in-

Fig. 4.18. Tunnel access elevators, Pennzoil Place. Houston.

spection and the granting of a thirty-year occupancy permit.[18] The city of Houston now publishes a tunnel-system master plan but lacks the means to direct its implementation. Although the first tunnel was constructed in 1947, over twenty years elapsed before the ad-hoc development process created some contiguous segments. This privately constructed and maintained system is accessible only from building lobbies during weekday business hours. Although available to the general public, it is not really a public pedestrian system. The tunnels are actually private-building corridors utilized to promote convenience and efficiency in business activities.

Houston's tunnel system succeeds economically and functionally despite its

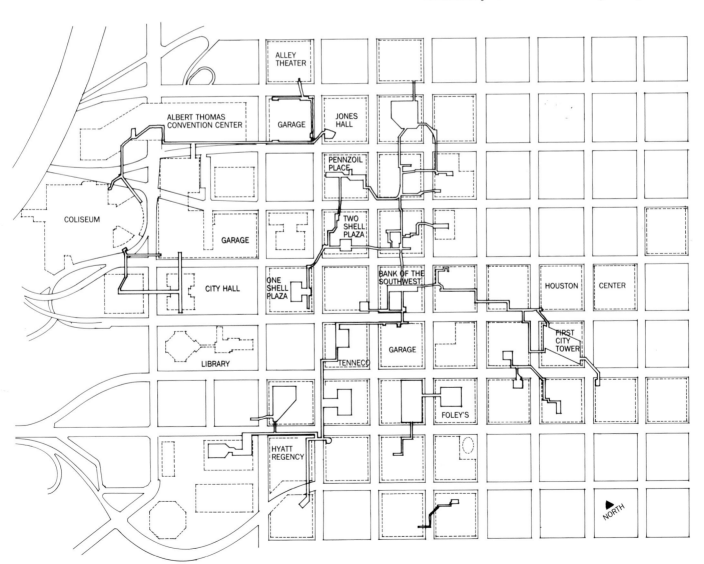
Fig. 4.19. Map of tunnel system. Houston.

lack of environmental quality. The rental premium for office space related to the system was between $2.25 and $4.00 per square foot in 1985, and this space was leased faster than space unrelated to the tunnel system.[19] Yet, due to utility relocations and difficult construction techniques, tunnels cost three times as much to build as do skyways. The tunnels are now the focus of virtually all center-city pedestrian activity related to shopping and eating—despite their inhospitable environment and the lack of spatial orientation and daylight. The tunnels are 10 to 14 feet (3 to 4.3 meters) wide and usually 10 feet (3 meters) high, with uniform surface treatments and inadequate signage. The city's 1977 report on the tunnel system recognizes these shortcomings and encourages building owners to foster a sense of environmental identity.[20]

Curiously, Houston also has segments of a skyway system: One segment links the Hyatt Regency Hotel to the surrounding office buildings. Another links together the nine blocks of phase one of Houston Center. This phase consists of four office towers, a hotel, two parking garages, and a retail center called The Park. This two-level linear shopping mall, with its half-vaulted skylight, is located in the middle of the nine blocks and is connected to the other elements by four skyway bridges.

The tunnel and skyway systems in Houston are not coordinated with each other. The result is redundancy and overlap. In a city with a mild climate for most of the year, every effort has been made to keep pedestrians from having to go outside. Needless to say, street life is virtually nonexistent, and the quality of the streetscape is a completely neglected urban-design issue. Whether the tunnels and skyways destroyed Houston's street life is debatable. However, as William Whyte points out, a version of Gresham's Law is in effect: when the streetscape is allowed to deteriorate, the off-street systems become more attractive.[21]

In three North American cities—Philadelphia, Toronto, and Montreal—concourse systems related to subway transit have developed into integrated interior pedestrian networks. These systems have gone far beyond the needs of servicing the subway system's pedestrian traffic and have achieved their own identity. In Philadelphia, the concept of a below-the-street pedestrian network at Penn Center has been extended into the development of Market East, which interrelates linearly many building functions and modes of transit (see pages 207–13). In Toronto, the extensive concourse system has produced a virtual underground city with usage that greatly exceeds the necessity to avoid the harsh winter climate (see pages 201–6). The third city is Montreal, which boasts a concourse system that rivals Toronto's in extent and quality.

Montreal's concourse system began with the construction in 1963 of a single, large project. Place Ville Marie, designed by I. M. Pei and developed by William Zeckendorf, is a forty-eight-story cruciform tower set off-center in a raised, seven-acre plaza defined by lower buildings along the street. Below are two levels of parking and one level of retail space (1.2 million square feet [111,480 square meters]). The tracks of the Canadian National Railroad pass underneath. The concourses are wide, orthogonal passages, which are lined with elegantly designed shop fronts. The concourses spatially relate to the plaza above through four skylit pavilions that cover sunken courts. These spaces—with ficus trees, granite paving, café furniture, and gracious stairs leading up to the plaza—are welcome points of visual release and orientation. After twenty-five years, the public spaces still look new and function superbly as locuses for pedestrian activity (see plate 43). The Royal Bank of Canada Tower brings the equivalent of forty-five acres of occupied offices to bear upon the concourse system—ensuring the required foot traffic for commercial viability. Additional pedestrian connections to the streets and the railroad station contribute to this pedestrian focus. The planning and design of Place Ville Marie set a high standard for Montreal's concourse system that has not been equaled in any subsequent project.

In 1967 the city of Montreal completed the first of sixty-eight Métro stations. This subway system has given great impetus to the development of central Montreal. Moreover, it has generated part of the rationale for an underground concourse system of commercial pedestrian routes. In 1967 planner Vincent Ponte prepared a master plan that called for the extension of the concourse system for ten kilometers (6.2 miles) within the area bounded by the Métro stations of Bonaventure, Victoria, McGill, and Peel.[22] Now, over twenty years later, this scheme has been substantially com-

pleted—with about one-half of the urban blocks in this area linked together. Place Ville Marie is linked south through the central railroad station to Place Bonaventure—a brutalist, multiuse megastructure. The concourse of Place Bonaventure has a two-story focal space surrounded by retail passages. Unlike the spaces in Place Ville Marie, Place Bonaventure's spaces are disappointing because of their lack of daylight and their lack of association with the street.

Between boulevard de Maisonneuve and rue Sainte-Catherine, Montreal's retail district has been extended by the development of retail centers on seven contiguous urban blocks: the new Cour Mont Royal (see page 82), the old Simpson's department store, the new Place Montreal Trust (see page 60), the recent Les Terrasses, the old Eaton's department store, the new Place de la Cathédrale, and the new La Bay (figure 4.20).

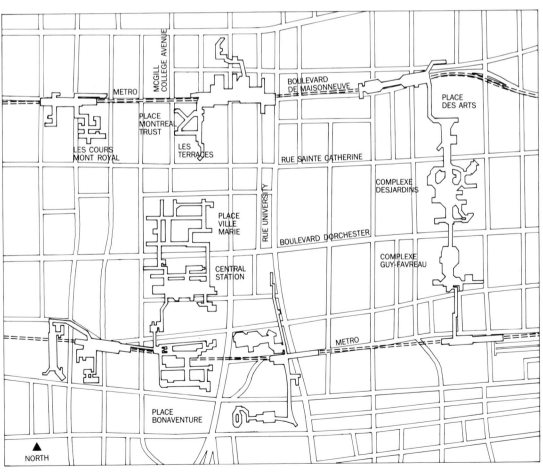

Fig. 4.20. Map of Underground Montreal.

Across the boulevard de Maisonneuve to the north are two additional retail centers—2020 University and Galeries 2001—with their shops, restaurants, cinemas, and a branch public library. These projects are all connected to each other by the streets and concourses. All are organized around atrium spaces of various plan and section configurations. The

newer of these centers are better designed than were the older ones; they are more spatially expansive, have more daylight, relate better to the outdoors, and provide better pedestrian amenities.

A few blocks to the east of this retail core, running north-south between the Place des Arts Métro station and the Place d'Armes Métro station, is the most rationally organized segment of the Montreal concourse system. The Place des Arts is a large cultural complex, consisting of three theaters for opera, ballet, and symphony. Its concourse leads directly under the rue Sainte-Catherine to the Complexe Desjardins, with its spectacular plaza-atrium. Three office towers and a hotel occupy the corners of this 200-meter-square (656-foot-square) superblock, which has a hollowed-out, four-story podium at its center. This plaza-atrium, surrounded by shops and services on three sides and hotel functions on the fourth, is covered by a huge concrete waffle-slab roof supported by four large, sculptural concrete columns (figure 4.21). The atrium floor is located at the concourse level and draws pedestrians into the space, up to the street level, and up further to the three surrounding galleries. At the atrium's center is a raised seating area and a large wooden mobile. The only significant design problem is the clerestory daylighting, which creates visual glare and causes the roof to appear heavy and confining. Also, the natural concrete surfaces have dirtied with age and do not reflect light well. Nevertheless, this is an atrium with the scale and character of an exterior plaza, with clear relationships to the streetscape.

Fig. 4.21. Atrium view, Complexe Desjardins. Montreal.

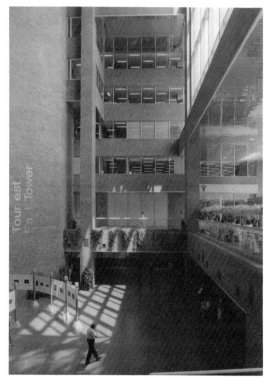

Fig. 4.22. Atrium view, Complexe Guy-Favreau. Montreal.

Continuing under boulevard Dorchester from the Complexe Desjardins, the pedestrian reaches the new national government office center called Complexe Guy-Favreau. The twin office towers surround an atrium that extends down to the concourse level (figure 4.22). Behind the towers is a café, overlooking both the concourse and a green space surrounded by housing. In this project, the shopping concourse extends under the entire site, thus providing a sheltered pedestrian system visually related to the exterior by means of the atrium. This is an excellent piece of urban design that relates housing and offices to a green space with shops and parking below. From this location, the concourse system continues south under a plaza to the Palais des Congrès, a high-tech convention center raised above the Ville Marie Expressway.

Montreal's concourse system has no identity or character of its own. Except for some of the new atria, most of the concourse spaces are environmentally banal. Its value as a system is in what it connects—the building complexes to the Métro stations. A continuity has been developed that gives it systemlike characteristics despite its idiosyncratic aspects. The shops and services along these routes have been sustained by the constant foot traffic between destinations. Of course, the pedestrian can avoid the concourses and enter the Métro stations directly from the street. But for most pedestrians, it is easier, safer, and shorter to use the concourses and avoid the climatic problems. ■

A SECOND CITY

Systems of skyways and concourses have been successfully utilized by pedestrians for their convenience—particularly in cities with extreme climates. Residents of skyway cities can travel from house, to attached garage, to car, to parking garage, to skyway to office without going outside. The trip home reverses this routine. At noon, people can bank, shop, and eat lunch on the skyway system. Such a routine is understandable during the work week in winter, when the weather and time put a premium on convenience. But is this a valid way of living on other days of the week and in other seasons of the year? Is the claim that one can live for days without wearing an overcoat in winter something to value? Are we not missing an important aspect of life by living entirely in controlled environments where our perceptions, movements, and activities have been totally organized by designers? Choice and freedom are limited in any controlled environment, and the potential to live as complete human beings is diminished.

People who live in cities with skyways or concourses must make difficult choices as to whether and when to use these interior walkways. Being creatures of habit who are often lazy, the tendency will be to follow a routine of convenience and use the skyways or concourses during all days of the year. Pedestrians who lived in a city before skyways and concourses were built retain some of the old patterns of use and switch between systems depending upon the weather. In Calgary, for example, there is an active street life in conjunction with the skyway system. Where the average winter daytime temperature is twenty-five degrees below zero (Fahrenheit), people appreciate good weather. The skyways are used in winter and the streets in summer. But what about future generations who have always known the skyways? Will they ever go outside when they are downtown?

Architect Elliot Willensky fears that our culture's support of skyways (and concourses) is a form of escapism:

My most serious concern with the skyway system is that we are toying with a second city. The skyway system is a second city as a way to avoid the problems of the first city, the city that we and our predecessors made. We made it, we used it, we enjoyed it and we tore it down as a matter of economic, political and social policy. We have now raised the ante about twenty-two feet six inches, plus or minus, to another level of the cityscape plane. We have left many of the problems on the ground level unresolved and have created new ones. It's fresh, fashionable and a bit kitschy. One day the skyway will no longer be kitschy, it will be something else.[23]

The creation of a "second city" has a compelling attraction to planners, for it affords a new frontier and a clean slate upon which to create an ordered plan. It has been undertaken in the centers of several major cities with good intentions: to escape harsh weather, for the sake of convenience, to provide security, and to facilitate pedestrian access. But with these positive results come negative consequences: decline in street-level activity, social stratification, aesthetic degradation of building facades, induced economic change, and the deterioration of the streetscape. Do the positives outweigh the negatives? Not in the long term, for eventually we must come to terms with the first city. As a culture, we are gradually realizing that our extensive efforts to escape the city for the sub-

urbs and country have not been completely successful. We are returning to rebuild our cities, but we must not make the same mistakes again. Using skyways and concourses as a means of escape will not work because the first city will always be there to prod our consciousness.

As interior pedestrian systems, skyways and concourses are applicable to the solution of urban pedestrian problems only under specific circumstances:

1. They are advantageous in cities during seasons when the climate is harsh, cold, windy, or snowy.

2. Concourses are viable in areas with underground transit systems as means for reaching or connecting stations.

3. In areas of abundant pedestrian density, skyways can alleviate sidewalk crowding by providing alternate pedestrian routes.

In all cases, thorough and careful design integration is essential between the grids above, below, and at the street level to produce a unified pedestrian network. ■

CHAPTER 5

URBAN-DESIGN CASE STUDIES

In his book of 1889, *The Art of Building Cities*, Viennese architect and critic Camillo Sitte sought to redirect the basis for designing cities from the geometry of road networks to the composition of urban space.[1] His method was to analyze the public squares of many Italian and German towns in order to derive principles of relationship among the open spaces, the buildings, and the monuments. Public squares, in Sitte's view, needed to be the focal points of towns; and he believed they should be designed based on artistic principles of spatial order. Sitte's approach to defining the elements of towns and establishing rules for their order has had an enormous influence on urban design—initially, in Europe and later in the United States.

Since Sitte's seminal treatise, several important urban-design practitioners and theorists have sought to define the elements of towns and their lawful relationships. For example, in *Town Planning in Practice*, published in 1909, Raymond Unwin analyzed in detail the components of historic towns to derive principles for their arrangement in developing a town plan.[2] In *Image of the City*, Kevin Lynch's innovative book of 1960, the author derived five types of elements referable to physical forms—paths, edges, districts, nodes, and landmarks—that comprise the content of city images.[3] More recently, in his book *Urban Space*, published in 1979, architect Rob Krier has returned to the legacy of Sitte with his comprehensive graphic analysis of the morphology of urban spaces and his critique of their erosion.[4] Theorist Leon Krier has defined the primary elements of the city as streets, squares, and quarters and has restated the primacy of urban space as the organizing element of urban morphology.[5]

This historical background is intended to emphasize the importance of urban space—particularly pedestrian space—as a component of urban design. The definition of streets, squares, and parks always has been fundamental to the design of cities. These are the spaces in which people walk, meet, and recreate; they are experienced directly throughout the hours of the day and the seasons of the year. Urban spaces are the counterparts of a city's buildings and give the city its form, continuity, stability, and image.

Urban space as an important component of city design has been considered historically as exterior space—the space between buildings. In a 1970 definition of the scope of urban design, a report by the Royal Institute of British Architects stated, "Its [urban design's] major characteristic is the arrangement of the physical objects and human activities which make up the environment; this space and the relationships of elements in it is essentially external, as distinct from internal space."[6] Rob Krier substantiates the prevalence of this viewpoint:

> The polarity of internal-external space is constantly in evidence . . ., since both obey very similar laws not only in function but also in form. Internal space, shielded from weather and environment is an effective symbol of privacy; external space is seen as open, unobstructed space for movement in the open air, with public, semi-public and private zones.[7]

The classical definition may indeed consider urban space as external and public—that is, freely available for pedestrian use. The viewpoint put forth in this book is that exterior space need not be considered as the city's only pedestrian space. Throughout the history of architecture and urban design, enclosed or covered spaces—such as stoa, markets, porticoes, colonnades, arcades, and atria—have had an important role in giving form to cities. I suggest that the definition of urban space should be extended to include significant interior public and semipublic places (much as Nolli considered such spaces in his map of Rome [see page 12]). Usually semipublic in nature, interior places have grown in variety and abundance in recent years—making them a significant component of the pedestrian realm of the city.

The urban-design case studies in this chapter will illustrate the role of interior pedestrian places in forming the spatial character of city centers. In the ancient city of Chester, England, historic and contemporary pedestrian places are well integrated as vital components of a thriving milieu. Washington, D.C., is extending its tradition of interior places with many new examples that are directly related to the traditional streetscape and parks. The underground concourse system in Toronto forms the matrix for a system of public atria and shopping centers that are the primary pedestrian components of this livable city. The redevelopment of the Market Street corridor in the center of Philadelphia is a significant example of interrelating several levels of interior public space to the existing streets. In each case study, the critical concern is the system of pedestrian spaces and the relationship of multilevels of interior space to traditional exterior spaces. ■

CASE STUDY: CHESTER, ENGLAND

For the tourist, Chester is a picturesque northwestern British town of well-preserved, black-and-white, half-timbered, Tudor-style architecture. For the shopper, Chester offers a wealth of opportunities—from department stores to tiny shops selling everything from luxury goods to local crafts in both exterior and interior environments. But for the urban designer, Chester represents a truly outstanding example of an integrated pedestrian environment that has been shaped over seven centuries. This combination of a traditional streetscape, second-level walkways (the Rows), a skylit Edwardian arcade, and a contemporary shopping mall has few comparisons for its qualities of human scale, physical continuity, and architectural character.

Chester was a Roman town, founded in A.D. 79 as a military base. The juncture of the town's two main streets, which cross at the center, is marked by a High Cross dating from 1407. There, the town crier still holds forth at noon everyday. The town's streets emanated from this crossing in a gridded sequence to their intersection with the defensive wall surrounding the town. In the tenth century, the Saxons rebuilt the Roman walls on the north and east sides and built new walls on the south and west sides in order to enlarge the town to three times its area. These walls were restored in 1701–8, and the four medieval gates were replaced later with arches spanning the streets.[8] The tops of the walls now form a wonderful two-mile (3.2-kilometer) promenade, from which the pedestrian can enjoy vistas of the countryside and overlooks to the town's center (figure 5.1).

Chester grew into a prominent trading city, and the Rows were created in about the thirteenth century. Their specific origins are, however, disputed.[9] One theory holds that during the Middle Ages arcaded buildings were built on top of and in front of the Roman ruins. Later, the basements of these buildings were excavated to create the present street levels with their elevated Rows. Another theory holds that the Rows were initially at grade on high ground. As the town grew, they were kept at a constant elevation, while the street level changed according to the topography. Both theories can be

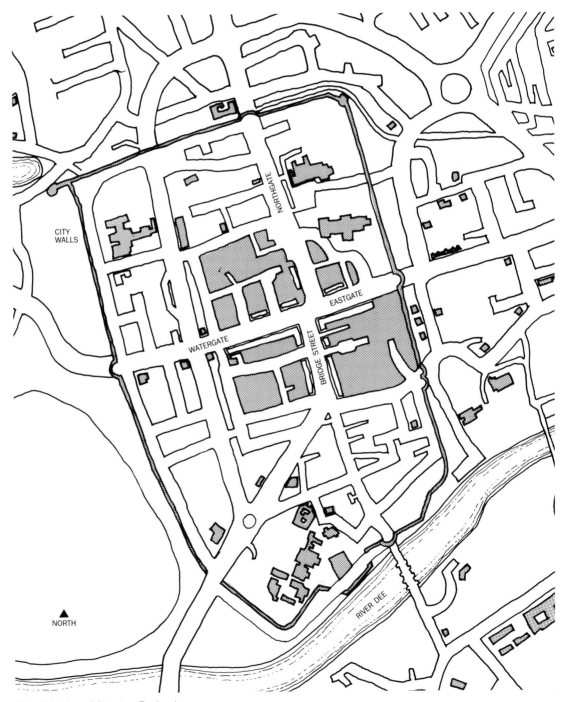

Fig. 5.1. Map of Chester, England.

Fig. 5.2. View of Eastgate Rows. Chester, England.

substantiated by existing physical evidence. In either case, the residences originally occupied the pedestrian level of the Rows and the floor above, with shops and storage below. It is only in the last 150 years that shops have expanded into the Rows themselves. Even as rebuilding proceeded in the Georgian and Victorian eras, these elevated public passageways were preserved and extended (figure 5.2).

The Rows of Chester form a unique system of elevated pedestrian passages, the viability of which has survived the test of time. They extend on both sides of the street through the second levels of four long urban blocks. Access is by stairs at frequent intervals along the street, and prominent entrances are located at street corners and at St. Michael's Row (see plate 44). Since the Rows are less than ten feet (three meters) above the street, the access stairs cause little difficulty. Walking along these passageways, the pedestrian is protected from the traffic as well as the rain. Nevertheless, the prohibition of cars on two blocks of these street frontages has made this area an even more enjoyable pedestrian environment. The remaining two blocks should be equally treated.

The architectural characteristics of the Rows come from every era of Chester's history. The variations in materials, colors, and ornamentation lend variety and uniqueness to the pedestrian's experience. The Rows themselves are considered as public rights-of-way through private property, and their maintenance is required of each owner. Their widths vary slightly, as do the ceiling heights and the floor levels. One constant feature is the 4-foot-wide (1.2-meter-wide) band of space that separates the walkway from the street facade. Its purpose is to display goods for viewing by those walking by as well as by pedestrians on the street or on the opposite Row. It also serves as a space to step out of the way in order to socialize (figure 5.3). Most of the display space is in

Fig. 5.3. View of Chester Row. Chester, England.

Fig. 5.4. St. Michael's Arcade. Chester, England.

shop windows or in recessed shop entries. The totality of this spatial arrangement enriches the pedestrian's opportunities of window-shopping or socializing. The intimate, personal quality of the Rows and their varying levels of daylight is a memorable milieu.

Beginning in the eighteenth century, the local Grosvenor family (the dukes of Westminster) became active in the town's development. In 1910 they sponsored the construction of St. Michael's Row, a one-block-long Edwardian shopping arcade opening off of the Row on the east side of Bridge Street. In 1965 they continued their development of the southeast quadrant of the town center with the construction of an enclosed shopping center, the Grosvenor Precinct, named after the family.

T. M. Lockwood designed St. Michael's Row as a three-story project—with Turkish baths at the street level, shops at the Row level, and commercial space above. Only the upper two levels are covered with a gabled skylight (figure 5.4). The one-block arcade has an entrance stair up from Bridge Street and a direct connection to the shopping center. Originally, the exterior was of Renaissance design with white Doulton tiles. But even in 1910, the townsfolk resisted this noncontextual design, and the facade was changed above the street level to the familiar black-and-white Tudor half-timber.[10] The interior retains its original, delicately detailed Renaissance design, which makes an interesting transition between the Tudor Rows and the modern shopping center.

When the Grosvenor Precinct shopping center opened in 1965, it was one of the first enclosed centers in England. Its real uniqueness was, however, its construction on back-land at the center of the block. Grosvenor Precinct was designed and built between and around an existing church, a department store, a hotel, shops, and the arcade—with street frontage for rental offices on Pepper

Street (figure 5.5). The center has three pedestrian entrances: Eastgate Street leading to Newgate Row, Pepper Street leading to Paddock Row, and Bridge Street via St. Michael's Row to St. Michael's Square. The pedestrian levels (except for Newgate Row) are above the street. Truck-service and storage areas are located at street level, and car parking is on the roof. Although the shopping center contains 173,000 square feet (16,072 square meters) of gross leasable area and 514 parking spaces, it has virtually no visible presence in the city—a commendable characteristic in a sensitive historic context.

In 1965 the complete refurbishment of Grosvenor Precinct was completed in three phases. The center's appearance had become dated, and there was a need to change the tenant mix as the twenty-one-year leases expired. In addition, the shops were relocated in response to contemporary shopping patterns and altered pedestrian routes.[11]

The refurbished center is based on a fashion-marketing concept. The elimination of a supermarket and the relocation of a furniture store enabled the management to relocate clothing stores and footware and jewelry shops along Newgate Row and around St. Michael's Square.

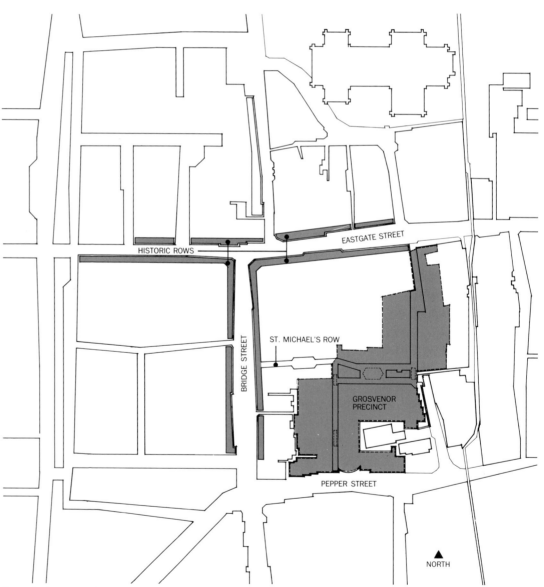

Fig. 5.5. Site plan, Grosvenor Precinct. Chester, England.

New shop fronts—featuring large expanses of glass, simple geometry, and controlled signage—showcase the merchandise. Shopping in historic Chester is primarily a leisure-time activity. This trend was acknowledged in the redesign by placing a café in the center of St. Michael's Square, by shortening the length of Paddock Row, and by improving the connection to the car park with a centrally located stair. The standards followed in the redesign of the public spaces included a uniform metal-ceiling pattern, cream-colored marble floors, mirrored-glass spandrels, and a limited use of plants. Newgate Row was covered with a gabled skylight, and the old paving was left intact (see plate 45).

The significance of Grosvenor Precinct is not its interior design but rather the high level of integration with its context. The entrances relate well to established walkways, enabling convenient circulation through the shopping center. The spatial focus of St. Michael's Square is important for pedestrian orientation. A continuous pattern of daylight, as in the old St. Michael's Arcade and the new portion of Newgate Row, was desirable; although it was not feasible due to the overhead car park. The refurbishment has reaped considerable economic benefits: a 30 percent increase in pedestrian flows, reduced tenant turnover, significantly higher rents, and increased sales.

In virtually all respects, Chester represents an idealized model for an urban-shopping precinct. The opportunity for a variety of pedestrian movement is remarkable. In addition to the promenade on top of the town walls and the traditional sidewalks, there are numerous alleys and squares. The Rows complement the exterior pedestrian system by being removed from the traffic level yet constantly oriented to it—with excellent connections between the two. The interior mall and the historic arcade afford yet another kind of shopping environment to complement the others. Pedestrians can choose a variety of routes based on their own inclinations or on the weather. They can also seek out certain kinds of shops, which have tended to locate in groups: food, services, and restaurants along the street; leather and clothing along the Rows; high fashion and jewelry in the mall. Some shops are organized vertically, while others are organized horizontally—allowing multiple access points. The shops vary in size, from small craft shops to large department stores.

In shopping, the quality of the pedestrian experience is as important as the shops. Chester's architectural character—with its balance of stylistic continuity and historic variety—is a pleasure to behold. All of the town's buildings share railings, columns, stairs, windows, and doors of similar scale and detail, allowing the buildings to relate well to each other. People respond positively to this setting. Being in an actively used environment that spans nineteen centuries is a rare human experience. The result is a pedestrian environment that is profound and stimulating, joyful and intense, and social and personal.

The urban-design lessons to be learned from Chester are many: The value of continuity between exterior and interior pedestrian systems through multiple access points is one such lesson. The development of these systems over centuries based on the voluntary cooperation of individuals is another. My colleague, Warren Boeschenstein, has pointed out the value of comparing Chester's system of elevated walkways with recent skywalk systems in the United States.[12] Chester's system maintains a constant relationship with the street for purposes of orientation and view; whereas the usual skywalk system crosses the street and penetrates into the building block, thus minimizing public exposure. Chester bears continued referral and study as a valuable urban design model with historic continuity. ■

More than any other American city, Washington, D.C., has a strong legacy of significant interior pedestrian places. Many are located in the monumental buildings of the federal government—beginning with the Capitol, with its colossal rotunda and its halls representing streets. Although not truly a pedestrian space, the 100-foot-diameter (30.5-meter-diameter) domed reading room of the Library of Congress is a spectacular interior public space. Daniel Burnham's Union Station, with its newly added marketplace, features a grand hall and circulation spaces based on classical Roman precedent. Nearby is the stilted white-marble atrium of the Hart Senate Office Building, with its enormous black stabile-mobile by Alexander Calder. The grandest space of all is located in the 1887 Pension Building (now the National Building Museum), the site of numerous inaugural balls (see page 130). Other non-federal government buildings with large interior public spaces include the International Monetary Fund, located at 19th and G streets, N.W., with its formal, eleven-story atrium measuring 105 feet by 120 feet (32.0 by 36.6 meters). Further north at 14th and U streets, N.W., is the recently completed Franklin D. Reeves Center of Municipal Affairs, with its handsome entry and linear atrium spaces (see page 133).

The museums of Washington, D.C., are another locus of significant interior public places. The rotunda, the galleries, and the garden courts in the National Gallery of Art are among the most elegantly composed sequences of interior places in any American building. The Corcoran Gallery and School of Art, built in 1897 and designed by Ernest Flagg, contains a pair of skylit, two-story atria—around which are arranged wonderfully daylit art galleries. Along the Mall, both the Museum of Natural History and the Arts and Industries Building incorporate rotundas from different architectural periods. The Arts and Industries Building also contains wonderful linear, skylit exhibit spaces much like those of the National Portrait Gallery. Museums recently constructed along the Mall have added immeasurably to the aforementioned legacy. The triangular atrium of the National Gallery of Art's East Building is certainly among the most memorable museum atria in the United States (see pages 134–35). The Air and Space Museum's three atria, which accommodate suspended airplanes, are the most unique of these spaces. Other recent examples are the mostly underground spaces of the Sackler Gallery of Asian Art and the Museum of African Art.

These are just the interior pedestrian places in Washington, D.C.'s government and cultural buildings. There are many more examples in hotels and in office and commercial buildings. Why are there more than twenty buildings with significant atria in Washington, D.C.? Do they relate to one another in terms of a pedestrian network? The answers to these questions are specific to each project, although there are some general responses that are possible.

Tradition and legacy are certainly strong contributing factors to this plethora of interior pedestrian places. Virtually all buildings built before the twentieth century were based on the demands of daylighting and often were designed around large courtyards for this purpose. With the advent of skylights, these courtyards were easily converted to public atria by covering them over. Grand entry halls and rotundas were long established as component spaces of government and cultural buildings of classic design. This legacy was not necessarily unique to Washington, D.C.; only the concentration is greater.

Climate is a contributing factor in the creation of interior pedestrian spaces (see pages 22–26). Washington, D.C., has hot, humid summers and cold, windy winters. There is considerable rainfall throughout the year, and significant snowfalls can occur. The fall and spring can be quite pleasant, with moderate temperatures and sunny skies. While there are not climatic extremes, the characteristics of a four-season climate are evident. There is reason to have the comfort and assurance of interior pedestrian systems but also the desire to enjoy the outdoors.

In a series of six articles exploring the atrium buildings of the city, Roger K. Lewis argues that urban-design principles are the primary catalyst for their presence.[13] Pierre L'Enfant's master plan for the capital city called for blocks between 300 and 500 feet (91 and 152 meters) wide—often of interesting geometric shape, resulting from the intersections of orthogonal and diagonal street systems. In 1910 building-height limits were established in order to preserve sunlight, fresh air, and views. These limits related to the street widths: for example, 60 feet, 90 feet, 110 feet, 130 feet, and 160 feet (18.3, 27.4, 33.5, 39.6, and 48.8 meters) along Pennsylvania Avenue, N.W. A secondary effect was to maintain the hierarchy of the Capitol as the highest building, thus assuring views to it from many parts of the city. Unlike other North American cities, Washington, D.C., has no towers or skyscrapers. Instead, it is a city where height limits establish hierarchical significance and meaning within an overall urban form.

Recent American urban-zoning regulations establish buildable-floor-area-to-site-area ratios (FAR) and/or percentage of site coverage. The usual floor-to-area ratio in the urban core of Washington, D.C., is ten, permitting eleven- to thirteen-story (130-foot to 160-foot [39.6- to 48.8-meter]) buildings. As a result, some of the site must be left unbuilt—in the form of plazas, courtyards, or atria (the latter being considered as unbuilt area). An aerial view of the city reveals that the buildings take the form of alphabetical characters—such as O, B, C, E, H, or L. The courtyards and atria formed by these plan shapes articulate the masses of these large buildings, while providing daylight and user amenities.

Another important aspect of the city's urban-design scheme is the quantity and quality of open spaces. The broad avenues with their generous sidewalks are defined by strong building planes at the street line; and these planes ensure the integrity of the streetscape. Within L'Enfant's plan are many squares and circles—open spaces that are defined with clarity and strength by the surrounding building facades. L'Enfant's two-dimensional mapped plan has been manifested in the third dimension by the responsible stewardship of generations of architects and planners.

International Square, completed in 1982, exemplifies the urban design scheme of Washington, D.C. It occupies three-quarters of the block between Eye and K and 18th and 19th streets, N.W. This building, designed by Washington architect Vlastimil Koubek and developed by the Oliver T. Carr Company, has eleven stories of offices, a Metro-level retail area, and two levels of parking underneath. One reason for its design success is the 8,000-square-foot (743-square-meter) atrium that effectively interrelates all floors of the project and also provides abundant daylight. There is a large central fountain with benches and plants surrounded by a crowded food court on the atrium floor, which is located one level below the street (see plate 46). Another reason is the direct connection to the Farragut West Metro station along Eye Street, accessed from both the street and the atrium. The project has excellent pedestrian connections; recessed entrances at the corners of 18th and Eye and 19th and K streets lead to a diagonal, brick-paved concourse. The shops at street level have entries from both sides, thus enlivening the sidewalk as well as the atrium. In spite of a few upper-level recesses and the eroded corner entrances, the banal concrete-and-strip-window ex-

Fig. 5.6. Exterior view, International Square. Washington, D.C.

terior facades succeed in strongly defining the street plane (figure 5.6).

The greatest concentration of buildings with interior pedestrian places is located in the rapidly developing area east of 15th Street, between Pennsylvania and New York avenues (figure 5.7). Although each of these projects was built independently, there is a semblance of coordination created by a continuity of developers and/or one architect responding to the design of another. The Grand Hyatt Hotel (see page 116) relates across H Street to the Convention Center with its gigantic exhibition spaces. At the south end of this block, the atrium of the Grand Hyatt connects to Washington

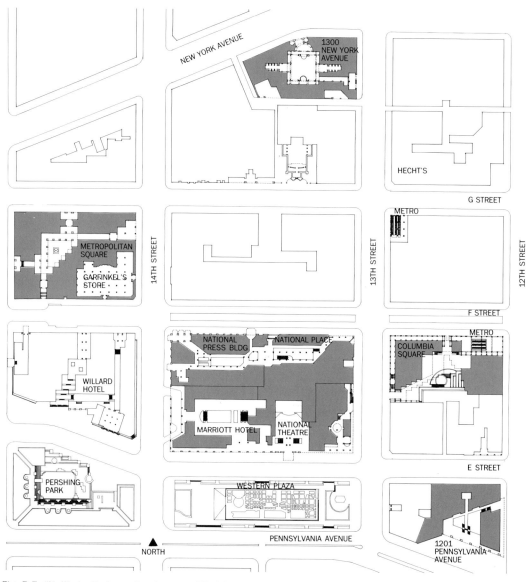

Fig. 5.7. "Nolli plan" of new development. Washington, D.C.

Fig. 5.8. Atrium view, Old Post Office Building. Washington, D.C.

Fig. 5.9. Atrium view, 1201 Pennsylvania Avenue. Washington, D.C.

Center, an adaptive-use office building that has an atrium facing 11th Street. A couple of blocks west, the office building at 1300 New York Avenue (see page 119) features a unique atrium that has a six-story waterfall and a terrace level that overlooks the Church of the Epiphany located on G Street. Adjacent to the church is the new Hecht's department store, and one block east is the restored Woodward & Lothrop department store. These department store interior spaces, although not noteworthy, are part of the pedestrian environment of those who shop and work in this area of the city.

On opposite sides of Pennsylvania Avenue at 12th Street are located the Old Post Office and 1201 Pennsylvania Avenue. The 1899 Post Office Building, with its powerful Romanesque massing, was renovated in 1983. Eight of the building's floors now are used as offices by the federal government, and the building's beautiful cortile was converted to an atrium with a new rooftop skylight (figure 5.8). The bottom two floors of the building accommodate fifty shops and restaurants, collectively called The Pavilion. This space provides a welcome respite for weary tourists and workers. The office building at 1201 Pennsylvania Avenue, completed in 1981, has a triangular, skylit atrium that is accessed from a shallow plaza (figure 5.9). The building accommodates retail shops at grade level and at below-grade level, two floors of parking, and twelve floors of exclusive offices. The top two floors are recessed to form a terrace along Pennsylvania Avenue. These two interior places complement each other well, despite the difficulty of relating across the breadth of Pennsylvania Avenue.

The three blocks between E and F streets and 15th and 12th streets contain several recent projects with significant interior places that relate closely to each other: Columbia Square is an elegant office building along F Street with an open, south-facing skylit atrium. It was designed by I. M. Pei and developed by Gerald D. Hines (see plate 47). National Place is a small three-level shopping center, managed by the Rouse Company. The office building is located above the center, which necessitates many structural columns and requires daylight to enter only from the sides (figure 5.10). The National Press Building is a renovated building adjacent and connected to National Place. It has three levels of retail space and eleven stories of offices around a skylit atrium. The National Press Club is located on the top floor. Here, only the old, exposed trusses add architectural interest between the banal atrium facades (figure 5.11). Metropolitan Square is a twelve-story office building with an atrium in the middle of the block. Developed by the Oliver T. Carr Company and designed by Skidmore, Owings & Merrill, it shares the block with the renovated Keith Albee Building (see plate 48).

The interesting aspect of this group of projects is not their individual design but rather the system of interior urban places generated by them. National Place and the National Press Building occupy the same block as the new Marriott Hotel and the restored National Theater. The diagonal pedestrian space of National Place leads to the lobby of the Marriott Hotel—as do the pedestrian areas of the National Press Building. To the west, on the adjacent block, is the magnificently restored and enlarged Willard Hotel, with its sumptuous lobby and stately passages. Both of these hotels front onto significant open spaces along Pennsylvania Avenue, Pershing Park, and Western Plaza, respectively. Columbia and Metropolitan squares are at the periphery of the node formed by these projects but are related through entrances across intervening streets. This entire series of buildings, with their direct street entrances, creates a rich and varied set of

Fig. 5.10. Atrium view, National Place. Washington, D.C.

Fig. 5.11. Atrium view, National Press Building. Washington, D.C.

Fig. 5.12. Corner of F and 13th streets. Washington, D.C.

pedestrian routes and experiences—both interior and exterior. The buildings share the common datum plane of the surrounding streets and sidewalks, which is reinforced by the open spaces of Pershing Park and Western Plaza. The designs of these two exterior spaces manipulate the pedestrian plane above and below the street level as a means of validating the common ground of the Ellipse and the Mall.

The Washington, D.C., of today is a collection of buildings related by a strong pattern of streets and open spaces. The relationship between the city's interior places always is across exterior open spaces that serve as intermediaries. This is an appropriate urban relationship, for it reiterates the function of the exterior spaces as the traditional public realm. In order to strengthen this concept, the interior spaces of future projects need to be expressed on the exterior—to invite people inside. The design of entrances relative to the streetscape and the relationship of entrances to each other should continue to be fostered (figure 5.12). In this way a positive spatial continuity between the interior and the exterior will be maintained.

The duality of exterior and interior pedestrian systems evident in Toronto, Montreal, Houston, and Minneapolis is not yet a problem in Washington, D.C.; and such a design direction is not likely to occur. As Roger Lewis states:

> If the atrium-making trend continues, Washington could someday become a city where automobiles dominate the streetscape as people thread their way from one building to another, from one atrium "square" to another, perhaps through underground tunnels or overhead covered bridges. Fortunately, the capital's climate and L'Enfant's plan are too hospitable to move everything indoors.[14] ∎

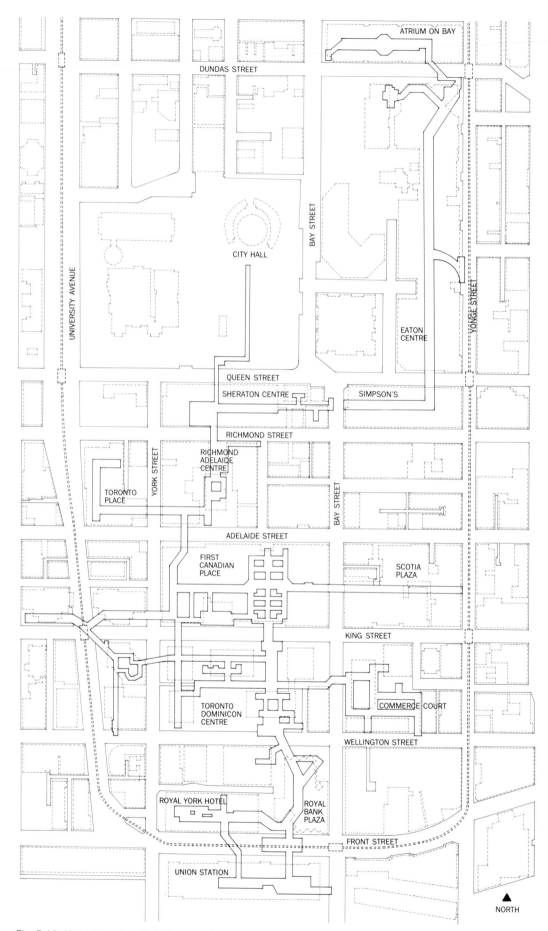

Fig. 5.13. Map of the Toronto Underground.

The Toronto Underground is arguably the best-integrated pedestrian concourse system in the world. It also is the most extensive: running 10 kilometers (6.2 miles) beneath the center of the city; providing access to 350,000 square meters (3,766,000 square feet) of retail space with another kilometer (.6 mile) of walkways; accessing 100,000 square meters (1,076,000 square feet) of retail space, planned for completion by 1991.[15] The system connects thirty office towers, three hotels, the railroad terminal, and thousands of parking spaces. An efficient, quiet, and clean subway forms a perimeter loop around the concourse system, affording direct access from six stations. The Toronto Underground grew northward, from the old Union Station on Front Street to the new city hall six blocks away. Most recently, it has grown even further north along Yonge Street, through Eaton Centre and on to the Atrium on Bay. Along this north-south course are many east-west laterals that knit the surrounding blocks together (figure 5.13).

Toronto's concourse system was proposed in the late 1950s as a means for relieving the city's overcrowded streets. The first sections to be completed in 1967 were the Toronto Dominion Centre and the Richmond/Adelaide Centre, which include below-grade shopping malls and at-grade plazas. These areas were built to attract tenants to the offices above, since this below-grade space was not calculated in the allowable building area. Subsequently, the city decided to participate in the construction of additional concourse elements, which eventually led to an integrated system connected with the subway stations. Since 1976, the implicit incentive to build concourse space has been terminated, but the city still encourages appropriate extensions to the system—which is now virtually all privately financed. Now that the concourse system is well established, developers are eager to cooperate. In fact, access to the system is worth about $2 per square foot in increased retail and office rents.[16]

The southernmost section of the Toronto Underground relates to the Union Station subway stop. It extends under the 850-foot-long (259-meter-long) monumental railroad station, built in 1927, and across Front Street to the grand Royal York Hotel, built in 1929. Both were designed by Ross & MacDonald Architects.[17] Another tunnel extends under Front Street to the Royal Bank Plaza, built in 1977, as designed by the firm of Webb Zerafa Menkes Housden Partnership, Architects. This pair of triangular towers (twenty-six and forty-one stories respectively), with their gold-tinted mirrored facades, are joined by a twelve-story atrium that extends down through two banking floors to engage two concourse levels. As an atrium it attracts attention because of its scale and not its design, which juxtaposes flat office-tower facades with awkwardly stepping atrium walls. The atrium draws the attention of the pedestrian visually and spatially up into the towering banking hall, where there is a sculpture of white-and-yellow rods forming hanging planes (figure 5.14). Separate exterior entrances are provided for both the banking levels and the concourse. A minor interior

Fig. 5.14. Atrium view, Royal Bank Plaza. Toronto.

connection between the concourse and the bank can be sealed off. The daylight reflected in the granite fountain is a welcome point of orientation and association with the exterior. A small, adjacent skylit atrium provides a similar focal point for the food court.

Proceeding north under Wellington Street, the pedestrian reaches Toronto Dominion Centre, one of the earliest of Toronto's high-rise office developments.

Fig. 5.15. Concourse view, Toronto Dominion Centre. Toronto.

Fig. 5.16. Concourse café, Toronto Dominion Centre. Toronto.

Designed by Ludwig Mies van der Rohe and built in the years 1964–71, these three meticulously detailed prismatic towers are set in a superblock of green spaces. The entrances to the concourse are located at the sidewalk's edge. The concourses are orthogonal corridors with uniform treatments of floors, ceilings, and shop fronts (figure 5.15). The focal space is a café located under a pavilion, which provides a welcome area of daylight and visual contact with the plazas above (figure 5.16).

To the east of Toronto Dominion Centre (across Bay Street) is Commerce Court, designed by I. M. Pei & Partners and built in the years 1968–72. This center is best known for its well-ordered exterior court. The court is sited between an old skyscraper, two new low buildings, and the new fifty-seven-story, steel-and-glass tower with its three-story glass base. Similar to the Toronto Dominion Centre, the concourse system is a rather bland set of identical orthogonal corridors that lacks the spatial variety and relationship to the street found in new projects to the north.

Most of the city block bounded by King, York, Adelaide, and Bay streets has been integrated into a three-level (concourse, street, and mezzanine) commercial center—known as First Canadian Place (figure 5.17). The block is anchored at the corner of King and Bay streets by the seventy-two-story Bank of Montreal Tower, designed by Edward Durell Stone and built in 1971. At the opposite corner is the Exchange Tower, and behind it is the Toronto Stock Exchange. In between is the office tower of First Canadian Place, which is surrounded by the three-level commercial center. Adjacent to the Exchange Tower is a street-level, cross-block passage and a handsome, small park on King Street. The other cross-block passage runs through and around the lobby of the First Canadian Place Tower to the focal space at the rear. This center, in which are located 160 shops,

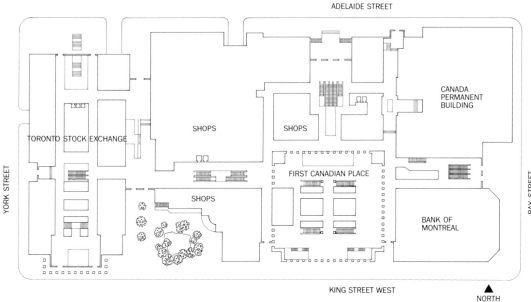

ADELAIDE STREET

CANADA PERMANENT BUILDING

TORONTO STOCK EXCHANGE

SHOPS

SHOPS

FIRST CANADIAN PLACE

SHOPS

BANK OF MONTREAL

YORK STREET

BAY STREET

KING STREET WEST

NORTH

Fig. 5.17. Street-level plan, First Canadian Place. Toronto.

Fig. 5.18. Teuscher Shop, adjacent to entry of First Canadian Place. Toronto.

Fig. 5.19. Atrium view, First Canadian Place. Toronto.

services, and cafés, is heavily trafficked by employees from the office buildings that share this city block.

First Canadian Place is notable because of its highly integrated pedestrian system and the quality of its public spaces. The multiple street-level entrances along each street afford direct access to the commercial areas (figure 5.18). The importance of these entrances cannot be overemphasized, for they draw people into the center and develop a high volume of foot traffic. Within, there are several escalator banks that provide convenient connections between the three levels. The connection from the tunnel concourse under King Street is excellent. There, the pedestrian enters directly into the lobby of the First Canadian Place Tower. The three-level focal space behind the elevator banks has a water cascade that provides both spatial and aural orientation (figure 5.19). With their white-marble walls, gray-marble floors, and white-plaster ceilings, the pedestrian areas are light and expansive even under artificial lights. The variety of entrances, connections, paths, and light levels has made this city block a highly successful element in Toronto's underground pedestrian system.

Between Adelaide and Queen streets, the concourse system becomes somewhat confused. The connection to the Richmond/Adelaide Centre through the Toronto Stock Exchange is indirect. The Richmond/Adelaide Centre office tower has a well-defined plaza raised above the street. Unfortunately, an excellent entry to the concourse, opens directly onto a crowded food court. Narrow concourse passages connect under Richmond Street north to Sheraton Centre, a hotel-conference center with a partial atrium at the entry and a spectacular garden court. Additional narrow concourse passages lined with shops extend to the east under Simpson's Tower and into Simpson's department store, which is joined via a pedestrian bridge to Eaton Centre across Queen Street (figure 5.20).

Eaton Centre is certainly the pièce de résistance of the Toronto concourse system. Here, the concourse becomes the lower level of the 860-foot-long and 90-foot-high (262- by 27.4-meter) linear atrium of Eaton Centre (see pages 55–60). This spectacular space—flooded with daylight and crowded with people—is actually overwhelming after the confined experience of the concourses (figure 5.21). Linear passage from one end to the other is virtually impossible because the space is so intriguing spatially that pedestrians inevitably depart from a direct route. Three vertical nodes spatially relate the complex's levels, and escalators connect the shopping levels. Direct linkages to subway stations are located along

Fig. 5.20. South entrance, Eaton Centre. Toronto.

Fig. 5.21. Concourse-level view, Eaton Centre. Toronto.

Fig. 5.22. Atrium view, Atrium on Bay. Toronto.

Yonge Street at Queen and Dundas streets. Five street-level entrances afford ready access to the galleria.

If and when the pedestrian reaches the northern end of Eaton Centre, he or she passes through Eaton's department store to arrive in a new pavilion at Dundas and Yonge streets. This glass structure brings together the entrances of the department store, the office tower, and the subway station. At this juncture, the concourse system extends under Dundas Street to the Atrium on Bay development, which occupies almost the entire block over to Edward Street. This new project features twelve stories of offices above the street, as well as concourse-level commercial space surrounding a full-height atrium. Elevators located in the center are the atrium's dominant feature (figure 5.22). The atrium—with its traditional colors, furnishings, and materials—is somewhat incongruous when compared to the elegant, high-tech ambience of Eaton Centre. Pedestrian traffic is minimal—possibly due to its newness, the awkward concourse linkage, or the atrium's general lack of attraction. A few blocks north is a concourse system that connects three blocks of enclosed specialty shopping centers along Bloor Street. These blocks, however, have not yet been linked to the main concourse.

The success of Toronto's Underground has grown as the system itself has grown and developed over the last two decades. There is now a "critical mass" of over one-thousand shops, services, and restaurants coordinated into a highly integrated pedestrian system with a multiplicity of street entrances and elevator accesses from the office towers above. Downtown employees are the primary users of the services along the system's routes. They frequent the doctors' and dentists' offices, the grocery stores and bakeries, the drug stores and stationers, the men's and women's fashion stores, the jewelers, and the many restaurants. The foot traffic peaks at lunchtime, with an additional concentration of use after work hours. Most shops are open on Saturday and some on Sunday, but foot traffic diminishes on the weekends. Even when the shops are closed, for pedestrian convenience and for those using the subway the concourses remain open. A notable characteristic of all these spaces is their cleanliness and high level of maintenance.

Part of the reason for the success of this pedestrian system appears to be cultural. The threat of street crime is not apparent. (One can only speculate that this reflects an unspecified behavioral agreement to act respectful toward one's fellow citizens.) There are fewer guards and more open access than in American concourses. In fact, the lobbies of banks and office buildings remain open and unguarded even on the weekends.

During the last two decades, the design of the concourses also has evolved in terms of pedestrian quality. The narrow, straight, uniform corridors of the earlier schemes have been replaced by passages of varying widths and configurations. The surfaces are lighter in color, and the light levels are higher—making the spaces appear larger. The points of vertical orientation and the connections to office atria and lobbies have become more dramatic—through the use of daylighting, fountains, plantings, and artworks. The entrances from the streets are more direct and gracious. By 1989 a coordinated system of signage and directories, funded jointly by the city and the buildings' owners, will aid the pedestrian in wayfinding and orientation. This coordination also will enable the system to be viewed as a coordinated enterprise for purposes of marketing and promotion.

In some respects, the concourse system has become too successful—thereby reducing the pedestrian life on the streets and squares. What began as a system of convenience due to the cold, wet, windy winters has become a system of habit. On a beautiful sunny day in August, there were at least twice as many people in the concourses as on the streets. However, the squares—such as Nathan Phillips Square in front of city hall, Commerce Court, the lawns of Toronto Dominion Centre, the plaza at the Sun Life Centre, and the plaza at Richmond/Adelaide Centre—were being well utilized. It seems that the concourses have replaced the streets as the preferred means for moving around, despite the city's effort to create a continuous, midblock, exterior pedestrian way from city hall to Union Station. The concourses are air conditioned and are, therefore, more comfortable than the sidewalks on a warm summer day. It is more convenient for an office worker to descend via elevator to the concourse and not worry about the weather, a habit developed during the difficult winters.

Toronto's city government is concerned with the diminished degree of sidewalk activity. From the beginning, the city viewed the below-grade system as one component of an overall pedestrian network—that includes sidewalks, plazas, squares, and parks. A 1969 city report stated:

> This does not imply an underground pedestrian system which is totally excluded from the natural and city environments. By establishing open spaces adjacent to the pedestrian routes . . . sunlight, sky, snow, trees, city-scape and street activity can and must be made accessible (visually and physically) to pedestrians.[18]

In working with developers, the city government encourages provisions for connecting spaces. Since 1976 the city also has tried to encourage the development of more street-level retail areas through density-bonus incentives, but without much success. As city planner Mal Williams observes, "developers show a preference for bland banking halls and office lobbies on the street level and an active shopping mall below. Once in motion, the trend to go underground has proved very difficult to reverse."[19]

Downtown Toronto represents a fully developed model of a new system of urban pedestrian activity. The perimeter subway loop provides convenient access to a well-integrated underground concourse system lined with shops and services. Atria and lobbies in office towers plug into this system, which is linked together by tunnels located below the streets. An open-air midblock pedestrian system affords access to numerous pedestrian plazas and green spaces. Although the traditional sidewalks are not inhospitable, the alternative systems are preferred for their convenience and pedestrian amenities. The pedestrian in Toronto's downtown is indeed fortunate to enjoy a choice of appealing pedestrian routes and places. ■

One of Edmund Bacon's important contributions to the theory and practice of urban design is the concept of simultaneous-movement systems—that is, the planned coordination of various modes of movement to produce a coherent urban form.

> A basic design structure is the binding together of perception sequences shared by large numbers of people, thereby developing a group image from shared experiences and so giving a sense of underlying order to which individual freedom and variety are related.[20]

Cities of the past were designed to be perceived by people on foot, on horseback, or in a carriage. The rate of movement was slow, and the vantage point was usually from the earth's surface. Cities of the present must be designed to be perceived by people in cars (at various speeds), in trains, in subways, in buses, on foot and at vantage points from below the ground to high above it. The design of integrated-movement systems brought together at transfer points and manifested in urban architecture is a necessity in developing a city that can be coherently perceived and clearly comprehended.

In the 1950s, when Edmund Bacon served as Philadelphia's planning director, the implementation of this design concept was begun at Penn Center along West Market Street. The pedestrian plane below the street was extended as a concourse from the subway station to provide direct interior access to the elevator lobbies of office towers. At certain points, small courts were created to bring light and air to this new pedestrian system. At the Municipal Services Building near city hall, the two-story lobby actually extends down below the street to engage the new concourse level.

In the 1960s, Bacon set in motion the planning for Market East, a project east of city hall that would link the burgeoning activity at Penn Center with the redevelopment of the historic Society Hill area and the three department stores on Eighth Street.[21] The basic design concept was to develop this linkage through retail activity at three levels—the street, the concourse, and above the street. The project would integrate the below-grade subway with the above-grade commuter trains at Reading Terminal, as well as with the bus station and parking garages. The primary pedestrian datum plane would be below the street, as at Penn Center; and additional terraces, promenades, and walkways would be installed above the street. Willo von Moltke's initial conceptual scheme called for a three-story, linear retail area. After a negative economic analysis, this scheme was abandoned. In 1963 architect Romaldo Giurgola developed a second scheme, which featured a dominant enclosed pedestrian esplanade one level above the street. After his plan was rejected by the department-store owners, Giurgola developed yet another, in which the dominant pedestrian plane would be located below street level (figure 5.23). The primary organizational element was a six-story, linear space. The subway and the shops were to be located along the street on the south; the buses, trains, and cars to the north; and the office towers above. The traditional street system accommodating pedestrians and vehicles would remain intact, and the cross

Fig. 5.23. Section drawing, Market East. Philadelphia.

streets would penetrate the six-story linear space on glass-enclosed bridges. Following further analysis and review, Skidmore, Owings & Merrill developed a refined version of Giurgola's conceptual scheme for the Philadelphia Redevelopment Authority.

By the early 1970s, Market Street East had developed into a primary location for transit arrival and transfer. Commuter trains arriving at Reading Terminal were connected via a tunnel to Penn Station at 30th Street. The major east-west subway line ran along Market Street, with a station at 9th Street. Overhead ramps from the Vine Street expressway allowed easy access for buses. Plans for several parking garages (providing sixteen hundred spaces) to be built along Filbert Street, one block north of Market Street, would enable passenger cars to access the new development directly.

Phase one of the five-block Market East project was completed in 1977, as designed by Bower & Fradley Architects (figure 5.24). Gallery I is a four-level enclosed shopping center of 200,000 square feet (18,580 square meters) anchored by the renovated Strawbridge & Clothier department store and the new Gimbel's department store. The gallery's major entrance, a glazed form with pyramidal

skylights that steps in both plan and section, is at the corner of 9th and Market streets. The entrance is recessed from the corner and has a plaza that steps down to the concourse level. Unfortunately, this makes it difficult either to perceive or reach the entrance from the street (figure 5.25). Located at this entry is a vertical circulation node as well as a social space enlivened by a fountain, trees, and a mobile. The mall space is linked under and over 9th Street to a smaller vertical space that contains two feature elevators adjacent to the Strawbridge & Clothier store. To the west, the mall extends behind the Gimbel's store (now Stern's). However, the linkage to Gallery II is only at the concourse level, since the department store extends back through the block to Filbert Street. Market Street's primary frontage is occupied by the department store, which breaks the tradition of facade design by presenting an austere concrete wall to the street. In contrast, the section of Gallery I along 9th Street has awning-covered shop windows along the street.

Phase two of Market Street East, called Gallery II, was completed in 1983 as designed by a joint venture of Bower Lewis Thrower/Architects and Cope Linder Associates. The new section adds

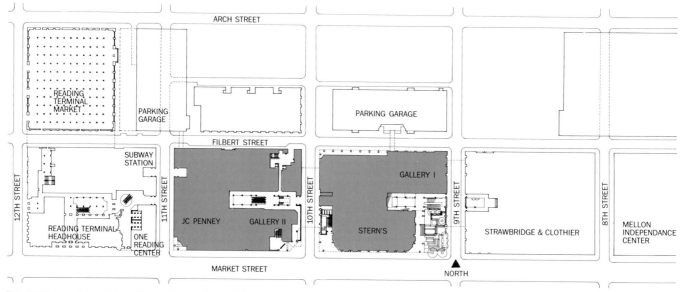

Fig. 5.24. Street-level plan, Market Street East. Philadelphia.

Fig. 5.25. Exterior view, Gallery I entry, Market Street East. Philadelphia.

another 200,000 square feet (18,580 square meters) of shops and a Penney's department store. There is a recessed entrance at 10th and Market streets, which leads to the mall space. Here, Penney's blocks the continuity of the mall space at all levels—except at the concourse level. However, Penney's did install awning-covered shop windows along Market Street. Additional entrances directly into the mall area are provided along the side streets.

The interior pedestrian areas of Gallery I and Gallery II are organized by a four-story, linear atrium, or mall space, at the middle of the block, which has a truck-service street below. Pedestrian continuity is afforded only at the concourse level, located below the street level, due to the presence of the two intervening department stores. Traffic continues along 9th and 10th streets, and pedestrian connections were built above and below these streets. The spatial and visual discontinuity of the pedestrian areas creates a lack of coherent relationships among the mall space, the stores, and the streets. However, the entry from the street at the second level of the mall does facilitate vertical pedestrian distribution. The linear atrium has continuous skylights and a stepped transverse section that maximizes the daylight at each gallery level. The unadorned, modern architectural detailing allows the color and variety of the shops and shoppers to visually dominate. The concourse level of the four-story space is treated as a pedestrian street, featuring brick pavers, trees, fountains, banners, and landscaping (figure 5.26).

The Gallery has been an economic success for its retail tenants. Due to its central location and the superb mass-transit connections, The Gallery attracts enough shoppers to be financially viable. After the first year of operation, gross sales per square foot were reported to be more than twice the average for suburban shopping malls.[22] These sales were primarily to middle-class residents of Philadelphia—the target market of the three department stores and the other shops. Such a stable base of shoppers is

Fig. 5.26. Gallery II view, Market Street East. Philadelphia.

significant for the center's long-term viability, since it will not have to depend on tourist trade.

The Gallery also has brought economic advantages for the city of Philadelphia. The public investment in mass-transit facilities and the construction of the exterior structure of this center is paying off in additional development along the once-blighted East Market Street. Adjacent to Penney's at 11th Street is One Reading Center, a thirty-one-story office building related to the 1893 Reading Terminal (figure 5.27). Behind the headhouse building is the Reading Terminal Market, which is famed for its great variety of produce and foods. This is a center of genuine urban vitality. North across Arch Street, the city is planning the construction of a convention center, which will utilize the old Reading train shed. A new convention hotel adjacent to the Reading Terminal is also planned on Market Street.

The Market Street block between 7th and 8th streets was occupied for decades by the Lit Brothers department store. The store was composed of at least twelve nineteenth-century buildings, which had been threatened with demolition since the closing of the department store in 1977. A heroic renovation and restoration effort has converted this group of buildings into the Mellon Independence Center, with 660,000 square feet (61,314

square meters) of space for the Mellon Bank and 220,000 square feet (20,438 square meters) of retail area. The main entrance from Market Street leads to a 40-foot by 60-foot (12.2- by 18.3 meter) atrium, which is surrounded by three levels of offices and three levels of shops (see plate 49). A street-level arcade connects 7th and 8th streets. A diagonal passage at the concourse level from the subway station in front of Strawbridge & Clothier forms the only internal connection to the nearby Gallery. The public areas, with their tricolored marble floors, marble wainscoting, paneled columns, and ornamental spandrels, have been designed with considerable finesse. Another important element in the grand scheme for Market Street East has been completed so as to contribute to the pedestrian vitality of this district.

The development of Market Street East is an important case study in the evolutionary development of interior pedestrian places. The grand concept of an internal pedestrian spine paralleling Market Street between city hall and Independence Mall has now come to fruition—albeit in a different form than had been originally envisioned. The initial pedestrian components of Gallery I and Gallery II are now extended to Reading Terminal and the Mellon Independence Center. Additional connections to the convention center and to hotels are being

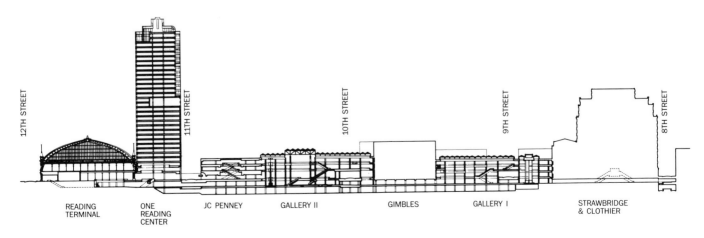

Fig. 5.27. Master site section, Market Street East. Philadelphia.

Fig. 5.28. Exterior view, Mellon Independence Center. Philadelphia.

planned. Although the physical linkages are workable and form interesting pedestrian sequences, discontinuity continues to plague the system. The pedestrian can get lost and disoriented, leading to some degree of frustration. Giurgola's original design avoided this problem by establishing a coherent linear space with more direct visual orientation to Market Street.

Another unresolved aspect of this grand concept is the horizontal and vertical displacement of the pedestrian system from Market Street. In Gallery I and Gallery II, the vital pedestrian activity of shopping has been moved from the street to the middle of the block. The shops have entrances only from this interior mall. The result is the devitalization of the role of the shopping street; the *market* has been removed from Market Street. Moreover, the mall's main level has been lowered to below the street to better relate to the subway stations and to allow pedestrian connections under the cross streets. Although the latter aspect further dissociates the mall from the street, it provides pedestrian convenience and may be partially responsible for the retail center's economic success. Fortunately, the negative effects of introversion have been recognized: Gallery II has shop windows and more street entrances, and the Mellon Independence Center features stores with entrances and shop windows along the street (figure 5.28).

Interestingly, now that many of the internal pedestrian places in Market Street East have been completed, Market Street itself is being revitalized as an important exterior urban space. It is being reconstructed between Juniper and Fifth streets as a more comfortable pedestrian environment. In this street-improvement project, the sidewalks are being widened by removing the parking lanes; drop-off zones are being created; trees are being planted for shade; new bus shelters are being provided (figure 5.29). Market Street East may once again become a vibrant pedestrian street. It will also contribute to the physical and spatial continuity of the projects nearby, since it is the common public denominator for them all. The devitalization of Market Street by the creation of internal streetlike environments is being countered by enhancing the quality of

Fig. 5.29. View of East Market Street. Philadelphia.

the street itself. With the addition of more pedestrians from increased business, shopping, convention, and tourist activity, both the internal and the external systems will be more vital. Most importantly, people will have choice and variety in their pedestrian experiences.

The Philadelphia City Planning Commission's 1988 *Plan for Center City* emphasizes the urban-design principle of developing well-formed active streets as a means for creating a high-quality urban environment. The plan outlines the following criteria:

1. Buildings should be designed to form street walls that define the street and its sidewalks as a coherent urban place.

2. Open spaces built as part of development projects should be consciously shaped and include public amenities.

3. The ground levels of buildings along streets should include retail space to promote traditional street activity.

4. Building entrances should be celebrated and scaled to relate to adjacent buildings.[23]

The plan recommends that the zoning bonus system be replaced by a series of mandatory development controls. The one related to pedestrian space would require that at least 30 percent of the site area be devoted to open areas, plazas, gardens, winter gardens, atria, and public rooms—with prescribed standards for access, seating, and landscaping. In this plan for the future of Philadelphia's center city, the planning commission and its design consultants, Robert Geddes and Robert Brown of Geddes Brecher Qualls Cunningham: Architects, have returned to the historic tradition of well-designed public spaces as the basis for creating a high-quality urban environment. ■

CHAPTER 6

FUTURE DESIGN DIRECTIONS

A resurgence has occurred in the development of interior pedestrian places. Retail arcades, shopping centers, atrium buildings, festival marketplaces, plaza-atria, winter gardens, skyways, and concourses are being designed and built in greater numbers than ever before. Often based on historic prototypes, these interior places have brought a new vitality to city centers. As the spatial organizers of retail, business, convention, and cultural functions, they have improved the pedestrian life of urban centers.

One view of the reasons for this resurgence is that this is the most recent stage in the evolutionary effort to deal with the congestion of circulation in the city. As Barry Maitland explains in *Shopping Malls*, the construction of interior urban places was an attempt "to define discrete areas of pedestrian circulation free from the hazards of wheeled traffic, which, long before the invention of the internal combustion engine, had become a major obstacle to movement on foot."[1] Contemporary interior urban places are responses to the complexity and density of traffic in the city brought about by passenger vehicles, delivery trucks, and transit systems. They are a means of separating pedestrians from traffic in order to promote safety and efficiency of movement. Interior urban places afford the experience of spatial continuity between protected interior places and traffic-free exterior pedestrian zones.

Another view of the reasons for the resurgence in development is that interior places are intended to encourage pedestrians to return to the city center—by providing them with convenience and attractive amenities. People who live in the suburbs have become accustomed to conveniently located, free parking; climate-controlled shopping; and the amenities of landscaping, sculptures, fountains, and public events. These positive features of interiorization have not been readily available in the urban centers. Privatization has been both a means and a consequence of developing these protected pedestrian spaces. Interior places attract people by providing opportunities for occasions and gatherings—that is, for participation in traditional sociological functions that had become less common in the downtown areas.

Since World War II, there has been considerable experience in designing, building, and using interior urban places in the cities of Western Europe and North America. It is time for an evaluation. Interior places are well established as valuable spatial forms that are certain to play a significant role in the continuing redevelopment of our cities. What will this role be, and how will it relate to the existing city? What design concepts and directions should architects and urban designers follow?

This chapter develops design concepts for interior pedestrian places as they relate to three urban-design criteria: preserving the existing, valuable context; strengthening street life; and developing pedestrian connections between blocks.

These criteria are supported by the writings of many noted urban-design critics and theorists, such as Kevin Lynch, Jane Jacobs, Edmund Bacon, Bernard Rudofsky, Colin Rowe, Rob Krier, and William Whyte.[2] Interior pedestrian places that contribute to the preservation of context, revitalization of street life, and the development of pedestrian connections will create a more vital city. ■

DESIGN CONCEPTS

The first important urban-design criterion is the preservation of the existing context. The preservation movement has demonstrated the validity of preserving and adapting valuable buildings and contexts as a basis for maintaining the historic continuity of urban settings. One problem with many new projects is the difficulty of blending them into the existing contexts without destroying them. The design concept of back-land development, whereby only land in the centers of already built-up blocks is utilized, acknowledges this problem. Where back-land is utilized, the building forms and interior pedestrian spaces often are unusual in their organization and geometry due to the irregularity in the configuration of these sites. Variations in site topography can lead to vertical changes throughout the pedestrian sequence. The formal geometry of the ideal shopping center must be adjusted to accommodate the contextual variation of the existing site. The resulting design can be either chaotic or ordered, depending upon the designer's ability to work within these parameters.

The concept of back-land development has been used extensively in the urban centers of Great Britain, where the only available land is often located behind historic street-front buildings that must be preserved. For example, the Grosvenor Precinct in Chester was built behind beautiful, historic buildings and was linked to their second-floor walkways, or Rows (see pages 191–93). In Wakefield, the Ridings Centre was built behind existing shops, which were then enlarged and given entrances from the new interior place (see pages 87–88). In both of these examples, the back-land design concept has been successfully executed. The exterior-to-interior relationships of pedestrian spaces in these commercial centers are exemplary for their continuity—despite the numerous plan and section adjustments. Other examples in Great Britain are the Royal Priors in Leamington Spa; Orchard Square in Fargate, Sheffield; and The Lanes Centre in Carlisle. Virtually every small city in England now has such a new retail center where the propensity for commercial development has been carefully balanced to preserve the existing townscape.[3]

The second important urban-design criterion is the strengthening of street life. Many projects based upon interior pedestrian places cause inversion—that is, pedestrian activity is displaced from the street to the middle of the block, causing a decline in street life. This happens when the suburban shopping-center model is utilized in an urban context with little design modification. In these cases, reversals of frontage occur when the active pedestrian spaces are located within the block. The blank facades fronting on the streets and the exposure of service areas interrupt the continuity of street life relative to adjacent blocks. When these commercial developments are large in scale, several blocks of dead street space can produce a stultifying exterior image. This is the case at Plaza Pasadena in California, where the abstract brick forms along Colorado Boulevard disrupt the visual and pedestrian continuity of this important street (see page 62). Similarly, at The Gallery in Philadelphia (figure 6.1) bland concrete facades, lacking fenestration, face the once-active Market Street (see page 209). The department stores are the worst offenders—being large, bulky masses without windows often occupying street corners.

The problem of inversion occurs to some extent in all urban shopping centers. Although shop windows somewhat alleviate the street deadening, one effective solution is double frontage—entrances to the stores along both the street and in the mall. Both frontages are thus

energized with activity, and the pass-through traffic sometimes generates new patterns of pedestrian movement. Traditional urban department stores always had entrances along each street in a block in an effort to maximize accessibility. Although it is more costly to have two entrances, in the long run enhanced accessibility should offset this expense. At International Square in Washington, D.C., the shops have both street and atrium entrances. The result is increased foot traffic and sales (see page 104). Another approach to providing double frontage is to have separate stores along the street and along the mall, as at Eaton Centre in Toronto.

Although the tendency in designing interior pedestrian places has been to make them inward oriented, they also can be designed to be outward oriented and thus relate to the development on adjacent blocks; to the surrounding streetscape; or to open, exterior spaces. Large, glazed facades and/or entrances accomplish this purpose. At First Montreal Trust, the central atrium—with its food court and restaurants—faces McGill College Avenue through a glazed facade (see page 61). The Gallery at Harborplace in Baltimore has a large, glazed corner entrance that allows pedestrians to see inside and shoppers to see outside via café terraces (see page 109). These are but two examples of a design concept that seeks to integrate exterior and interior pedestrian space through visual transparency.

A new design concept termed the *edge-atrium* is intended to better relate the traditional centroidal atrium to the street by extending the atrium to a building's facade, thus enlivening the street with visual activity and access. This concept is being employed by RTKL Associates at the A&S Plaza in Manhattan, the renovation of a former Gimbel's department store designed by Daniel Burnham in 1909. In this scheme, the face of the nine-story, T-shaped atrium dominates

Fig. 6.1. Market Street facade, The Gallery. Philadelphia.

ment, activity, and people. At the street scale, the edge-atrium enables pedestrians to see directly into this dramatic space, to comprehend the scope of the center, and to view the shops and food court within (figure 6.2). At the sidewalk scale, the character of the interior place invites pedestrians inside with architectural elements and granite paving that extend through the glass facade. Because of the prominence of this site and the boldness of the design, this project should have a significant impact on the design of future retail centers.

The third criterion is developing pedestrian connections between city blocks. In the Western world, the city traditionally has been laid out in a grid pattern of streets, which form blocks of land for buildings. Pedestrian circulation and the entrances to buildings usually are located around the perimeters of these blocks. In the nineteenth century, the inhospitable streets and the need for additional shop space to market goods led to the creation of arcades, which connected the streetside to the block interior and related across adjacent streets to adjoining blocks (see pages 31–47). Although the nineteenth-century form of arcade has not been built during most of the twentieth century, some recent projects have been based on a similar concept.

In 1984, at The Courtyards in Fort Wayne, Indiana, architect Eric Kuhne proposed the renovation of an intact block of commercial buildings by glazing over the interstitial spaces (figure 6.3). Kuhne planned to convert the residual service courts and alleys of this block of stone-and-brick buildings to three-story-high arcades and atria. The arcades would be extended to the street, and a glazed entry court would be located at one corner of the block. Shop windows along the street would be recessed to form a perimeter colonnade leading to the interior places. Thus, the traditional streetscape and shop fronts would be preserved—while

Fig. 6.2. Model of A&S Plaza. New York City.

the Sixth Avenue facade, and the stem of the T extends pedestrian space to the new department store at the back of the block. Looking out through the edge-atrium, shoppers have constant orientation to Sixth Avenue, and each shop has a share of street presence. The design's intent is to make a strong exterior statement that will enable this retail center to be perceived at three scaler levels. At the distant vantage point, or city scale, the 100-foot-tall (30.5-meter-tall), clear glass windows animate the facade with move-

Fig. 6.3. Aerial perspective, The Courtyards. Fort Wayne, Indiana.

new interior frontage would be created for shops, restaurants, and offices. Although Kuhne's proposal was not executed for political and economic reasons, his concept is amenable to many urban contexts.

A similar project is indeed being executed in Harrisburg, Pennsylvania. Strawberry Square, as designed by Beyer Blinder Belle Architects & Planners, involves the renovation of eleven vacant historic buildings located adjacent to the state capitol. To integrate these different buildings, a four-story, two-block-long, skylit arcade provides an interior pedestrian system. The arcade creates connections between buildings and locations for new street-level shops with office space above (see plate 50). The streetscape improvements and shop-front renovations will enable the street-side pedestrian zone to function better in conjunction with the interior passage.

In Ottawa, Ontario, an innovative application of the arcade concept has been implemented along several blocks of Rideau Street. Here, glazed perimeter half-arcades were built on opposite sides of the street, thus enclosing the sidewalks and providing entrances to the existing shops (figure 6.4). These half-arcades also create an entrance to the shopping mall in Rideau Centre, a rather conventional series of interior shopping galleries. Since Rideau Street also functions as a bus terminal, shelters with interior and exterior waiting areas have been built into these arcades—along with benches, phone booths, directories, and plantings. The construction system of white-painted steel and clear glazing creates bright, sunlit spaces that can be ventilated in good weather by opening sliding doors. In bad weather, the half-arcades, which are tempered by passive solar heating, are welcome shelters from the wind and snow. This ingenious piece of urban infrastructure knits together the existing buildings, streets, and sidewalks—giving them a coherent form and image while enhancing their pedestrian vitality.

The arcade as a covered pedestrian street has the potential for widespread application in the development of urban pedestrian systems. In fact, in many urban-design competitions and in visionary city proposals, the arcade continues to appear as an important spatial concept. However, due to disparate land ownership and varied building configurations, the number of arcades actually built has been limited. The most significant value of arcades is the potential for continuity with existing at-grade pedestrian spaces and retail frontages. Completely introverted frontages that are detached from the street must be avoided. The economic value of extending and creating frontages at-grade and above is undoubtedly one of the reasons for the continuing appeal of this design strategy.

Another approach to developing pedestrian connections between city blocks is the nodal-atrium model, which is based on the linkage of interior places at the center of each block to adjacent blocks by grade-level arcades, overhead skyways, or subterranean concourses. The derivation of this model is based on Richard Newcourt's plan for rebuilding London after the great fire of 1666.[4] In Newcourt's scheme, four small blocks were grouped around an open, central square containing a church. These modules were joined to the surrounding roads by small intersecting streets but were separated from other modules by these roads (figure 6.5).

Fig. 6.4. Rideau Street arcades. Ottawa, Ontario.

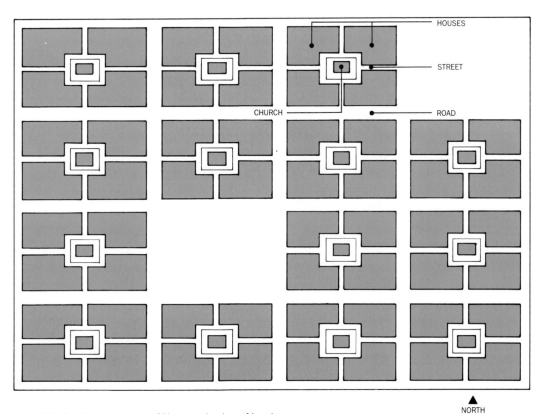

Fig. 6.5. Southwest quarter of Newcourt's plan of London.

(Such a plan was, in fact, realized by James Edward Oglethorpe, founder of the colony of Georgia, in Savannah, Georgia, in 1733.) Maitland explains the importance of this model:

> Newcourt's plan thus inverted the gradations of social and economic value implicit in the other London plans, locating foci at the centre, rather that the edges, of blocks of development and providing an abstract model of the medieval organization of Venice on the one hand and of the modern urban mall on the other.[5]

The realization of the nodal-atrium model—utilizing an interior instead of an exterior space to integrate the buildings around a block—can be seen in several North American cities. In both Toronto and Montreal, nodal places are connected via subterranean concourses, which run under the intervening streets to create a continuous pedestrian system. Buildings have been grouped around these nodal atria, thus creating vertically oriented places used for social gathering (see pages 201–6). Perhaps the best example to date is located in Montreal—between the three superblocks of the Place des Arts, the Complexe Desjardins, and the Complexe Guy-Favreau (see pages 182–84). The Complexe Desjardins—with its four corner towers forming a covered urban square that is linked both to the sidewalks and the concourses—is the purest statement of this design concept.

In St. Paul and Minneapolis, skyways are the primary means of horizontal connection between developments with nodal atria (see pages 146–59). This design concept can be seen in St. Paul, where the retail centers of Town Court and Town Square are linked via skyways to Galtier Plaza, a multiuse center that includes apartments. In Minneapolis, the nodal atria at IDS Center, City Center, and Gaviidae Common are linked via skyways to nodal atria in the Opus Building, the Norwest Center, the Pillsbury Center, and the Government Center—thus, joining retail, office, and government functions. Without the nodal atria, the skyway system is but a maze of corridors and bridges; with them, there are places of arrival and meeting.

Washington, D.C., is the only city where the existing sidewalks directly connect a series of nodal atria (see pages 194–199). For example, Columbia Square, National Place, the National Press Club Building, and Metropolitan Square are located on adjacent blocks of F Street, which serves to physically relate the nodal atria within these projects. Nodal atria in buildings on other blocks also are indirectly related to each other through the common system of sidewalks and open spaces. As demonstrated in Washington, D.C., newly constructed linkages do not need to be constantly created to link nodal atria because a viable sidewalk system already exists.

Atria need not be nodal to entire blocks in order to relate to each other. Except in those cases where entire blocks are being developed, atria usually relate only to a given building. In some cases, bridging atria are employed to relate a historic and a new building to each other. Additional partially enclosed spaces, such as colonnades, pavilions, porticoes, and covered streets, can be provided to give continuity to the pedestrian sequence. Thus, pedestrian systems can be designed to provide both a physical linkage and a visual relationship between the centers of blocks and their perimeters, as well as between interior and exterior pedestrian places.

A proposed project that addresses all three of these urban-design criteria is the Pittsburgh Centre, designed by RTKL Associates. This mixed-use project will occupy two primary blocks in the center of Pittsburgh between Forbes and Fourth

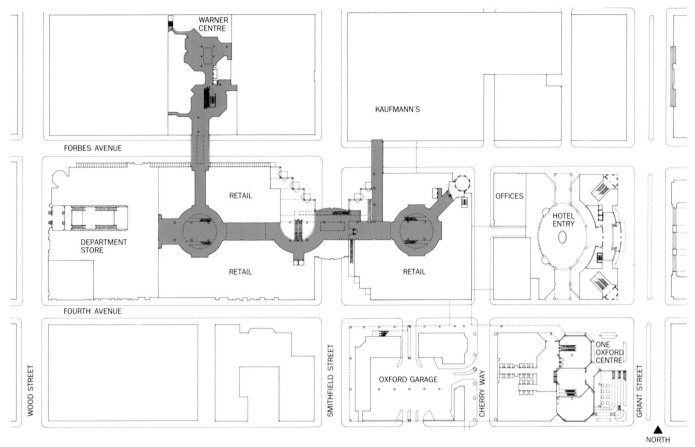

Fig. 6.6. First mall-level diagram, Pittsburgh Centre. Pittsburgh.

avenues. The project will include two new department stores, an atrium hotel above an existing department store, a kiosk retail center, multiplex cinemas, a shopping center, and several levels of underground parking (figure 6.6). Efforts to preserve the existing context include incorporating five small, existing buildings and eight historic facades. The street life along Forbes Avenue will be enhanced by a street-level kiosk retail area called the New Diamond Market, to be located behind glazed storefronts. Pedestrian connections will be developed by locating the major entrances, glazed partial atria, where the project crosses Smithfield Street. A four-level bridge with glazed facades will join the two blocks and will also reveal the internal activity. Additional pedestrian skyways will provide pedestrian linkage to the adjoining blocks. Thus, the old and new street-level entrances and retail activity will be retained. The design of this project is exemplary in its efforts to satisfy these important criteria, in addition to creating a modulated series of interior pedestrian places. ■

Since World War II, a war against the street has been waged in the United States by virtually everyone responsible for the street's stewardship. In his new book, *City: Rediscovering the Center*, urbanologist William H. Whyte, a leading crusader for saving the cities' streets, portrays the battle ground:

> The war against the street gains force. Not only have planners and architects been lining it with blank walls and garages; they have been leveling blocks of old buildings for parking lots, de-mapping streets for megastructures. Now they are going the next step. They are taking the principal functions of the street and putting them almost anywhere but on street level. They are putting them in underground concourses and shopping malls, in skyways and upper-level galleries. Ultimately, they may get the pedestrian off the street altogether.[6]

Those who favor relocation of urban activities away from the streets argue that the increased intensity of traffic in the city center has produced chaotic streets full of noise, pollution, and danger. They contend that increased building density has created crowding—leading to street crime, vandalism, and litter. They believe that vulnerable pedestrians must be protected from these inhospitable conditions by removing them from the streets to safe harbors—that is, to interior and exterior pedestrian spaces that are joined together by systems dedicated to efficient pedestrian movement. These proponents claim that such a strategy will enable the city center to compete with the suburban supermall, which already offers these pedestrian assurances.

This argument is rational if one accepts the premises. However, there are alternative solutions: Traffic congestion could be controlled by restricting private automobiles and on-street parking in the city center, while improving public transit. In addition, traffic could be restricted to perimeter zones and deliveries allowed only during off hours. Limitations on building density would reduce conditions of crowding, but crowding by itself does not cause street crime. In fact, streets filled with pedestrians are often safer than lonely streets. Vandalism and littering are the results of a lack of regard for the public realm—a social outlook that can be improved only through public education.

Now, after forty years of this war against the streets, there are signs that the streets of many cities are being preserved and/or redeveloped: Toronto has withdrawn its incentives for developing concourses in order to encourage street-level retail activity. New York, Philadelphia, and Washington, D.C., have changed their zoning ordinances either to require or encourage street-level commercial space. In Baltimore's Charles Center, the ineffective second-level walkways are being removed. And in Philadelphia, an extensive streetscape program on East Market Street is re-creating the street as a prominent shopping destination. These signs are hopeful but not yet extensive enough to significantly rejuvenate pedestrian life on the streets of the city. The tide of the battle has not yet completely turned.

A certain kind of nostalgia for the qualities of historic streets has also been growing in the American culture. The new resort town of Seaside, Florida, designed by architects Andres Duany and Elizabeth Plater-Zyberk, has initiated a renewed interest in town planning based on concepts of nineteenth-century streets. The design trends in renovating suburban shopping centers also are turning to more urban concepts. Thomas Fisher, writing in *Progressive Architecture*, acknowledges this trend:

> One of the most dramatic changes being made to older malls is the in-

crease in light levels and the introduction of daylight. The effect is to make malls more like urban streets, open to the sky and to shift the emphasis from the stores to the public spaces. Complementing that street-like character is the increased use of fountains, planters, and seating.[7]

Even the shops within suburban malls are being reconfigured as village streets—with stalls and kiosks, landscaping, and street furniture (figure 6.7). Another indicator of the changing attitude is reflected in television and magazine advertisements, where urban street scenes and a glamorizing of the urbane lifestyle are now featured.

Many city streets are being reclaimed and renovated as valued urban spaces. Virtually every American city now has a rejuvenated historic area that features the urban ambience of its streetscape: Georgetown in Washington, D.C.; Shockoe Slip in Richmond; Lowertown in St Paul; Society Hill in Philadelphia; and Latimer Square in Denver. Other cities have retained, intensified, and extended their pedestrian malls, developing them into specialized shopping and entertainment districts (figure 6.8). The festival-marketplace concept also draws upon this renewed interest in historic urban areas.

Historically, streets have been the dominant physical organizing infrastructure of the city, and they will continue to assume this role. In recent de-

Fig. 6.7. Georgetown Store, White Flint Mall. Rockville, Maryland.

Fig. 6.8. Pedestrian mall. Charlottesville, Virginia.

cades, we have seen a greater differentiation of street types: service streets, pedestrian streets, transit-only streets, even covered streets. (Recently, a street in Miami and one in Germany have been covered with fabric.) We have also seen the elimination of many streets through the creation of superblocks or the construction of multiblock megastructures. In some cases, the streets have been incorporated into buildings, by passing through them on bridges or in tubes. Through all of this, the primacy of the street as a public vehicular and pedestrian space has persevered. The street is and always will be the most important spatial and functional element of the city.

In the last analysis, all interior pedestrian places should be considered as adjunct spaces to the pubic sidewalks, parks, and plazas of the city. They should be directly related to them in physical, spatial, and visual terms. The connections between open and enclosed pedestrian spaces should be carefully designed to accomodate smooth transitions. Interior places should be urban in scale, materials, and furnishings and should visually relate to the exterior through the use of horizontal and vertical glazing, which provides daylighting and views. Forms of public control over use and activities should be obtained and exercised to guard against excessive privatization. If all of this is done, the urban pedestrian will be enriched with a diversity of choice in routes, activities, and amenities. Only through this comprehensive approach can there be an inherent continuity in the city's pedestrian places—the kind of continuity originally envisioned in Nolli's plan of baroque Rome. ■

CREDITS

Fig. 1.2: Delineation by Starling Keene

Fig. 1.8: Photograph by Gary Okerlund

Fig. 1.11: Courtesy of the Louisiana Superdome

Fig. 1.13: Reproduced courtesy of the Trustees of the British Museum

Fig. 2.4: Courtesy of Irving B. Haynes & Associates

Fig. 2.7: Photograph by Gary Okerlund

Fig. 2.9: Courtesy of Cleveland Arcade Management (redrawn)

Fig. 2.10: Courtesy of Skidmore, Owings & Merrill, San Francisco

Plate 7: Photograph by Jane Lidz

Fig. 2.11: Courtesy of Sixth Street Marketplace (redrawn)

Plate 8: Photograph by Eric Oxendorf Studio; courtesy of ELS/Elbasani & Logan Architects

Fig. 2.14: Courtesy of ELS/Elbasani & Logan Architects (redrawn)

Fig. 2.20: Photograph by Barbara Martin; courtesy of Hellmuth, Obata & Kassabaum, Inc.

Fig. 2.21: Photograph by Warren Reynolds; courtesy of Gruen Associates

Fig. 2.22: Courtesy of RTKL Associates Inc. (redrawn)

Plate 13: Photograph by Hedrich/Blessing; courtesy of RTKL Associates Inc.

Fig. 2.25: Courtesy of Zeidler Roberts Partnership, Architects

Fig. 2.28: Photograph by Balthazar Korab

Fig. 2.30: Courtesy of Zeidler Roberts Partnership, Architects (redrawn)

Plate 15: Photograph by Peter Christopher; courtesy of Zeidler Roberts Partnership, Architects

Fig. 2.35: Photograph by Balthazar Korab

Fig. 2.36: Photograph by Nick Wheeler; courtesy of Urban Design Group

Plate 17: Photograph by David Whitaker, courtesy of Les Cours Mont Royal

Plate 18: Photograph by David Whitaker, courtesy of Les Cours Mont Royal

Fig. 2.39: Courtesy of Lorenz & Williams, Architects

Plate 19: Photograph by Carol M. Highsmith

Fig. 2.40: Photograph by Fiona Spalding-Smith

Fig. 2.41: Courtesy of Eldon Square (redrawn)

Fig. 2.49: Photograph by Steve Rosenthal © 1977

Plate 21: Photograph by Steve Rosenthal © 1977

Plate 22: Photograph by Balthazar Korab

Fig. 2.56: Courtesy of Hellmuth, Obata & Kassabaum, Inc.

Plate 23: Courtesy of Hellmuth, Obata & Kassabaum, Inc.

Fig. 2.58: Photograph by Alexandre Georges; courtesy of Thompson, Ventulett, Stainback & Associates, Inc.

Fig. 2.59: Courtesy of Oliver T. Carr Company (redrawn)

Fig. 2.60: Courtesy of Johnson/Burgee Architects (redrawn)

Plate 24: Photograph by Richard Payne, AIA © 1984

Fig. 2.62: Courtesy of Thompson, Ventulett, Stainback & Associates, Inc.

Fig. 2.63: Photograph by E. Alan McGee; courtesy of Thompson, Ventulett, Stainback & Associates, Inc.

Fig. 2.64. Courtesy of Forest City Development

Plate 25: Photograph by Balthazar Korab

Fig. 3.2: Courtesy of John Portman & Associates

Plate 26: Courtesy of John Portman & Associates

Fig. 3.3: Courtesy of Thompson, Ventulett, Stainback & Associates, Inc.

Plate 27: Photograph by R. Greg Hursley

Plate 29: Photograph by Victoria Lefcourt

Fig. 3.6: Courtesy of Hellmuth, Obata & Kassabaum, Inc.

Fig. 3.7: Photograph by Norman McGrath

Fig. 3.8: Courtesy of Kohn Pedersen Fox Associates, PC

Fig. 3.9: Courtesy of Cope Linder Associates (redrawn)

Fig. 3.10: Photography © by Lawrence S. Williams, Inc.

Fig. 3.13: Photography © by Richard Payne, AIA

Plate 31: Courtesy of Arthur Cotton Moore Associates

Fig. 3.19: Photograph by Harlan Hambright; courtesy of Sasaki Associates, Inc.

Plate 32: Photograph by James Steinkamp; courtesy of Murphy/Jahn Architects

Plate 33: Photograph by Richard Guy Wilson

Fig. 3.23: Photograph by Ronald Livieri, courtesy of Kevin Roche John Dinkeloo and Associates

Fig. 3.25: Photograph by Allen Rokach; courtesy of The New York Botanical Garden

Plate 35: Courtesy of PPG Industries, Inc.

Plate 36: Photograph by Cervin Robinson

Plate 37: Photograph by Norman McGrath

Fig. 3.26: Photograph by Timothy Hursley, The Arkansas Office; courtesy of Cesar Pelli & Associates

Plate 38: Photograph by Timothy Hursley, The Arkansas Office; courtesy of Cesar Pelli & Associates

Fig. 4.2: Courtesy of City of Minneapolis Planning Department

Fig. 4.3: Courtesy of BRW, Inc.

Fig. 4.9: Photograph by Balthazar Korab

Fig. 4.13: Courtesy of St. Paul Department of Planning

Fig. 4.14: Courtesy of Calgary Planning and Building Department

Fig. 4.19: Courtesy of Houston Department of Planning (redrawn)

Fig. 4.20: Delineated by Paul Thompson

Fig. 5.1: Delineated by Paul Thompson

Fig. 5.5: Courtesy of Grosvenor Developments (redrawn)

Fig. 5.7: Courtesy of Joseph R. Passanneau, FAIA; delineated by Starling Keene

Fig. 5.13: Delineated by Paul Thompson

Fig. 5.17: Delineated by Starling Keene

Fig. 5.23: Courtesy of Mitchell/Giurgola Architects

Fig. 5.24: Courtesy of Bower Lewis Thrower/Architects (redrawn)

Fig. 5.26: Photograph by David Gentry; courtesy of Bower Lewis Thrower/Architects

Fig. 5.27: Courtesy of Bower Lewis Thrower/Architects

Plate 49: Photograph by Tom Crane; courtesy of Burt Hill Kosar Rittelmann Associates

Fig. 5.28: Photograph by Tom Crane; courtesy of Burt Hill Kosar Rittelmann Associates

Fig. 6.2: Courtesy of RTKL Associates Inc.

Fig. 6.3: Drawing © 1986 by Eric R. Kuhne; courtesy of Eric R. Kuhne & Associates

Plate 50: Photograph by Arch Currie; courtesy of Beyer Blinder Belle Architects & Planners

Fig. 6.5: Delineated by Paul Thompson

Fig. 6.6: Courtesy of RTKL Associates Inc. (redrawn)

NOTES

PREFACE

1. Michael J. Bednar, *The New Atrium* (New York: McGraw-Hill, 1986).

CHAPTER 1

1. Edmund Bacon, *Design of Cities* (N.Y.: Viking Press, 1967), 147.
2. Colin Rowe, "I Stood in Venice on the Bridge of Sighs," *Design Quarterly* 129 (1985): 11.
3. Johann Friedrich Geist, *Arcades* (Cambridge: MIT Press, 1983), 62.
4. Klaus Uhlig, *Pedestrian Areas* (New York: Architectural Book Publishing, 1979).
5. Ibid., 28.
6. Samuel Langhorne Clemens, *A Tramp Abroad* (1880), 119.
7. Bernard Rudofsky, *Streets for People* (Garden City, N.Y.: Doubleday, 1969), 94.
8. William H. Whyte, *The Social Life of Small Urban Spaces* (Washington, D.C.: Conservation Foundation, 1980), 79.
9. Donlyn Lyndon, "Does the Vision Stick?" *Places* 3, no. 4 (1986): 32.
10. James Sanders, "Toward a Return of the Public Place: An American Survey," *Architectural Record* (April 1985): 87–95.
11. Paul Goldberger, "Plazas, Like Computers, Are Best If User-Friendly," *New York Times*, 22 Nov. 1987, sec. H.
12. Robert Venturi, *Complexity and Contradiction in Architecture* (New York: Museum of Modern Art, 1966), 133.
13. Paul Zucker, *Town and Square* (Cambridge: MIT Press, 1959), 1.
14. J. B. Jackson, "Forum Follows Function," in *The Public Face of Architecture*, ed. Nathan Glazer and Mark Lilla (New York: The Free Press, 1987), 119.
15. Ibid., 118.
16. Richard Sennett, "The Public Domain," in *The Public Face of Architecture*, ed. Nathan Glazer and Mark Lilla (New York: The Free Press, 1987), 27.
17. Nathan Glazer and Mark Lilla, eds., *The Public Face of Architecture* (New York: The Free Press, 1987), xiv.
18. R. Buckminster Fuller and Robert Marks, *The Dymaxion World of Buckminster Fuller* (Garden City, N.Y.: Anchor Press, 1971), 234.
19. Nikolaus Pevsner, *A History of Building Types* (Princeton, N.J.: Princeton University Press, 1976), 244.
20. Goldberger, "Plazas, Like Computers, Are Best If User-Friendly," H40.
21. William H. Whyte, *CITY: Rediscovering the Center* (Garden City, N.Y.: Doubleday, 1988), 210.
22. Sam Bass Warner, "The Liberal City," *Design Quarterly* 129 (1985): 18.
23. Robert A. M. Stern, *Pride of Place* (Boston: Houghton Mifflin, 1986), 238.
24. Sanders, "Toward a Return of the Public Place," 95.

CHAPTER 2

1. Geist, *Arcades*, 4.
2. Ibid., 12.

3. Ibid., 70.

4. Margaret MacKeith, *The History and Conservation of Shopping Arcades* (London: Mansell Publishing, 1986), 38.

5. Ibid., 75.

6. Ibid., 44.

7. Ibid., 58.

8. Donald Canty, "Glazed Gallery behind an Elegant Tower," *AIA Journal* (May 1983): 180.

9. R. H. Melton, "Sales Encourage Officials at Richmond Marketplace," *Washington Post*, 31 August 1987.

10. Whyte, *Social Life*, 79.

11. Kenneth Frampton, "Generic Street as a Continuous Built Form," in *On Streets*, ed. Stanford Anderson (Cambridge: MIT Press, 1978), 327.

12. Stern, *Pride of Place*, 230–31.

13. Meredith L. Clausen, "The Department Store—Development of a Type," *Journal of Architectural Education* (Fall 1985): 20–29.

14. Ibid., 24.

15. Stern, *Pride of Place*, 230.

16. Barry Maitland, *Shopping Malls* (London: Construction Press, 1985), 23–63.

17. Ibid., 11–13.

18. Ibid., 13.

19. Ibid., 59.

20. John Morris Dixon, "Procession in Pasadena," *Progressive Architecture* (July 1981): 94–97.

21. John Morris Dixon, "Piazza, American Style," *Progressive Architecture*, (June 1976): 64–69.

22. William Severini Kowinski, *The Malling of America* (New York: William Morrow and Company, 1985), 271.

23. Maitland, *Shopping Malls*, 67.

24. Paul Goldberger, *On The Rise* (New York: Penguin Books, 1983), 144.

25. Jim Murphy, "Under Glass," *Progressive Architecture* (November 1980): 106–110.

26. Frank Kuznik, "Collosal Comeback," *Historic Preservation* (September/October 1988): 64–69.

27. Maitland, *Shopping Malls*, 94.

28. Maitland, *Shopping Malls*, 66.

29. "A Boom in Recycled Buildings," *Business Week*, 31 October 1977, 101.

30. Robert Campbell, "Evaluation: Boston's 'Upper of Urbanity,'" *AIA Journal* (June 1981): 24–31.

31. Jane Thompson, "Boston's Faneuil Hall," *Urban Design International* 1, no. 1 (November-December 1979): 12–16.

32. "A New Market Complex with the Vitality of an Old Landmark: Harborplace in Baltimore," *Architectural Record* (October 1980): 100–105.

33. Michael Demerest, "He Digs Downtown," *Time*, 24 August 1981, 44.

34. "Down to the Sea in Shops," *Architectural Record* (January 1984): 98–107.

35. David S. Hilzenrath, "Festival Marketplaces Have Fewer Developers Cheering," *Washington Post*, 1 October 1988, sec. E, pp. 14–16.

36. Campbell, "Evaluation," 25.

37. Eberhard H. Zeidler, *Multi-Use Architecture in the Urban Context* (Stuttgart: Karl Kramer Verlag, 1983), 9.

38. Ibid., 9.

39. Stern, *Pride of Place*, 241.

40. "Spirit of St. Louis," *Progressive Architecture* (November 1985): 83–93.

41. Kevin Klose, "Detroit Center Edges Away from Insolvency," *Washington Post*, 18 October 1983.

42. Bruce N. Wright, "Megaform Comes to Motown," *Progressive Architecture* (February 1978): 57–61.

43. Bednar, *New Atrium*, 53.

44. Ibid., 53–55.

45. David Morton, "Water Tower Place," *Progressive Architecture* (December 1975): 48–51.

46. Grace Anderson "Democracy at Work," *Architectural Record* (August 1986): 114–23.

CHAPTER 3

1. Bednar, *New Atrium*, 63.
2. Stern, *Pride of Place*, 231.
3. Ibid., 233.
4. William Marlin, "An Outside, Inside," *Architectural Forum* (November 1973): 47.
5. Calvin Trillin, "Atlanta, Ga., a Travelling Person Marooned on a Cocktail Island," *The New Yorker*, 29 March 1976.
6. Bednar, *New Atrium*, 18.
7. James T. Burns and C. Ray Smith, "Charity Begins at Home," *Progressive Architecture* (February 1968): 100.
8. Bednar, *New Atrium*, 63–65.
9. Goldberger, *On the Rise*, 114.
10. Pilar Viladas, "Equitable: Art for All," *Progressive Architecture* (May 1986): 25–26.
11. Peter Papademetriou, "Is 'Wow!' Enough?" *Progressive Architecture* (August 1977): 66–73.
12. Janet Nairn, "Urban Botanical Park Glassed In at ChemCourt," *Architectural Record* (December 1982): 20–21.
13. Kaplan · McLaughlin · Diaz, "Tall Buildings, Tight Streets," (San Francisco, 1985).
14. Stern, *Pride of Place*, 215.
15. Ibid., 220.
16. Goldberger, *On the Rise*, 122–23.
17. Stanley Tigerman, "A Critique of the Language Employed in the Design of the State of Illinois Office Building," *Places* 3, no. 4 (1986): 34–35.
18. Lyndon, "Does the Vision Stick?," 33.
19. Editors, "P/A on Pei: Roundtable on a Trapezoid," *Progressive Architecture* (October 1978): 49–59.
20. Ibid., 52, 55.
21. Ibid., 55.
22. Ibid.
23. Thomas Matthews, "The Controversial Musée d'Orsay," *Progressive Architecture* (February 1987): 35–36.
24. David Morton, "Tipping the Scales," *Progressive Architecture* (May 1979): 98–101.
25. George Kohlmaier and Barna von Sartory, *Houses of Glass* (Cambridge: MIT Press, 1986), 37.
26. Ibid.
27. Ibid. 354.
28. Eleni M. Constantine, "Restoring a Victorian Botanical Conservatory," *Architectural Record* (October 1980): 72–77.
29. See Bednar, *New Atrium*, 103–138; and Richard Saxon, *Atrium Buildings*, (New York: Van Nostrand Reinhold, 1983), 71–168.
30. Daralice Boles, "Turned to Stone," *Progressive Architecture* (February 1984): 76–81.
31. Paula Deitz, "The IBM Garden Plaza," *Architectural Record* (May 1984): 154–155.
32. Cervin Robinson, "A Triumphal Arch, a Gateway, and a Garden," *AIA Journal* (Mid-May 1979): 114–117.
33. Stern, *Pride of Place*, 241.
34. Ibid., 242.

CHAPTER 4

1. Jaquelin, Robertson "Private Space in the Public Realm," *Design Quarterly* 129 (1985): 4.
2. Lawrence M. Irvin, "The Minneapolis Skyway System" (Minneapolis: City of Minneapolis, 1982), 3.
3. Ibid., 7.
4. Bruce N. Wright, "Coping with a Legendary Winter Climate," *AIA Journal* (March 1981): 62.
5. Irvin, "Minneapolis Skyway System," 19.
6. Ibid., 8.
7. Bernard Jacob and Carol Morphew, "Skyway Typology Minneapolis" (Washington, D.C.: AIA Press, 1984), 33.
8. Wright, "Coping," 65.

9. Department of Planning, "The Saint Paul Skyway System" (St. Paul, Minn. 1982).

10. Glenn Lyons, Don Sinclair, and Sophia Lum, "Calgary's +15: Twenty Years of Development," *Plan Canada* (January 1988): 268–76.

11. Ibid., 269.

12. Victor Caliandro, "Street Form and Use," in *On Streets*, ed. Stanford Anderson (Cambridge: MIT Press, 1978), 181.

13. Sarah Williams, "Conference Report: Bringing the Mall Back Home," *Architectural Record* (September 1985): 75.

14. David Dillon, "Conference Looks at the Benefits and Problems of 'Skyways,'" *Architecture* (June 1985): 13.

15. Caliandro, "Street Form and Use," 183.

16. Rowe, "I Stood In Venice," 14.

17. Zeidler, *Multi-Use Architecture*, 22.

18. Houston City Planning Department, "Houston Downtown Tunnel System" (Houston, 1987), 6.

19. David Dillon, "Dallas: A Case Study in Skyway Economics," *Design Quarterly* 129 (1985): 24–27.

20. Ibid., 10–13.

21. Whyte, *CITY*, 204–5.

22. Maitland, *Shopping Malls*, 151.

23. Elliot Willensky, "Essay," *Design Quarterly* 129 (1985): 14–15.

CHAPTER 5

1. Camillo Sitte, *The Art of Building Cities* (1889, Reprint, New York: Reinhold, 1945).

2. Raymond Unwin, *Town Planning in Practice* (London: T. F. Unwin, 1909).

3. Kevin Lynch, *Image of the City*, (Cambridge: MIT Press, 1960).

4. Rob Krier, *Urban Space* (New York: Rizzoli, 1979).

5. Leon Krier, *Houses, Palaces, Cities*, ed. Demetri Porphyrios (London: Architectural Design Editions, 1984).

6. Royal Institute of British Architects Board of Education, "Report of the Urban Design Diploma Working Group," May 1970 (London: Royal Institute of British Architects, 1970), 3.

7. Rob Krier, *Urban Space*, 15

8. Warren Boeschenstein, "Chester, England: Urban Design Ideas from an Ancient Source," *Places 2*, no. 4 (1985), 3–16.

9. Ibid., 5.

10. MacKeith, *History and Conservation*, 110.

11. Grosvenor Developments, "The Refurbishment of the Grosvenor Precinct, Chester 1984–86" (London, 1986).

12. Boeschenstein, "Chester, England," 15.

13. Roger K. Lewis, "Shaping the City," *Washington Post*, 24 August 1985, 7 September 1985, 14 September 1985, 21 September 1985, 28 September 1985, 5 October 1985.

14. Ibid., 5 October 1985.

15. Judy Morgan, letter to author, 19 October 1988.

16. Ibid.

17. Patricia McHugh, *Toronto Architecture, A City Guide* (Toronto: Mercury Books, 1985), 103–4.

18. Toronto Planning Board, "On Foot Downtown" (City of Toronto, Ontario, 1969).

19. Mal Williams, "The Underground City," *City Planning* (Toronto) (Fall 1984): 24–29.

20. Bacon, *Design of Cities*, 243.

21. Ibid., 253.

22. David Morton, "Suburban Shopping Downtown?" *Progressive Architecture* (December 1978): 64–67.

23. Philadelphia City Planning Commission, *The Plan for Center City* (City of Philadelphia, 1988).

CHAPTER 6

1. Maitland, *Shopping Malls*, 115.

2. See Lynch, *Image of the City*; Jane Jacobs, *The Death and Life of Great American Cities* (New York: Random House, 1961); Beacon, *Design of Cities*; Rudofsky, *Streets for People*; Colin Rowe and Fred Koetter, *Collage City* (Cambridge: MIT Press, 1978); Rob Krier, *Urban Space*; and Whyte, *Social Life*.

3. For additional examples and an excellent analysis of back-land development, see Maitland, *Shopping Malls*, 94–108.

4. Norman G. Brett-James, *The Growth of Stuart London* (London: George Allen & Unwin, 1935), 299.

5. Maitland, *Shopping Malls*, 124.

6. Whyte, *CITY*, 193.

7. Thomas Fisher, "Remaking Malls," *Progressive Architecture* (November 1988): 96–101.

INDEX